1987

Studies in Natural Language Processing
Sponsored by the Association for Computational Linguistics

Semantic interpretation and the resolution of ambiguity

Studies in Natural Language Processing

Executive Editor: Aravind K. Joshi

This series publishes monographs, texts, and edited volumes within the interdisciplinary field of computational linguistics. Sponsored by the Association for Computational Linguistics, the series will represent the range of topics of concern to the scholars working in this increasingly important field, whether their background is in formal linguistics, psycholinguistics, cognitive psychology, or artificial intelligence.

Semantic interpretation
and the resolution of ambiguity

GRAEME HIRST
Department of Computer Science, University of Toronto

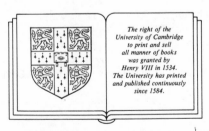

*The right of the
University of Cambridge
to print and sell
all manner of books
was granted by
Henry VIII in 1534.
The University has printed
and published continuously
since 1584.*

CAMBRIDGE UNIVERSITY PRESS

CAMBRIDGE

LONDON   NEW YORK   NEW ROCHELLE

MELBOURNE   SYDNEY

Published by the Press Syndicate of the University of Cambridge
The Pitt Building, Trumpington Street, Cambridge CB2 1RP
32 East 57th Street, New York, NY 10022, USA
10 Stamford Road, Oakleigh, Victoria 3166, Australia

First published 1987

Printed in Great Britain at the University Press, Cambridge

British Library cataloguing in publication data
Hirst, Graeme
Semantic interpretation and the resolution of ambiguity.–
(Studies in natural language processing)
1. Semantics–Data processing
I. Title   II. Series
412   P325.5.D38

Library of Congress cataloguing in publication data
Hirst, Graeme
Semantic interpretation and the resolution of ambiguity.
(Studies in natural language processing)
Bibliography.
Includes indexes.
1. Semantics–Data processing. 2. Ambiguity–Data processing. 3. Psycholinguistics–Data
processing. I. Title   II. Series
P325.5.D38H57   1986   415´.028´5   85-18978

ISBN 0 521 32203 0

Table of contents

Part III   STRUCTURAL DISAMBIGUATION

Part IV   CONCLUSION

For Nadia,
who made it possible.

Preface

This book is based on my doctoral dissertation at Brown University, submitted in December 1983. I have revised it extensively; in particular, I have kept the literature reviews up to date, and tried to take account of related work on the same topic that has been published since the original dissertation.

The work herein is interdisciplinary, and is perhaps best described as being in cognitive science. It takes in artificial intelligence, computational linguistics, and psycholinguistics, and I believe that it will be of interest to researchers in all three areas. Accordingly, I have tried to make it comprehensible to all by not assuming too much knowledge on the reader's part about any field. The incorporation of complete introductory courses was, however, impractical, and the reader may wish to occasionally consult introductory texts outside his or her main research area.[1]

Organization of the book

Chapter 1 is an introductory chapter that sets out the topic of the work and the general approach. The problems of semantic interpretation, lexical disambiguation, and structural disambiguation are explained. For readers who haven't come across them before, there are also brief overviews of frame systems and case theories of language; people who already know it all can skip this. I then describe the research, and in particular the Frail frame language and the Paragram parser, that was the starting point for the present work.

Chapters 2 and 3 form Part I, on semantic interpretation. Chapter 2 is a detailed examination of past research on the topic, and discusses properties desirable in a semantic interpreter. Chapter 3 describes Absity, a compositional semantic interpreter whose output is expressions in the frame language Frail and which has many of the desirable properties discussed in chapter 2.

---

[1] Here is a non-exhaustive list: Good introductions to artificial intelligence are Boden 1977 and Charniak and McDermott 1985. For frames and knowledge representation, see Brachman and Levesque 1985, or, for a short introduction, the paper by Fikes and Kehler 1985. An introduction to transformational syntax may be had from Akmajian and Heny 1975 or Baker 1978. I don't know of a good non-partisan introduction to semantics, but JD Fodor 1977 or Kempson 1977 and Dowty, Wall, and Peters 1981 may be read for separate introductions to each side. For psycholinguistics see Foss and Hakes 1978 or Clark and Clark 1977.

Chapters 4 and 5 comprise Part II, on lexical disambiguation. Chapter 4 describes what is necessary for lexical disambiguation and the approaches that have previously been taken to the problem. The chapter also reviews current psycholinguistic research on lexical disambiguation. Chapter 5 describes my lexical disambiguation system, which has two cooperating processes: marker passing in a network of frames and Polaroid Word procedures, one per word, that gather and apply disambiguating information. The system works in concert with the Absity system described in chapter 3.

Chapters 6 and 7, Part III, are on structural disambiguation. Chapter 6 reviews the problem, and catalogues the different types of structural ambiguity that a language-understanding system has to deal with. It also presents previous approaches to structural disambiguation, and current linguistic theories. Chapter 7 is on the Semantic Enquiry Desk, a mechanism that helps a parser choose among the possible parses of a structurally ambiguous sentence. Like Polaroid Words, the Semantic Enquiry Desk works in concert with Absity.

Part IV, chapter 8, recapitulates the main points of the work, emphasizing the operation of the approaches developed in the previous parts as an integrated system. The work is compared with other current research in the same area. The book closes with the usual "problems for future research" (chapter 9), including a number of random thoughts and half-baked ideas that I hope will interest others.

Subject and name indexes and an extensive bibliography are provided for the comfort and convenience of the reader.

> Persons attempting to find a motive in this narrative will be prosecuted; persons attempting to find a moral in it will be banished; persons attempting to find a plot in it will be shot.
> —Mark Twain[2]

Notation

Although I often talk about "natural language", this book is primarily about English, though of course I hope that most of the general principles I put forward will be true of all languages. In both the example sentences and the language of the book itself, I have tried to remain independent of any particular dialect of English (an interesting task for an Australian revising in Canada for a British publisher a manuscript originally written in the north-eastern U.S.). On those occasions where a dialect choice had to be made (in particular, in the case of spelling), I have usually chosen American English, which was the language of the university to which the original dissertation was submitted.

A few totally conventional abbreviations are employed. *AI* means *artificial intelligence* and *NLU* means *natural language understanding*. Table 0.1 shows the

---

[2]TWAIN, Mark. *The Adventures of Huckleberry Finn*. 1884.

Table 0.1. *Abbreviations for syntactic categories*

ABBREV	MEANING	ABBREV	MEANING
ADJ	adjective	NP	noun phrase
ADJP	adjective phrase	PP	prepositional phrase
ADV	adverb	PREP	preposition
AUX	auxiliary	S	sentence
DET	determiner	V	verb
N	noun	VP	verb phrase

abbreviations used for syntactic categories. A superscript asterisk on a symbol means that the symbol may be repeated zero or more times; thus *ADJ** represents as many adjectives as you like—or possibly none at all.

Italics are used in the usual metalinguistic manner and boldface is used to give names to meanings; thus, I might write "the **badly-made-car** meaning of *lemon*". Case names appear in small caps. Roman small caps are also used for emphasis, and when a new term is being defined. A "typewriter" font is used for the Frail frame language and for frame objects in general; it is also used occasionally for other computer input and output. Underlining is used in examples to draw attention to the important word or words. An asterisk in front of an example text means that it is syntactically ill-formed, and a hash mark ("#") means that it is syntactically well-formed but semantically anomalous. For instance:

(0-1)   *Ross and Nadia is the main actors of these chronicle.

(0-2)   #My toothbrush sings five-part madrigals.

By *I*, I mean myself, Graeme Hirst, and by *you* I mean you, the reader. When I say *we*, as when I say "we see that . . . ", I mean you and me together.

When a string of citations is offered to bolster a point, the intent is usually that the reader wishing to consult the literature need find but one of them, not all of them; by offering a long list, I am thoughtfully maximizing the reader's chances of physically obtaining a relevant publication.

Acknowledgements

This work grew out of many discussions with my dissertation advisor, Eugene Charniak, and many of the ideas herein are from seeds that he planted and fertilized. I am grateful to him for the time, patience, and thought that he gave me throughout my stay at Brown University.

I am grateful also to my external examiner, James Allen of the University of Rochester, and to Trina Avery for her expert copyediting of the dissertation.

Many other people also read and commented on some or all of the manuscript in its various stages, helped me in discussions to develop and clarify my ideas, pointed me to relevant work, or gave me other valuable advice during the course of the research. I am indebted to Robert Amsler, Emmon Bach, Barb Brunson, Penny Carter, Carole Chaski, Gennaro Chierchia, Robin Cohen, Stephen Crain, Meredyth Daneman, Marilyn Ford, Mike Gavin, Tom Grossi, Phil Hayes, Jim Hendler, Jennifer Holbrook, Susan Hudson, Polly Jacobson, Margery Lucas, Stephen Lupker, Tony Maida, Susan McRoy, Amy Rakowsky, Anonymous Referee, Stu Shieber, Nadia Talent, Yuriy (George) Tarnawsky, and Doug Wong.

The Brown University Department of Computer Science was my home for four and a half years. The excitement of just being in the department was due in no small way to the then-chairman, Andy van Dam, who turned the department from a neonate to one of the leading U.S. computer science departments in an amazingly short time. I also appreciate the work of those who really ran the department: Trina Avery, Mary Agren, Ginny Desmond, Gail Farias, and Jennet Kirschenbaum. My fellow inmates in 018, Steve Feiner and Jim Hendler, were a constant source of inspiration and humor throughout the writing of the dissertation.

At the University of Toronto, where I turned the dissertation into a book, Ralph Hill and Jean-François Lamy helped to revise a large package of TEX macros, and Jean-François made TEX talk to a PostScript™ typesetter. Joanne Mager typed new sections faster than I ever could, and helped in innumerable ways.

At Cambridge University Press, Penny Carter, my editor, put up with my tendencies to lateness and perfectionism with good grace, and Philip Riley skillfully copyedited the final manuscript.

At Brown University, financial support for this work was provided in part by the U.S. Office of Naval Research under contract number N00014–79–C–0592 (Eugene Charniak, Principal Investigator). At the University of Toronto, I was supported by grants from the University and from the Natural Sciences and Engineering Research Council of Canada.

I am grateful to my parents for encouraging and supporting me throughout my education, to Robin Stanton for convincing me that I too could be a graduate student, and to my best friend, Nadia Talent, for putting up with all this silliness.

September 1986

1   Introduction

> Like all other scientists, linguists wish they were physicists. They dream of
> performing classic feats like dropping grapefruits off the Leaning Tower of
> Pisa, of stunning the world with pithy truths like $F = ma$ ... [But instead,]
> the modern linguist spends his or her time starring or unstarring terse unlikely
> sentences like "John, Bill, and Tom killed each other", which seethe with re-
> pressed frustration and are difficult to work into a conversation.
> —Joseph D Becker[1]

WHEN I TOOK my first linguistics course, freshman transformational syntax, in
1974, we were taught that syntax was now basically under control. Sure, people
still argued over particular transformations, and this was still all new and exciting
stuff, but there was general agreement on the approach. Semantics, on the other
hand, was a difficult and tenuous territory; no one yet understood what a semantic
was. Semantics was said to have the same qualities as God or Mind—fun to argue
about, but inherently unknowable. The study of semantics was left, therefore, until
junior year.

Given linguists with attitudes like those toward semantics, it is not surprising
that consumers of linguistic theory, such as researchers in natural language understanding, took semantic matters into their own hands. The result was approaches
to semantics that were exemplary in their own terms but lacked a firm theoretical
basis and hence were inadequate in their relationship to other aspects of language
and to wider issues of meaning and representation of meaning. The best example
of this is the dissertation of Woods (1967), which I will discuss in some detail in
section 2.3.1.

But times are changing. Linguists are much braver than they used to be, and
exciting new things are happening in the study of linguistic semantics. Probably
the most important is Montague semantics (Montague 1973), which remained for
several years a small and arcane area, but which has now attracted a large amount
of interest. It is therefore time to start importing modern semantic theories into
NLU and examining them to see how they can be applied, how they need to be
adapted, and what their limitations are.

---

[1] Becker 1975: 70.

It is the goal of this work to do just this, with a particular emphasis on semantic interpretation. I will be using new approaches to semantics to help put NLU semantic interpretation onto a firmer and more theoretical foundation, and, in the framework thereby set up, to look at issues of lexical and structural disambiguation.

1.1 The problems

The problems discussed in this monograph can be divided into three distinct (but, of course, related) areas: semantic interpretation, word sense disambiguation, and structural disambiguation. In this section I explain each of these problem areas.

1.1.1 Semantic interpretation

By SEMANTIC INTERPRETATION we mean the process of mapping a syntactically analyzed text of natural language to a representation of its meaning. The input to a semantic interpreter is a parse tree, but we do not require that it represent a complete sentence; we allow well-formed subtrees such as noun phrases and even single words (labeled with their part of speech and syntactic features) as input. The output of a semantic interpreter is the meaning of the input text, or a suitable representation thereof. I will discuss in chapters 2 and 3 what such a representation might be; for the present, we will just observe that the natural language input text itself is a representation of its meaning, but not a "suitable" one.

I exclude from semantic interpretation all aspects of syntactic analysis; rather, I assume the existence of a parser that performs morphological and syntactic analysis upon an input text before it is passed to the semantic interpreter. This is not in any sense a logical necessity; systems have been built in which syntactic analysis and semantic interpretation have been completely integrated—*e.g.*, Riesbeck 1974, 1975; Riesbeck and Schank 1978; Hendrix 1977a, 1977b; Cater 1981, 1982. However, this approach becomes very messy when complex syntactic constructions are considered. Keeping syntactic and semantic analysis separate is well motivated merely by basic computer science principles of modularity. Moreover, it is my observation that those who argue for the integration of syntactic and semantic processing are usually disparaging the role of syntax,[2] a position that I reject (see

---

[2] "The theory of syntax is an artifact that cannot be used as a foundation for parsing; stereotypic patterns of lexical interactions cannot account for the highly particular nature of context and usage" (Small 1980: 12).

"Syntactic and semantic processing is *[sic]* done at the same time, with the primacy of semantics over syntax ... Syntax is used only when it helps in semantic analysis" (Gershman (1979: 11), describing Riesbeck's parser).

See also Schank and Birnbaum 1980.

also Charniak 1983b), and one which has been found to be unworkable[3] and, probably, psychologically unreal (Marslen-Wilson and Tyler 1980: 62–66; Tanenhaus and Donnenwerth-Nolan 1984) *(see section 2.4)*. This is not to say that parsing is possible without semantic help; in chapters 6 and 7 we will see many situations, such as prepositional phrase and relative clause attachment, in which the parser must call on semantic knowledge. In this book, I will show that syntax and semantics may work together well and yet remain distinct modules.[4]

Lytinen (1984) argues for a "compromise" position. It seems to me, however, that his position is much closer to the separation camp, in which he places the present work, than the integration camp. He states five principles regarding the interaction of syntax and semantics (1984: 4–5), and I am in agreement with about 4.3 of them:

1. Syntactic and semantic processing of text should proceed at the same time.

2. Syntactic decisions must be made with full access to semantic processing; that is, communication between syntax and semantics is high.

3. [Only] a limited amount of syntactic representation [need] be built during text understanding.

4. Knowledge about syntax and semantics is largely separate. Syntactic knowledge should be expressed in the parser's knowledge base as a largely separate body of knowledge, but this knowledge should have references to semantics, telling the system how semantic representations are built from these syntactic rules.

5. Semantics guides the parsing process, but relies on syntactic rules to make sure that it is making the right decisions.

---

[3] "The conclusion that must be drawn from [these experiments] is that if a semantic parser operates without a complete syntactic parse of its input, it is difficult, if not impossible, to prevent it finding readings which do not in fact exist" (Tait 1982, comparing the parsers of Boguraev 1979 and Cater 1981).

"It is fair to say that none of these 'semantically based' approaches has succeeded in producing anything like the clear, communicable framework that seems to be offered by a syntactic parser sitting together with a semantic interpreter. As a result, people are continuing to write new and better syntactic parsers, and more and more complete grammars to be used with them in two-part natural language processing systems. The advantages of modularity and portability to new application areas seem to outweigh any other arguments that there may be" (Mellish 1982a).

"[The] basic assumption [of Riesbeck's parser] that every part of the input sentence has to be specifically expected by some previously built structure does not always work" (Gershman 1979: 11). (Gershman adapted Riesbeck's parser by adding two new modes of processing, with much more syntactic knowledge.)

"The [not-much-syntax] models that have been presented to date . . . are and will remain fundamentally inadequate to handle the range of grammatical phenomena well known and understood within the linguistics community for the last ten years" (Marcus 1984: 254).

See also chapter 4 of Lytinen 1984 for a critique of integrating syntax and semantics.

[4] Mellish (1982a) suggests the possibility of a system in which separate syntactic and semantic modules are automatically compiled into an efficient unified system. Hendler and Phillips (1981) suggest object-oriented computing to achieve this goal.

The system I will develop in this book is in full accord with principles 1, 2, and 5. I will not quite meet principle 4; rather, we shall see that the relationship between syntactic and semantic rules need not be quite so explicit. Principle 3 is usually true; the internal structure of a syntactic constituent at any level is almost never used once it and its semantic representation have been built, and it may be immediately discarded. There are, however, two good reasons for constructing a full parse tree anyway:

- **Programming:** It is easier to discard the whole tree at the end of the parse than do it piece by piece during the parse, and it is useful to retain the tree for purposes of debugging the program.

- **Theoretical:** Sentences in which apparently-closed constituents are re-opened are widely acceptable *(see section 6.2.5)*; the internal structure must be retained just in case.[5]

I also exclude from semantic interpretation any consideration of discourse pragmatics; rather, discourse pragmatics operates upon the output of the semantic interpreter. Thus, semantic interpretation does not include the resolution in context of anaphors or definite reference, or of deictic or indexical expressions, or the recognition and comprehension of speech acts, irony and sarcasm, metaphor, or other non-literal meanings.[6] These exclusions should not be thought of as uncontroversial; while few would advocate making speech-act interpretation part of semantic interpretation, Moore (1981) argues that definite reference resolution, as well as certain "local" pragmatic matters, must be resolved during semantic interpretation, and Plantinga (1986) argues that metaphor comprehension cannot be divorced from other aspects of language comprehension.

1.1.2 Word sense and case slot disambiguation

Many words of English have more than one meaning, and many quite common words have a very large number of meanings. Table 1.1 lists the words of English

---

[5]Moreover, there are sentences that require the surface form to be retained—for example those with SURFACE COUNT ANAPHORS (Hirst 1981a):

(i)   When connecting the toe pin to the ankle rod, make sure that the latter goes underneath the former.

(ii)   When the ankle rod is connected to the toe pin, make sure that the former goes underneath the latter.

and it may be that there are sentences that, similarly, refer into their structure. (I have not been able to find any examples.)

[6]For a discussion of anaphors, definite reference, and their resolution in context, see Hirst 1981a, 1981b. Deictics and indexicals are discussed by Fillmore 1975, Kaplan 1978, 1979, and Levinson 1983. Some useful starting points for reading about the role of speech acts in language are Searle 1969, Cole and Morgan 1975, Boyd and Ferrara 1979, and Levinson 1983. For work in AI on recognizing and understanding speech acts, see Allen 1979, 1983a, 1983b, Allen and Perrault 1980, Perrault and Allen 1980, Brown 1979, 1980.

Table 1.1. *Words with the greatest number of senses in the* Merriam-Webster Pocket Dictionary *(data from Amsler 1980: 55–57)*

WORD	CATEGORY	NO. OF SENSES	WORD	CATEGORY	NO. OF SENSES
go	verb	63	take	verb	24
fall	verb	35	dead	adj	21
run	verb	35	good	adj	21
turn	verb	31	have	verb	21
way	noun	31	line	noun	21
work	verb	31	pass	verb	21
do	verb	30	touch	verb	21
draw	verb	30	dry	adj	20
play	verb	29	wing	noun	20
get	verb	26	draft	noun	19
form	noun	24	give	verb	19
make	verb	24	turn	noun	19
strike	verb	24			

that Amsler (1980, 1981, 1982a) found to have the greatest number of senses listed in *The Merriam-Webster pocket dictionary*. Any practical NLU system must be able to disambiguate words with multiple meanings, and the method used to do this must necessarily work with the methods of semantic interpretation and knowledge representation used in the system.

There are three types of lexical ambiguity: POLYSEMY, HOMONYMY, and CATEGORIAL AMBIGUITY. Polysemous words are those whose several meanings are related to one another. For example, the verb *open* has many senses concerning unfolding, expanding, revealing, moving to an open position, making openings in, and so on. Conversely, homonymous words have meanings with no relationship one to another.[7] For example, *bark* means both **the noise a dog makes** and **the stuff on the outside of a tree**. A word may be both polysemous and homonymous; the adjective *right* has several senses concerning correctness and righteousness, but also senses concerning the right-hand side.[8] There is no clear line between

---

[7] The terminology in this area can be a little confusing. Strictly speaking, since we are interested in written language, the homonymous words we are concerned with are HOMOGRAPHS, that is words where many meanings are associated with the same lexeme, though different meanings may have different pronunciations. For example, the vowel varies in *row* depending on whether it means **a line of objects** or **a commotion**, but this fact is of no consequence when dealing with written language. If we were concerned with speech recognition, the type of homonyms we would worry about would be HOMOPHONES—words that are pronounced the same but possibly spelled differently, such as *four* and *fore*. A HETERONYM is a non-homophonic homograph (Drury 1983).

[8] A common etymology does not preclude the senses being distinct enough to be considered homony-

polysemy, homonymy, and metaphor; today's metaphor may be tomorrow's polysemy or homonymy. For example, there is an obvious relationship between *mouth* in the sense of **a person's mouth** and in the sense of **the mouth of a river**, but for practical purposes they are quite separate concepts, and it is not clear into which category *mouth* should therefore be placed.

Categorially ambiguous words are those whose syntactic category may vary. For example, *sink* can be a noun describing a **plumbing fixture** or a verb meaning **become submerged**. Clearly, categorial ambiguity is orthogonal to the other types: the ambiguity of *respect* is categorial and polysemous, as its noun and verb meanings are related, but that of *sink* is categorial and homonymous, as its noun and verb meanings are not related. Categorial ambiguity is mainly a problem in parsing, and I will say no more about it in this monograph, except where it interacts with other types of ambiguity. (See Milne 1980, 1986 for a discussion of handling categorial ambiguity in a deterministic parser.)

Generally, verbs tend to polysemy while nouns tend to homonymy, though of course there are many homonymous verbs and polysemous nouns.[9] This is consistent with the suggestion of Gentner (1981a, 1981b) that verbs are more "adjustable" than nouns; that is, nouns tend to refer to fixed entities, while verb meanings are easily adjusted to fit the context, with frequent adjustments becoming lexicalized as new but related senses of the original verb.

Panman (1982) argues that although experiments, including his own, have shown that people's intuitions do distinguish between polysemy and homonymy, it is difficult and probably unnecessary to maintain the distinction at the level of linguistic theory. While it seems strange that a cognitively real linguistic phenomenon should have no place in linguistic theory, I too will make little use of it in this work. The semantic objects we will be using are discrete entities,[10] and if a word maps to more than one such entity, it will generally (but not always) be a matter of indifference how closely related those two entities are.

For an NLU system to be able to disambiguate words,[11] it is necessary that it use both the discourse context in which the word occurs and local cues within the sentence itself. In this book, I discuss how this may best be done in conjunction with my approach to semantic interpretation, although the techniques will not be limited to use solely within my approach.

---

mous in everyday modern usage.

[9] In general, adjectives show less ambiguity than nouns and verbs, and this is reflected in Table 1.1.

[10] There are those who would argue that this fact immediately damns the whole approach. But there are no well-developed models yet for any form of non-discrete semantics in AI, though current research in fine-grained connectionist systems may change this.

[11] It is not always the case that an NLU system need worry about disambiguation at all; in some applications, such as machine translation, it is acceptable to ask the user for help (Tomita 1984) or simply preserve the ambiguity in the system's output (Hirst 1981a[1]:68, fn 11; 1981b:90, fn 10; Pericliev 1984).

Ideally, an NLU system should be able to go beyond polysemy and into metaphor. In the most general case, this is an extremely difficult task, and I do not attempt it in this research. For a discussion of metaphor in NLU, see Russell 1976, Wilks 1977, Browse 1978, Hobbs 1979, Carbonell 1981, and Plantinga 1986.[12]

A problem closely related to lexical disambiguation is case slot disambiguation. Case theories of language are generally associated with the work of Fillmore (1968, 1977). In its most basic form, case theory views a sentence as an assertion whose predicate is denoted by the verb of the sentence and whose arguments are denoted by the noun phrases. For example:

(1-1)   Nadia tickled Ross with a feather.

Here, *Nadia* is the AGENT of the verb *tickle*, and we say that *Nadia* FILLS THE SLOT of the AGENT CASE. Similarly, *Ross* fills the the PATIENT slot, and *a feather* is in the INSTRUMENT case. We say that the INSTRUMENT case is FLAGGED by the preposition *with*; the AGENT and PATIENT cases are flagged by subject and object position respectively.

There is no rigid one-to-one mapping between flags and cases, however; that is, case flags are not unambiguous. For example, *with* can also flag the cases MANNER[13] and ACCOMPANIER:

(1-2)   Nadia tickled Ross <u>with</u> glee.

(1-3)   Ross flew to Casablanca <u>with</u> Nadia.

Also, a case may have more than one flag, often varying with different verbs. For example, some verbs allow the INSTRUMENT in the subject position when no AGENT is specified:

(1-4)   <u>The feather</u> tickled Ross.

Thus, different verbs take different cases and different flag-to-case mappings; however, there is still a great degree of regularity in case systems that we will be able to use.

This explanation of cases is greatly simplified, and a few extra points should be made. First, not all prepositional phrases are case-flags and fillers; PPs can qualify nouns as well as verbs. Second, an adverb can act as a combined case-flag and filler:

(1-5)   Nadia tickled Ross <u>gleefully</u>.

---

[12]Also of interest here is the work of Granger (1977; Granger, Staros, Taylor and Yoshii 1983) on determining the meaning of an unknown word from context. If it has been determined that a particular instance of a word does not accord with its normal usage, techniques such as Granger's may be applied. Metaphor, of course, provides more semantic constraints than are available in the general case of a hapax legomenon.

[13]Strictly speaking, MANNER is not a case at all but a verb modifier; see footnote 15.

In this example, *gleefully* behaves exactly as *with glee* does in (1-2).[14] Third, subordinate clauses also exhibit case behavior, with the conjunction as the flag and the sentence as the filler:

(1-6)   <u>Because Ross couldn't bring himself to touch the geranium</u>, Nadia put it in an old shoe box for him.

The word *because* flags the REASON case here. Fourth, there are good linguistic reasons (*e.g.*, Bresnan 1982b) for distinguishing between cases and certain VERB-MODIFYING PPs that describe such things as the time or place at which an action occurs:

(1-7)   Nadia tickled Ross <u>on Friday</u> <u>at the Art Museum</u>.

In the present research, this distinction will not in general be necessary, and we will usually be able to treat all verb-attached PPs in the same way.[15]

Clearly, the assignment of a case to a flag depends on the meaning of the potential slot-filler; we know that in (1-4) *the feather* is not in the AGENT case because

---

[14] In English, we can think of the suffix *-ly* as a flag for the MANNER case. However, English morphology is not quite regular enough to permit a general morphological analysis of case-flags in adverbs; rather, we just think of both the flag and the case-filler being bundled up together in the word's meaning.

[15] An example of the linguistic distinction between case-fillers and verb modifiers is that PP verb modifiers are sensitive to adverb movement and may be put at the start of the sentence, while PP case-fillers must usually follow the verb unless topicalized. Thus it sounds strange to say (i) instead of (ii):

(i)   *On the boat, Ross put his luggage.

(ii)   Ross put his luggage on the boat.

where *on the boat* is in the LOCATION case, but one can say both (iii) and (iv):

(iii)   On the boat, Ross was having fun.

(iv)   Ross was having fun on the boat.

where *on the boat* is a PLACE verb qualifier. Also, modifiers may sometimes not come between the verb and true case-fillers. Thus one can say (v) but not (vi):

(v)   Ross put his luggage on the boat on Tuesday.

(vi)   *Ross put his luggage on Tuesday on the boat.

But:

(vii)   Ross threatened Nadia with a wrench in the park.

(viii) Ross threatened Nadia in the park with a wrench.

(Barbara Brunson, personal communication). The most important difference, however, is the BIU-NIQUENESS CONDITION (Bresnan 1982b): each case may appear at most once in a sentence, while there is no restriction on how many times each modifier type may appear. Thus one may not have two INSTRUMENT cases; if more than one INSTRUMENT has to be specified, conjunction must be used with a single flag; examples from Bresnan 1982b:

(ix)   *Ross escaped from prison with dynamite with a machine gun.

(x)   Ross escaped from prison with dynamite and a machine gun.

On the other hand, (xi) (also from Bresnan 1982b) contains three MANNERs, three TIMEs and two PLACEs:

AGENTs must be conscious animate entities. Thus the problem of determining which case slot a particular preposition or syntactic position flags is very similar to that of lexical disambiguation: in each, semantic information is necessary to decide which one of a set of meanings is to be assigned to a particular token. In the present research, I will show how the two tasks may indeed be accomplished by very similar mechanisms.

1.1.3 Syntactic disambiguation

Although many sentences of English have more than one parse,[16] there is usually a unique preferred parse for a sentence after semantics and discourse context are considered. For example, in (1-8):

(1-8)   Nadia left the university on the wrong bus.

we do not take *the university on the wrong bus* as a single noun phrase; rather, we apply the knowledge that universities seldom ride buses. That is, there is a SEMANTIC BIAS to one of the parses. Bias may also come from context; the parse of a sentence such as (1-9):

(1-9)   They're cooking apples.

depends on whether it answers the question *What are they doing in the kitchen?* or *What kind of apples are those?*

In addition, the English language often exhibits certain preferences—SYNTACTIC BIASES—in choosing among several possible parses. Thus (1-10) was judged silly by informants:

(1-10)   The landlord painted all the walls with cracks.[17]

(xi)   Ross deftly handed a toy to the baby by reaching behind his back over lunch at noon in a restaurant last Sunday in the Back Bay without interrupting the discussion.

Nevertheless, there are certain restrictions on using the same flag twice in the same way, even for modifiers; thus *with* can't be used twice in the same sentence for MANNER:

(xii)   *Ross chaired the meeting with tact with dignity.

(xiii)   Ross chaired the meeting with tact and dignity.

The apparent exception (xiv) may be explained as an elliptical form of (xv):
(xiv)   Ross chaired the meeting with tact and with dignity.

(xv)   Ross chaired the meeting with tact and Ross chaired the meeting with dignity.

See also Somers 1984 and Brunson 1986a.

[16]Church and Patil (1982) point out that some sentences can have parses numbering in the hundreds if semantic constraints are not considered.

[17]From Rayner, Carlson, and Frazier (1983), who took it to be semantically well-formed.

who generally said that though the intent was clear, it sounded like either the walls were painted with a crack-like pattern or that cracks were being used to paint the walls, readings that both have the prepositional phrase attached to the verb phrase of the sentence instead of to the object noun phrase. Similarly, (1-11):

(1-11)   Ross baked the cake in the freezer.

was taken by informants to mean that the baking in some bizarre way took place in the freezer, rather than that the particular cake known to have once been in the freezer was baked in a conventional manner.[18] PPs starting with *by* often sound like passives even when a locative reading makes more sense:

(1-12)   SHOESHINE BY ESCALATOR[19]

(1-13)   Ross was told what to do by the river.

Sentence (1-12) seems to be saying that the escalator shines one's shoes, and (1-13) sounds like Ross heard voices in the running water; even though the meaning in which Ross received instructions from an unspecified person on the river bank makes more sense, the parse that treats *the river* as the deep-structure subject is still preferred.[20] The following are reported by Cutler (1982b) as "slips of the ear":

(1-14)   You never actually see a forklift truck, let alone person.
           (Perceiver attempted to access a compound noun, forklift person, *as if a second occurrence of* forklift *had been deleted.)*

(1-15)   The result was recently replicated by someone at the University of Minnesota in children.
           (Perceiver assigned NP status to the University of Minnesota in children, *cf.* the University of California in Berkeley.*)*

Cutler attributes such errors to the hearer; I am inclined to say, rather, that the error was the speaker's in creating a sentence whose structure misled the speaker. The main point, however, is that the speaker WAS misled into an anomalous interpretation consistent with the sentence structure, despite the availability of a sensible interpretation "close by".

The source of syntactic bias is disputed. Frazier (1978; Frazier and JD Fodor 1978) has suggested two principles for the preferred placement of a constituent whose role is ambiguous:

---

[18]Sentence (1-11) and its test on informants is due to Barbara Brunson.

[19]Sign at American Airlines terminal, LaGuardia airport, New York, November 1984.

[20]Marcus (1980: 228–234) argues that, at least in some cases, when syntactic and semantic biases conflict and neither is strong enough to override the other, the sentence is judged ill-formed. The argument is based on subtleties of well-formedness that vary widely over idiolects, and I am not convinced of the generality of the hypothesis.

- Right Association (also called Low Right Attachment, Late Closure, or Local Association): A new constituent is attached as low and as far to the right in the parse tree as possible.[21]

- Minimal Attachment: A new constituent is attached to the parse tree using as few non-terminal nodes as possible.

These principles predict many of the syntactic biases of English; Frazier (1978:115; Frazier and Fodor 1978) shows that they are inherent consequences of a two-stage parsing model she presents, and Milne (1982a) has shown them to be a natural consequence of Marcus parsing *(see section 1.3.2)*. However, the principles sometimes conflict, or interact in complex ways. In cases such as prepositional phrase attachment, when both a noun phrase and its dominating verb phrase could receive the PP, Low Right Attachment suggests that the NP (the lowest, right-most node) should take it, while Minimal Attachment prefers the VP because NP attachment allegedly requires an extra NP node above the resulting complex NP.[22,23] Sentence (1-10) shows that common sense is not always used to resolve the conflict, and Ford, Bresnan, and Kaplan (1982) and Crain and Steedman (1985) have proposed a different set of principles, which I will discuss in detail in sections 6.3.3 and 6.3.4.

Many sentences that are structurally unambiguous are, however, LOCALLY AMBIGUOUS: they contain a point at which, in left-to-right parsing, the parser could take one of several paths, and the information that determines which is correct occurs only later in the sentence. In the case of parsers with limited lookahead, such as Marcus parsers *(see section 1.3.2)*, the disambiguating information may be out of sight and a choice may have to be made without it. If this choice is wrong, the parser will eventually find itself off in entirely the wrong direction, unable to find any correct parse. A sentence that can do this to a parser is said to be a SYNTACTIC GARDEN-PATH SENTENCE,[24] in that it leads the parser "down the garden path"; the unfortunate parser is said to have been "GARDEN-PATHED". Many well-formed sentences are garden paths for the human mental parsing mechanism:

(1-16)   The horse raced past the barn fell.[25]

---

[21] This principle was first suggested by Kimball (1973), and was modified by Frazier and Fodor; see Fodor and Frazier 1980 for discussion of the differences.

[22] This crucially assumes that noun phrases with PP modifiers are parsed as in (i) rather than (ii):

(i)   [$_{NP}$ [$_{NP}$ the noun phrase] [$_{PP}$ with [$_{NP}$ the prepositional phrase]]]

(ii)   [$_{NP}$ the noun phrase [$_{PP}$ with [$_{NP}$ the prepositional phrase]]]

Analysis (i) strikes me as dubious, and I use (ii) below.

[23] In Frazier's (1978) two-stage model, Minimal Attachment only occurs (in the second stage) if Right Association (a consequence of the first stage) fails to happen.

[24] In section 4.3.2, we will see that there are also semantic garden-path sentences.

[25] From Bever 1970:316.

(1-17)   The old dog the footsteps of the young.[26]

Most people have trouble with these sentences the first time they see them.[27] Marcus (1980) argues that it is no shame for a computational parser to be garden-pathed by sentences that also trip humans up, and that such behavior is in fact necessary if claims of cognitive modeling are to be made for the parser. I also take this viewpoint.

To find which parse is the one preferred in each particular case, a parser needs help from both world knowledge and discourse context, as well as knowledge about preferred attachments. In this research, I develop a method of providing such semantic information for a parser—a method that works in concert with the semantic interpretation and lexical disambiguation systems that I also develop.

1.2 Frames

The concept that unifies the approaches to the problems described in the previous section is that of the FRAME as a semantic object. I am using the word *frame* in the conventional AI sense: a data item that contains a collection of knowledge about a stereotyped topic (Charniak 1976, 1981a), or represents a concept. A frame is usually structured as a set of SLOTS or ROLES that may contain VALUES; often, a DEFAULT VALUE obtains for a slot if no other value is specified. A value may be almost any type of object: a number, a boolean value, another frame (or frame instance—see below), or a homogeneous set of such values. A slot may be marked with restrictions on what sort of values it allows.

Here are some examples. The first set, shown in figure 1.1, is based (loosely) on the frames in Wong 1981b for the task of reading a menu in a restaurant. (The formalism is that for the Frail frame system—*see section 1.3.1.*) The first frame defined is read. Its second line says that it is a ("ISA") particular type of the task frame, and as a consequence INHERITS all the properties of that frame. Thus, since tasks already have a slot for the agent performing the task, it is unnecessary to define the slot again in read. On the other hand, object is defined at this level of the FRAME HIERARCHY (or ISA HIERARCHY), because it is not true that all tasks have this slot. It is also specified that the filler of this slot must be something that can be read, namely reading-material. The facts clauses, not shown in detail here, describe the actions involved in reading, starting off with taking the item to be read.

---

[26] I believe this example is due to Yorick Wilks.

[27] Their meanings are, respectively:

(i)   The horse—the one that was raced past the barn—fell.

(ii)   The footsteps of the young are dogged by the old people.

```
frame:   read
  isa:   task
slots:   object (required) (reading-material)
facts:   (take ?agent ?object)
            ...

frame:   possibilities-list
  isa:   reading-material
slots:   type-of-possibilities

frame:   menu
  isa:   possibilities-list
facts:   (type-of-possibilities food)

instance:   menu34
    isa:    menu
```

Figure 1.1. Frail frames describing some of the knowledge necessary to understand the concept of reading a restaurant menu (from Wong 1981b).

The next frames define possibilities-list, menu, and also a particular INSTANCE of a menu, namely one given the arbitrary name menu34. Because menu34 has reading-material as an ancestor in the hierarchy, it will be allowed to fill the object slot in any instance of the read frame. An instance is necessarily a leaf in the frame hierarchy, and no other frame may be defined in terms of it. Nodes that are not instances are said to be GENERIC.

The second example set, in figure 1.2, is from KRL (DG Bobrow and Winograd 1977, 1979). (I have modified it slightly for this exposition.) First the BusinessTravel and Visit frames are defined, and then an item that is simultaneously an instance of both is given. The SELF clause gives the frame's parent in the frame hierarchy, from which properties may be inherited. The following clauses list slots, giving their names and restrictions on their fillers; for example, the visitor slot can only be filled by an instance of the Person frame. Event137 is an instance of the Visit frame, and particular values for the slots of Visit are given. It is also an instance of BusinessTravel; note that since a value is not given for the mode slot, it will take on the default value Plane. Because a KRL frame can be an instance of more than one frame, the frame hierarchy of KRL is a network, not just a tree as in Frail.

Thus we can think of a generic frame as a representation of a concept and an instance as one specific occurrence of the concept. Slots can be thought of as arguments or parameters of the concept, so that the filled slots of an instance describe or qualify that instance.

Many different frame systems have been developed in AI—another important one not mentioned above is KL-ONE (Brachman 1978)—and there is still much

```
[BusinessTravel UNIT
  ⟨SELF (an Event)⟩
  ⟨mode (OR Plane Auto Bus) DEFAULT Plane⟩
  ⟨destination (a City)⟩]

[Visit UNIT
  ⟨SELF (a SocialInteraction)⟩
  ⟨visitor (a Person)⟩
  ⟨visitees (SetOf (a Person))⟩]

[Event137 UNIT Individual
  ⟨SELF {
     (a Visit with
        visitor = Rusty
        visitees = (Items Danny Terry))
     (a BusinessTravel with
        destination = SanFrancisco) }⟩]
```

Figure 1.2. An example of frames in KRL, describing a trip from two different perspectives (from DG Bobrow and Winograd 1977).

controversy over how frames may best be organized and what their exact semantics should be (*e.g.* Brachman 1982, Brachman and Levesque 1982). Although the details of the present approach are tied to the Frail frame system (to be described in section 1.3.1), we try as far as possible to keep the basic ideas independent of any particular frame formalism.

The power of frame systems, the power that we will exploit in dealing with the problems described in the previous section, lies not merely in having a large hierarchy or network of frames but in being able to manipulate those frames and perform inferences upon them, prove theorems about them, do inductive, deductive, and abductive reasoning with them. A frame system is not just a static knowledge base containing a collection of pieces of information, but includes powerful procedures for using that information. Thus, when we say that we are using the concept of a frame as a semantic object, we are not simply defining a data structure; rather, we are adopting a whole system for representing, storing, retrieving, and using knowledge.

By using frames as semantic objects, we will be able to take the following approach to the problems under discussion:

- We will use a frame system as a well-defined semantics for natural language. By having a strong correspondence between lexical categories and elements of the frame system, we will be able to construct an elegant and compositional semantic interpreter.

- Because of this strong correspondence, well-formed subtrees of the input text will be mapped to well-defined items in the frame system, so whenever the parser needs semantic help in dealing with a subtree, it can draw upon the full power of the frame system for assistance.

- Similarly, because individual words also correspond to frame system entities, lexical disambiguation can use the knowledge of the frame system. By constructing the semantic interpreter so that it deals, whenever possible, with semantic objects by reference only to their type rather than their content, lexical disambiguation may proceed independently of semantic interpretation and structural disambiguation and yet supply word meanings to the other processes when necessary.

1.3 Artificial intelligence research at Brown University

The work described in this book began as a component of the artificial intelligence research in the Department of Computer Science, Brown University.[28] This section describes that work briefly, so that the reader may better understand the present work and its place in the overall project.

The top-level goal of the project is to study the use of common-sense knowledge in both language comprehension and problem solving. To this end, a knowledge representation suitable for both these tasks has been developed (Charniak 1981a). This representation incorporates features of both frame systems and predicate calculus; it forms the basis of the Frail frame language (Wong 1981a, 1981b).

Frail is used by Bruin (Wong 1981a, 1981b), a system that can both understand simple stories, making inferences from the story when necessary, and solve problems. Here are three examples that Bruin can handle:

(1-18)   A manufacturer used a molding machine in producing TV cabinets. The standard time for production was 0.025 hours per TV cabinet. The molding machine operated for 80 hours per week. The manufacturer delivers 2000 cabinets per week. The standard time for a setup change for the molding machine was 6.5 hours per lot. The setup change cost 3.50 dollars per hour. Storage of the TV cabinets cost 0.115 dollars per cabinet per week. Calculate the economic lot-size for inventory control of the TV cabinets.

(1-19)   There is a green block on a table. A red block is on the table. The red block has a blue block on it. Put the red block on the green block while putting the green block on the blue block.

(1-20)   Jack took a menu. He ordered a hamburger. He ate. He paid. He left.
          What did Jack eat? What did Jack do before paying? Did Jack read the menu? Why did Jack take the menu? What did Jack pay for?

Bruin contained a parser based on that of Marcus (1980) and a primitive semantic interpreter based on that of Woods (1967, 1968) to translate the English input into

---

[28] Eugene Charniak, Principal Investigator. Others who have contributed to the project are Michael Gavin, Tom Grossi, Jim Hendler, Doug Wong, and the present author.

assertions or commands in Frail.[29] A module called Pragmatics monitored the input to the Frail knowledge base and made inferences about likely consequences, on the basis of simple world knowledge. In (1-20), the assertion would be made, from a script about restaurants, that what Jack ate was the hamburger he ordered. A problem solver named NASL, based on that of Drew McDermott (1978), could answer questions, either by looking directly for an assertion that provided the answer, as in the case of finding out what Jack ate, or by using problem-solving techniques to find a solution, as in the TV cabinet economic lot-size problem.

This system is presently being redesigned and extended. A new version of Frail has been developed (Charniak, Gavin, and Hendler 1983), and work is proceeding in such areas as context recognition and discovering causal connections (Charniak 1981b, 1982) and problem solving (Hendler 1985, 1986a). Improvements to the natural language front-end include a new parser, Paragram (Charniak 1983a), and the work described in this volume. Since this work makes extensive use of Frail and Paragram, it is important that the reader understand their design and intent. In the next two subsections I describe each in turn.

1.3.1 The Frail frame language

Frail is a frame language that incorporates features of first-order predicate calculus. This section describes the most recent version, Frail 2.1 (Charniak, Gavin, and Hendler 1983). Frail is based on the deductive information retriever of Charniak, Riesbeck, and McDermott (1980: 140–161); an earlier implementation is described by Wong (1981a, 1981b); and the motivation for its design is described by Charniak (1981a).

Frail consists of a knowledge base of "true" statements, together with functions `assert`, `erase`, and `retrieve` to add, delete, and retrieve statements. The function `retrieve` takes a statement with variables in it—one may think of it as a pattern to be matched—and returns all assignments of values to those variables that make the statement "true" in the knowledge base. The truth of a statement to be retrieved may be determined by its literal presence in the knowledge base or may be INFERRED using BACKWARD-CHAINING RULES. These rules, also asserted to the knowledge base, tell Frail about valid inferences; for example, the rule (1-21) says "Nadia likes anything that is warm and fuzzy", *i.e.*, "One way to prove that Nadia likes something is to prove that it is warm and fuzzy":

```
(1-21)    (←(likes Nadia ?x)
              (and (warm ?x) (fuzzy ?x)))
```

Frail also permits the assertion of frame information. One may assert that something is a frame or is an instance of a frame, or that a frame has a particular set of slots, each with a particular restriction on its filler. Since frame statements are

---

[29]The parser was implemented by Tom Grossi and the interpreter by Graeme Hirst.

```
[frame:    purchase                            The action of buying
    isa:   action                              is a kind of action.
  slots:   buyer (person)                      The buyer and seller
           seller (person)                       must both be people.
           bought-item                         No restrictions on what is sold.
           money (negotiable-instrument)       Cash, check, or credit card.
   acts:   pay-step                            The components of the action.
           (give buyer money seller)           Paying for the item.
           get-item-step
           (give seller bought-item            Getting the item.
              buyer)]

[instance: purchase34                          A particular purchase action.
              (purchase
                 (buyer Nadia)                 The slot fillers.
                 (seller Ross)
                 (bought-item marmoset34)
                 (money twenty-dollars)]
```

Figure 1.3. A frame and an instance in Frail 2.1 describing (in very simple terms) the action of purchasing. Italics indicate comments. (Based on an example from Charniak, Gavin, and Hendler 1983.)

frequent in Frail, it provides a special syntax for their definition; an example may be seen in figure 1.3.

In the work described in this book, I make extensive use of FRAME DETERMIN-ERS. Although frame determiners are not a facility in Frail 2.1, but are instead programmed on top of it, I use them as if they were part of the frame system (as they may indeed be in future versions), so it is appropriate to discuss them here. A frame determiner is a function that, like `assert` and `retrieve`, adds or gets formulas from the database but, unlike those basic functions, takes into account notions of CONTEXT and FOCUS. The focus is basically the set of entities that the discourse has referred to recently—see Hirst 1981a, 1981b for a more precise characterization—and is where the referents of pronouns and other definite references are sought.

The two main frame determiners are `the` and `a`, and their semantics are what their names suggest. The `the` function is like `retrieve`, except that before searching the database it first looks in the focus for a matching instance that is ACTIVE in context (Hirst 1981a, 1981b). (It is an error if there is not either exactly one match in focus, or none in focus but exactly one in the database.) This implies that `the` has available to it a representation of a discourse focus and that there is a process that dynamically maintains this focus.[30] The `a` function asserts the

---

[30]In the present implementation, there is only a very primitive model of discourse context to maintain

existence of a new frame instance (and returns as a value its name), but allows the possibility that it may turn out to be identical to a pre-existing instance; in particular, if there are frame instances of the same type in focus, a will assume that its argument is identical to one of them.

For example, suppose the following are in focus, each an instance of the frame suggested by its name:

(1-22)   penguin34, penguin87, catch22, kiss88

Then the call (the ?x (kiss ?x)) will return kiss88; the call (a ?x (penguin ?x)) will return a new instance:

(1-23)   [instance: penguin99
          one-of: (penguin34 penguin87)][31]

and (a ?x (restaurant ?x)) will return a new restaurant instance with no restrictions on its being identical with other restaurant instances in the knowledge base. In each case, the instance returned will be added to the focus, or, if already there, be marked as again very recent.

The frame determiner question is used in questions. It is very close to a simple knowledge-base retrieval function, looking for an instance that matches its argument and not considering focus at all. It returns a list of matching instances, and if its argument included any free variables, it also gives the bindings of those variables for each instance it found.

Other frame determiners include some and the-pl, which are the plural forms of a and the; each deals with a set of instances instead of a single instance.

1.3.2 The Paragram parser

The Paragram parser (Charniak 1983a) is a deterministic parser with limited lookahead. That is, once it has made a decision about the structure of the input or the lexical category of a word, it is unable to change that decision. Further, it is restricted in how far beyond the point of current processing it is allowed to look for information that might help its decisions. In these respects, it is modeled on Marcus's well-known parser Parsifal (Marcus 1980, Sampson 1983).

A Marcus-type parser uses a set of grammar rules, an input buffer of limited length, and a work stack. Each grammar rule is a pattern–action pair. When the input buffer matches the pattern of a rule, that rule is executed. An example of a pattern is (1-24):

---

this focus (and even that is not yet operative), since this is not the primary thrust of the present work. Ideally, the focus should allow for references to items only implicitly in context—if a car is in focus, then any of its parts, for example, may also be referenced. Later versions may take into account focus and topic determination. For a discussion of the issues involved and some approaches, see Hirst 1981a, 1981b or Grosz 1977a, 1977b, 1978, 1981. This approach has mild psychological reality; *cf.* Guindon 1985.

[31] Frail does not yet permit implementation of this construction; *cf.* section 3.8.

(1-24)   [= np] [=* to] [= tnsless]

This pattern matches a buffer whose first element is a noun phrase, whose second is the word *to*, and whose third is marked as being tenseless. Rules are organized into PACKETS, and only rules whose packet is presently ACTIVE are considered. In addition, rules may be assigned PRIORITIES; if more than one rule matches, the one with highest priority is the one chosen.

The actions in a rule may include taking items out of the buffer and putting them on the stack, adding them to a partial parse tree that is on the stack, marking them with certain syntactic features, and so on. Rules may also activate and deactivate rule packets (including their own). As items are taken from the buffer to the stack or put back from the stack into the buffer, words from the input flow into or out of the buffer, so that it always contains the same number of items. An exception to this occurs during the processing of noun phrases, when the parser is allowed to look further ahead in the input than at other times.

Marcus parsers, being deterministic, stand in contrast to AUGMENTED TRANSITION NETWORK (ATN) parsers (Woods 1970, Bates 1978, Johnson 1983, Charniak and McDermott 1985). An ATN parser takes its grammar as a directed network whose nodes are states and whose arcs are labeled with tests that must be satisfied for their traversal and with actions that are performed if the arc is traversed. The parser itself is non-deterministic; if more than one arc may be traversed from a given state with a given input, it chooses one at random, and if it subsequently finds itself in a state from which it cannot proceed, it backs up and makes a different choice.

Although Paragram is a Marcus parser, there are several differences between it and Parsifal. First, although deterministic, Paragram is not "strictly" deterministic in the sense that Parsifal is; that is, unlike Parsifal, it is allowed in certain special cases to modify the parse tree that it is building. One of these is sentences that require lowering, such as (1-25):

(1-25)   Ross believes Nadia to have invented the three-ring binder.

in which the object, *Nadia*, is lowered into the verb complement sentence so that it can be parsed as (1-26):

(1-26)   Ross believes that Nadia invented the three-ring binder.

The second difference is in the type of grammar rules that each parser uses. Both parsers have grammars that are based quite closely on traditional standard transformational syntax (Chomsky 1965). However, Parsifal does not distinguish base-structure rules from transformational rules, but rather requires both types to be expressed in a single formalism (which is essentially a reverse transformation). On the other hand, like standard transformational grammars, Paragram maintains the distinction between the two types of rule, greatly simplifying the grammar. Unfortunately, the separation is not as clean as one would like, and the grammar writer cannot be blind to the fact that each base rule is actually converted by the grammar interpreter into a set of the other type of rule.

Third, Paragram can parse ill-formed sentences. If no rule pattern can be found that exactly matches the input buffer, Paragram attempts to find the nearest match, and proceeds from there. In the same situation, Parsifal simply gives up. I do not explicitly make use of this feature of Paragram in this work.

In using Paragram for the work described herein, it was necessary to modify its grammar somewhat. These changes will be described in the appropriate sections.

1.4 Policy statements

In addition to the biases mentioned elsewhere (such as my anti-anti-syntax position; *see section 1.1.1*), two other attitudes that pervade this book should be made explicit:

1. Psychological reality. The primary aim of the research is to build an artificial intelligence system; if the system performs as intended, then it has achieved its goal, regardless of whether or not any claims can be made for the system's being a model of human cognitive mechanisms. However, it is often a good strategy in AI to consider cognitive modeling anyway; finding out how people do something and trying to copy them is a good way to get a program to do the same thing (*cf.* Ringle 1983). Moreover, claims that can be made about the psychological reality of an AI program's mechanisms are interesting in their own right, even if they are not central to the research. For these reasons, therefore, we will where appropriate look at psycholinguistic research on how people deal with the language-understanding problems that we are trying to handle computationally.

2. Artificial difficulties. It is necessary in artificial intelligence to distinguish between genuine hard problems and artificial ones. A common form of argument in AI against the adequacy of a procedure or rule is to show that it cannot handle some particular hard case. Often, however, the cases cited are pathological ones that are not true counterexamples. For example, one can construct sentences with many horrible interacting ambiguities that will probably defy resolution by the mechanisms developed in this research. However, such sentences usually turn out to be "artificial"—that is, they are not sentences that would ever turn up in real, considerate discourse, and if, by accident, they did, they would probably defy resolution by the human sentence-understanding mechanism as well.

In general, people often misunderstand hard ambiguities. Sometimes their resolution mechanism notices the problem and applies conscious error-recovery procedures that we will not consider further herein. Sometimes the problem is not detected, and the mechanism confidently returns an answer that is wrong, or an answer that is correct but is so by luck rather than by science.[32] It would be wrong

---

[32]For examples of garden-path ambiguities that fool people, see section 4.3.2.

to expect an AI system to do better.[33] It is therefore necessary to be very careful when considering counterexamples to make sure that they are "genuine". At present, our only tool for this is our sharp, unbiased intuition.

---

[33]The reader familiar with it should note that my point here is NOT simply Wilks's (1975e) argument that "there will always be a counterexample for any AI system". For a discussion of Wilks's view, see Hirst 1976.

Part I

Semantic Interpretation

2   Semantic interpretation

2.1 Introduction

In this chapter, I look at previous approaches to semantics and semantic interpretation in linguistics and NLU. The work I will examine addresses one or more of the following questions:

- What kind of formalism, representation, or model can adequately capture the semantics of a natural language utterance? That is, what is a "semantic object"?

- What kind of process can map a natural language utterance to these semantic objects?

- Can these semantic objects be used in artificial intelligence applications? Once a sentence has been interpreted, how can its meaning be applied by the system to which it was input?

All three questions are of interest to AI researchers, but linguists care only about the first two and philosophers only about the first. We should therefore not be surprised or too disappointed if, in looking at work on semantics outside AI, we find that it stops short of where we wanted to go. Conversely, we may also find that a semantic theory is adequate for AI without satisfying the linguists or philosophers.

It is worth emphasizing the point that our concerns in semantics are not identical to everyone else's. We can identify two distinct (but obviously related) concerns (*cf.*Winograd 1984):

- The study of abstract meaning and its relation to language and the world.

- The study of how agents understand the meaning of a linguistic utterance in the world.

Too often the label *doing semantics* is used vaguely to mean one or the other of these, or some random, shifting mixture of both, and the word *semantics* is unwittingly used differently by different participants in discussions. In this research, our concern is the second of those above. We will, of course, look at work on the other, and try hard not to get ourselves too confused.

What exactly is it that we are looking for in a semantic theory? We can identify the following properties as desirable:[1]

- The semantic objects, whatever they are, must be amenable to computational manipulation, supporting inference and problem solving.

- The theory must account for the relationship between the meaning of a sentence and the meanings of its components; that is, the theory must be compositional.

- The theory must show what role syntactic structure plays in the meaning of a sentence (Tarnawsky 1982: 113).

- The theory should be able to deal with intensions, opaque contexts, generics, and the like.

- The theory must relate semantics to syntax in such a way as to be able to provide feedback to a parser. (Preferably, the theory should allow the earlier parts of a sentence to be interpreted even before the later parts are seen or heard, as human sentence comprehension clearly has this property.)

Most of these properties are self-explanatory once I have defined the terms; skip to the next section if you know the terms already. An INTENSION may best be thought of as a description, an individual instantiation of which is its EXTENSION. For example, in (2-1), the noun phrase *the president* refers to an intension:

(2-1)   The president is elected every four years.

That is, it doesn't follow from (2-1) that if George Washington is the president, then George Washington is elected every four years; (2-1) has a DE DICTO reading. In a different context, the same noun phrase can also refer to an extension, that is, have a DE RE reading:

(2-2)   The president was discussing foreign policy with his horse when a White House aide arrived with the bad news.

A sentence can have both an intensional and extensional reading; (2-3) could refer to whoever is president or to George Washington in particular:

(2-3)   The president has too much power.

An OPAQUE or OBLIQUE CONTEXT is one in which referential substitution cannot occur. For example, even if Nadia's pet unicorn is a Montague semanticist, we cannot conclude from (2-4):

(2-4)   Ross believes that Nadia's pet unicorn is persecuting him.

that (2-5) holds:

(2-5)   Ross believes that a Montague semanticist is persecuting him.

---

[1]Conspicuously missing from the desiderata is the requirement (Tarnawsky 1982) that the theory account for the processes of meaning acquisition and meaning extension. I will have nothing to say on these matters.

as Ross may be unaware of the unicorn's particular field of research.

A GENERIC noun phrase is one intended to refer to all members of the class of which it is an instance. Thus (2-6) is intended to be true of all golden tamarins and all cats:

(2-6)   The golden tamarin is smaller than a cat, but twice as cute.

By COMPOSITIONALITY we mean that the meaning of the whole is a systematic function of the meaning of the parts.[2] At first glance this sounds trivial; if the noun phrase *my pet penguin* denotes by itself some particular entity, namely the one sitting on my lap as I write this paragraph, then we do not expect it to refer to a different entity when it is embedded in the sentence *I love my pet penguin*, and a semantic system that did not reflect this would be a loser indeed. Yet there are alternatives to compositional semantics.

The first alternative is that the meaning of the whole is a function of not just the parts but also the situation in which the sentence is uttered. For example, the possessive in English is highly dependent upon pragmatics; the phrase *my penguin* could refer, in different circumstances, to the penguin that I own, to the one that I am now carrying but don't actually own, or to the one that I just bet on at the penguin races. My definition of semantic interpretation in section 1.1.1 excluded this sort of consideration, but this should not be regarded as uncontroversial.

The second alternative is that the meaning of the whole is not a *systematic* function of the parts in any reasonable sense of the word, but rather that the meaning of an individual word varies idiosyncratically with the other words in the same sentence. We will see an example of a semantic system with this property in section 2.3.1. Generally, non-compositional semantics can get very messy. Maintaining compositionality permits us to apply our semantic techniques, whatever they might be, recursively to a sentence and each of its components, in a uniform (and, we hope, elegant) manner. In section 3.8 we will examine some of the limitations of compositional semantics.

The requirement that the theory be able to interpret the first part of the sentence even before the rest is seen is not strictly necessary. It does, however, accord with our intuition on how people understand sentences (Swinney 1982; Marslen-Wilson and Tyler 1980) *(see section 2.4)*. The result of hearing (2-7):

(2-7)   Ross gave Nadia the ...

is some kind of mental structure representing Ross giving something to Nadia, and if the sentence broke off completely after the *the*, the hearer could still answer the question *Whom did Ross give something to?* To be able to provide an interpretation

---

[2]By *parts*, we mean of course syntactically well-formed parts. We do not expect there to be a meaning to the substrings *again Nadia* or *mother's industrial* in sentence (i):

(i)   If Ross brings that sheepdog to our meditation session again, Nadia is going to have to borrow her mother's industrial vacuum cleaner.

of a constituent as soon as it is complete seems also a desirable property for a computer NLU system, especially one that may have to use the context of the first part of the sentence to resolve ambiguity in a later part. A suitably compositional semantic theory should be able to meet this need.

2.2 Semantic interpretation and linguistic theory

In this section I look at two semantic theories from linguistics. The first is decompositional semantics, the second model-theoretic semantics.

2.2.1 Decompositional semantics

Theories of decompositional semantics[3] attempt to represent the meaning of each word by decomposing it into a set of semantic primitives. For example, the word *chair* could be represented as shown in (2-8) (Katz 1972, JD Fodor 1977: 148):

(2-8)   (Object), (Physical), (Non-living), (Artifact),
          (Furniture), (Portable), (Something with legs),
          (Something with a back), (Something with a seat),
          (Seat for one)

In practice, such a lexical decomposition program is problematic. It is extremely difficult, if not perhaps impossible in principle (see Kempson 1977: 96–101 for discussion), to find a suitable, linguistically universal collection of semantically primitive elements in which all words (of all languages) could be decomposed into their necessary properties. For example, not all the properties shown in (2-8) are defining features of a chair, or are even present in all modern chairs, and yet they seem necessary in distinguishing chairs from other seating equipment (JD Fodor 1977: 148). Even simple words whose meanings seem straightforward are extremely difficult to characterize (Winograd 1976). Decompositional semantics is also problematic in its notion of how a sentence is represented (JD Fodor 1977: 160–165). One cannot simply hang the representations of the individual words from the parse tree of a sentence and call the result the meaning, for that would predict that the slightest variation in syntactic structure changes the meaning of the sentence. But a "less structured" approach does not work well either; Katz and JA Fodor (1963) simply strung the word representations together in order thus:

---

[3] I do not attempt to list or catalogue here the many theories that come under the heading of decompositional semantics; perhaps the best-known versions are those of Katz and JA Fodor (1963) and Jackendoff (1972). JD Fodor 1977, Kempson 1977, and Tarnawsky 1982 may be consulted for detailed reviews of various theories. See also Nida 1975 for a detailed example of such a theory.

(2-9)   The man hits the colorful ball.
          ```
          [Some contextually definite] → (Physical Object) →
          (Human) → (Adult) → (Male) → (Action) → (Instancy)
          → (Intensity) → [Collides with an impact] →
          [Some contextually definite] → (Physical Object) →
          (Color) → [[Abounding in contrast and variety
          of bright colors] [Having globular shape]]
          ```

It is by no means clear what to do with a thing like that, but obviously it fails to satisfy the requirement that a semantic theory show the contribution to meaning of a sentence's syntactic structure.

In particular, these problems can be seen to be fatal in any consideration of the theory for use in NLU. Representing a word as a set of primitives is by itself useless when the theory can provide neither a suitable structure for putting them together to represent a sentence, nor methods for deep inference in context upon the resultant structures.[4] There have been attempts in AI to make decompositional semantics usable by adding these missing elements to the theory. Notable among these are the Preference Semantics system of Wilks (1973, 1975a, 1975b, 1975c, 1975d) and the early conceptual dependency representations of Schank (*e.g.*, 1973, 1975); in particular, Schank had a principled system for building his primitives into a structure that represented a sentence and performing inference upon it.[5] I will return to this point in section 2.3.3.

> The result of decomposition is usually compost.
> —Nadia Talent[6]

2.2.2 *Model-theoretic and truth-conditional semantics*

In his well-known "PTQ" paper (Montague 1973), Richard Montague presented the complete syntax and semantics for a small fragment of English. Although it was limited in vocabulary and syntactic complexity,[7] Montague's fragment dealt

---

[4]Nor does decompositional semantics even constitute an adequate semantic theory from a linguistic standpoint, since all that has happened in a decompositional analysis is that one set of symbols has been translated into another set, without any relationship being specified between the world and that new set. For critiques of decompositional semantics see Putnam 1970, Winograd 1976, and Tarnawsky 1982.

[5]As Waltz (1982) points out, Schank's set of primitives is incomplete and is unable to capture nuances of meaning; the embedding of conceptual dependency representations in Schank's newer, larger memory structures (*e.g.*, Schank and Abelson 1977, Schank 1982a, 1982b) is of no help. Waltz proposes a decompositional representation intended to capture subtle differences in verb meaning (see also DeJong and Waltz 1983).

[6]Personal communication, 22 February 1983.

[7]Hausser (1984) has significantly extended the fragment, much modifying the system in the process.

with such semantic problems as intensions and opaque contexts, different types of predication with the word *be*, and the "THE TEMPERATURE IS NINETY" PROBLEM.[8] Montague's formalism is exceedingly complex, and I make no attempt to present it here, discussing rather the formalism's important theoretical properties. The reader interested in the details will find Dowty, Wall, and Peters 1981 (hereafter *DWP*) a useful introduction.

Montague's theory is TRUTH-CONDITIONAL and MODEL-THEORETIC. By *truth-conditional* we mean that the meaning of a sentence is the set of necessary and sufficient conditions for the sentence to be TRUE, that is, to correspond to a state of affairs in the world (DWP 1981:4–6). By *model-theoretic* we mean that the theory uses a formal mathematical model of the world in order to set up relationships between linguistic elements and their meanings. Thus semantic objects will be entities in this model, namely individuals and set-theoretic constructs defined on entities. Since sentences are not limited to statements about the present world as it actually is, Montague employs a set of POSSIBLE WORLDS; the truth of a sentence is then relative to a chosen possible world and point in time (DWP 1981:10–13). A possible world–time pair is called an INDEX.

Montague takes the word to be the basic unit of meaning, assuming that for each index there is an entity in the model for each word of the language. The same entity could be represented by more than one word, of course: thus at some index, the words *unicorn* and *pigeon* could denote the same set of individuals— in particular, they could both denote the empty set. The converse, an ambiguous word representing different entities in different linguistic contexts but at the same index, was not allowed in Montague's formalism; this matter is dealt with at length in Part II of this book.

For Montague, then, semantic objects, the results of the semantic translation, are such things as INDIVIDUALS in (the model of) the world, INDIVIDUAL CONCEPTS (which are functions to individuals from the set of indexes), properties of individual concepts, and functions of functions of functions. At the top level, the meaning of a sentence is a truth condition relative to an index. These semantic objects are represented by expressions of an INTENSIONAL LOGIC; that is, instead of translating English directly into these objects, a sentence is first translated to an expression of intensional logic for which, in turn, there exists an interpretation in the model in terms of these semantic objects.

Montague has a strong THEORY OF TYPES for his semantic objects: a set of types that corresponds to types of syntactic constituents. Thus, given a particular syntactic category such as proper noun or adverb, Montague was able to say that the

---

[8] That is, to ensure that (i):

(i)   The temperature is 90 and the temperature is rising.

cannot lead to the inference (ii):

(ii)   90 is rising.

meaning of a constituent of that category is a semantic object of such and such a type.[9] Montague's system of types is recursively defined, with individuals, truth values, and intensions as primitives, and other types defined as functions from one type to another in such a manner that if syntactic category X is formed by adding category Y to category Z, then the type corresponding to Z is functions from senses of the type of Y to the type of X.[10]

Montague's system contains a set of syntactic rules and a set of semantic rules, and the two are in one-to-one correspondence. Each time a particular syntactic rule applies, so does the corresponding semantic rule; while the one operates on some syntactic elements to create a new element, the other operates on the corresponding semantic objects to create a new object that will correspond to the new syntactic element. Thus the two sets of rules operate in TANDEM.

The syntactic rules are a simple categorial (Ajdukiewicz) grammar (see DWP 1981: 182). A typical rule is (2-10), the rule for combining a noun and a determiner to make a noun phrase:

(2-10)   If ζ is a noun, then *every* ζ and *the* ζ are noun phrases, and so is *a* ζ or *an* ζ according as ζ takes *a* or *an*.

The words *every*, *the*, *a*, and *an* are said to be introduced by the rule SYNCATE-GOREMATICALLY. Many rules just concatenate constituents:

(2-11)   If δ is a sentence-taking verb phrase and β is a sentence, then $\delta\beta$ is an intransitive verb phrase. [Example: *believe that + John loves a unicorn*]

There are three types of semantic rule. The first type is basic rules that just provide translations of most individual words. The second type translates syntactic constituents with syncategorematic words in them. Here is the semantic rule that corresponds to the noun-phrase rule above:

(2-12)   If ζ translates into ζ', then *every* ζ translates into:
$$\lambda P \left[\forall x \left[\zeta'(x) \Rightarrow P\{x\}\right]\right];$$
the ζ translates into:
$$\lambda P \left[\exists y \left[\forall x \left[\zeta'(x) \Leftrightarrow x = y\right] \wedge P\{y\}\right]\right];$$
and *a* ζ and *an* ζ translate into:
$$\lambda P \left[\exists x \left[\zeta'(x) \wedge P\{x\}\right]\right],$$
where $P\{x\}$ denotes the application of the EXTENSION of P to x.

(You needn't be worried if this doesn't mean a great deal to you; all you need to notice is that the translation of the noun phrase is a function—in particular, a function in intensional logic—that includes the translation of the noun.) The third type of semantic rule is rules of functional application: the translation of the

---

[9]To be precise: the semantic type of a proper noun is *set of properties of individual concepts*; that of an adverb is *function between sets of individual concepts* (DWP 1981: 183, 187).

[10]For example, the semantic type of prepositions is *functions mapping senses of the semantic type of noun phrases to the semantic type of prepositional phrases*.

new constituent is formed by functionally applying the translation of one of its components to the other. The rule that corresponds to (2-11) is this:

(2-13)   If the translation of δ is the function δ′ and that of β is β′, then the translation of δβ is δ′(ˆβ′), where ˆβ′ denotes the intension of β′.

Because of the strong typing, the tandem operation of the two non-basic types of rule, and the fact that the output of a semantic rule is always a systematic function of its input, Montague semantics is compositional. (Because verb phrases are generally analyzed right to left, however, many constituents are uninterpreted until the sentence is complete.)

Although Montague semantics has much to recommend it, it is not possible to implement it directly in a practical NLU system, for two reasons. The first is that Montague semantics as currently formulated is computationally impractical. It throws around huge sets, infinite objects, functions of functions, and piles of possible worlds with great abandon. Friedman, Moran, and DS Warren (1978a) point out that in the smallest possible Montague system, one with two entities and two points of reference, there are, for example, $2^{2^{522}}$ elements in the class of possible denotations of prepositions, each element being a set containing 2^{512} ordered pairs.[11]

The second reason we can't use Montague semantics directly is that truth-conditional semantics is not useful in AI. We are interested not so much in whether a state of affairs is or could be true in some possible world, but rather in the state of affairs itself; thus AI uses KNOWLEDGE-BASE SEMANTICS in which semantic objects tend to be symbols or expressions in a declarative or procedural knowledge-representation system (*see section 2.3.2*). Moreover, truth-conditional semantics really only deals with declarative sentences (DWP 1981: 13) (though there has been work attempting to extend Montague's work to other types of sentence; *e.g.*, Hamblin 1973); a practical NLU system needs to be able to deal with commands and questions as well as declarative sentences.

There have, however, been attempts to take the intensional logic that Montague uses as an intermediate step in his translations and give it a new interpretation in terms of AI–type semantic objects, thus preserving all other aspects of Montague's approach; see, for example, the paper of Hobbs and Rosenschein (1977) and Smith's (1979) objections to their approach. There has also been interest in using the intensional logic itself (or something similar) as an AI representation[12] (*e.g.*, Moore 1981). But while it may be possible to make limited use of inten-

---

[11]Despite this problem, Friedman, Moran, and DS Warren (1978b, 1978c) have implemented Montague semantics computationally, using techniques for maintaining partially specified models. However, their system is intended as a tool for understanding Montague semantics better rather than as a usable NLU system (1978b: 26).

[12]Ironically, Montague regarded intensional logic merely as a convenience in specifying his translation, and one that was completely irrelevant to the substance of his semantic theories.

sional logic expressions,[13] there are many problems that need to be solved before intensional logic or other flavors of higher-order logical forms could support the type of inference and problem solving that AI requires of its semantic representations; see Moore 1981 for a useful discussion. Moreover, Gallin (1975) has shown Montague's intensional logic to be incomplete. (See also the discussion of work using logical forms, in section 8.3.1.)

Nevertheless, it is possible to use many aspects of Montague's approach to semantics in AI (*cf.* DS Warren 1985). The semantic interpreter that I will describe in Chapter 3 has several of the properties of Montague semantics that we described above, and I therefore refer to it as "Montague-inspired".

> If your thesis is utterly vacuous,
> Use first-order predicate calculus.
>   With sufficient formality,
>   The sheerest banality
> Will be hailed by all as miraculous.

> But for theses you fear indefensible,
> Reach for semantics intensional.
>   Your committee will stammer
>   Over Montague grammar,
> Not admitting it's incomprehensible.

> —Henry Kautz[14]

2.3 Semantic interpretation and artificial intelligence

The development of artificial intelligence has necessarily included much research on knowledge-representation formalisms and systems. Two major classes of representation have been used:

- Logical representations: predicate logic, higher-order logic, various forms of intensional logic (*e.g.*, Moore 1981, DS Warren 1983). A knowledge base consists of assertions in the formalism that are known to be true.

- Knowledge structures: semantic nets, frames, scripts, etc. (*e.g.*, Charniak 1976, Schank and Abelson 1977). A knowledge base consists of a set of data objects in a structure that denotes relationships between the objects.

The two classes are not antithetical; indeed, predicate calculus is isomorphic to a simple semantic network or frame system. Representations such as Frail, described in section 1.3.1, attempt a synthesis that provides the advantages of both classes. (Note, however, my remarks in the previous section about higher-order logic as an AI representation.)

---

[13]Godden (1981) in fact uses them for simple translation between Thai and English.

[14]Personal communication.

Regardless of the representation used, a knowledge base can be thought of as a model of a world in exactly the sense used in model-theoretic semantics *(see section 2.2.2)*.[15] That is, it provides a way of deciding the truth of a statement about the world that it represents: a true statement is one that is represented in the knowledge base or is provable from it, and a false statement is one whose negation is true. In practice, of course, incompleteness of the knowledge base or Gödelian orneriness will make some statements undecidable.

In this section I look at semantic theories from artificial intelligence. I will use three theories as representatives of AI: procedural semantics, knowledge semantics, and object-oriented semantics. The theories differ in the degree to which the entities that they use are INTERPRETED. Thus, the theories represent three points on a spectrum; many AI systems may be considered hybrids that fall elsewhere on the line.[16] I will be arguing that things are best at the object-oriented end (the interpreted end) of the line.

2.3.1 Procedural semantics and Woods's semantic interpreter

Research on semantic interpretation in artificial intelligence goes back to William Woods's dissertation (1967, 1968),[17] which introduced PROCEDURAL SEMANTICS to NLU in a natural-language front-end for an airline reservation system. Input sentences were translated into procedure calls that retrieved information from a database, and the meaning of a sentence was identified with the corresponding procedure call. For example:

(2-14)   AA-57 is non-stop from Boston to Chicago.
          `equal (numstops (aa-57, boston, chicago), 0)`

(2-15)   They serve breakfast on flight AA-57.
          `mealserv (aa-57, breakfast)`

(2-16)   Every flight that leaves Boston is a jet.
          `(for every X1/flight: depart (X1, boston); jet (X1))`

(2-17)   What is the departure time of AA-57 from Boston?
          `list (dtime (aa-57, boston))`

(2-18)   Does AA-57 belong to American Airlines?
          `test (equal (owner (aa-57), american-airlines))`

---

[15] This is not to say that the knowledge base will necessarily meet the formal requirements of a model for any particular model-theoretic system, such as Montague's.

[16] This spectrum is, in principle, independent of the two classes of representation mentioned above. In practice, however, frame systems tend to be at the interpreted end of the line, and logic systems closer to the other end.

[17] See section 1.2 of Woods 1967 for the relevant prehistory. See Simmons and Burger 1968 and Wilks 1968 for approaches contemporary to Woods's.

Thus the representation is essentially first-order. Note that the system accepted only questions for retrieval from the database, not declarative sentences for updating it, a point that will be important later. Nevertheless, for simplicity I follow Woods's style of showing most example sentences in a "raw" declarative form, rather than an interrogative form. The representation of the interrogative form was the declarative form given as an argument to the procedures `test` (for *yes/no* questions) or `list` (for *wh-* questions), which formatted the output accordingly. For example, in (2-18), the procedure `equal` will check for the equality of its arguments, and return `true` or `false`; the procedure `test` will then present the result to the user as *yes* or *no*.

Woods's system had rules with patterns that, when they matched part of the parsed input sentence, contributed a string to the semantic representation of the sentence. This string was usually constructed from the terminals of the matched parse tree fragment. The strings were combined to form the procedure call that, when evaluated, retrieved the appropriate database information. The rules were mostly rather ad hoc; they looked for certain key items in the parse tree, and their output was quite unconstrained. For example, the rule that applied to (2-14) was this:

```
(2-19)   1-(G1: flight((1)) and (2) = be) and
         2-(G4: (1) = non-stop) and
         3-(G3: (1) = from and place((2))) and
         4-(G3: (1) = to and place((2)))
         => equal (numstops (1-1, 3-2, 4-2), 0)
```

`G1`, `G3`, and `G4` are the names of partial parse-tree patterns; for example, `G1` is the partial S tree with an NP labeled `(1)` and a VP with a verb labeled `(2)`. The first line of the rule thus matches a sentence that starts with a noun phrase that is a **flight** and whose verb is *be*. The subsequent lines require an adjective phrase *non-stop* and two prepositional phrases, one with *from* and a **place**, the other with *to* and a **place**. If these conditions are satisfied, then the string specified in the last line of the rule results. In the string, items of the form $x-y$ are replaced by the yth node of the pattern matched on line x of the rule; thus $3-2$ will be replaced by the place name in the *from* PP. Note that the word *non-stop* does not appear in the output at all; rather, it has been syncategorematically changed into `equal (numstops (...), 0)` by the rule. The verb of the sentence does not appear in the output either, not even in disguise.

We can identify two major shortcomings of this system: as the above example suggests, it is ad hoc and non-compositional. Table 2.1 shows how the interpretation of the verb *depart* varies as different prepositional phrases are attached to it (Woods 1967: A-43–A-46).[18] This variation is possible because the rules are both

---

[18]I have simplified a little here in order to make my point. In fact, sentences like those with prepositional phrases in table 2.1 would actually cause the execution of two semantic rules: one for the

very specific and very powerful. For example, rule (2-19) could not handle sentence (2-14) if its verb were changed to a synonym, even though the verb itself is not used in the output:

(2-20)   AA-57 flies non-stop from Boston to Chicago.

(2-21)   AA-57 goes non-stop from Boston to Chicago.

The rule could, of course, be extended to look for these other verbs as well as *be*, but the point is that the system is inherently unable to handle such synonymy except by exhaustively listing synonyms in each rule in which they might occur. And (2-19) is also tied to a very particular sentence structure; separate rules would be needed for paraphrases:

(2-22)   AA-57 doesn't stop between Boston and Chicago.

Moreover, the output is not tied in any way to the input; a rule can ignore any or all of its input, or make syncategorematic changes that are quite inconsistent with those of other rules.[19]

Non-compositionality was necessitated by the particular set of primitives that Woods used, selected for being "atomic" concepts in the domain of discourse (1967: 7-4–7-11) rather than for promoting compositionality.[20] Woods's semantics could probably be made reasonably compositional by appropriate adjustment of the procedure calls into which sentences are translated. However, the system would still not be compositional BY DESIGN, and it would be easy to inadvertently lose compositionality again when extending the system. The problem is that the rules are too powerful.

Adding an ability to update the database would also be antithetical to compositionality in the system, for then either the meaning of a procedure would have to vary with context, or the translation of the whole sentence would have to vary with sentence form. To see the problem, consider the sentence (2-23):

(2-23)   AA-57 is non-stop from Boston to Chicago.

---

complete sentence, and one for the subsentence it happens to contain, *AA-57 departs from Boston*. The resulting interpretation would be the conjunction of the output from each rule (Woods 1967: 9-5):

(i)   AA-57 departs from Boston to Chicago.

(ii)   `depart (aa-57, boston) and connect (aa-57, boston, chicago)`

Woods left it open (1967: 9-7) as to how the semantic redundancy in such expressions should be handled, but one of his suggestions is a filter that would remove conjuncts implied by others, giving, in this case, the interpretations shown in table 2.1.

[19]Nor is there anything preventing the construction of rules that would result in conjunctions with conflicting, rather than merely redundant, terms.

[20]DS Warren (1983) points out that a first-order representation, such as Woods's, is inadequate in principle if both compositionality and a suitable typing are to be maintained.

Table 2.1. *Noncompositionality in Woods's system*

AA-57 departs from Boston.
```
depart (aa-57, boston)
```

AA-57 departs from Boston to Chicago.
```
connect (aa-57, boston, chicago)
```

AA-57 departs from Boston on Monday.
```
dday (aa-57, boston, monday)
```

AA-57 departs from Boston at 8:00 a.m.
```
equal (dtime (aa-57, boston), 8:00am)
```

AA-57 departs from Boston after 8:00 a.m.
```
greater (dtime (aa-57, boston), 8:00am)
```

AA-57 departs from Boston before 8:00 a.m.
```
greater (8:00am, dtime (aa-57, boston))
```

Previously, I said that the "raw" meaning of this sentence was (2-24):

(2-24)   equal (numstops (aa-57, boston, chicago), 0)

and that therefore the meaning of the interrogative form, (2-25):

(2-25)   Is AA-57 non-stop from Boston to Chicago?

is (2-26):

(2-26)   test (equal (numstops (aa-57, boston, chicago), 0))

But if we are to allow sentence (2-23) as input to modify the database, we have to think more carefully about its translation. Possibilities include its "raw" form, (2-24), and a form more analogous to (2-26), such as (2-27):

(2-27)   assert (equal (numstops (aa-57, boston, chicago), 0))

But in either case, the meaning of `equal` has suddenly changed; instead of being a predicate, it is now an assignment statement. The alternative is to translate (2-26) into an entirely different procedure call:

(2-28)   make-equal (numstops (aa-57, boston, chicago), 0)

We must thus choose from two unpalatable situations: one is to say that `equal` shall somehow be sensitive to the context in which it is called and adjust its behavior accordingly (a dubious idea both semantically and from a programming viewpoint); the other is to double the number of rules and predicates needed in the system, having one set for interrogative forms, another for declaratives, again defeating compositionality.[21]

Another problem with Woods's approach is that semantic interpretation necessarily occurs after the parsing of the sentence is complete, and so the interpretation of the first part of the sentence is not yet available to aid the parser if a structural ambiguity arises later in the sentence.[22] Some later versions (*e.g.*, that of Woods, Kaplan, and Nash-Webber 1972) had the parser keep all the information necessary to back up and look for a different parse if the first one found turned out to be semantically unacceptable *(see section 6.3.1)*.

The status of procedural semantics itself as a theory of semantics has been a matter of considerable controversy (Woods 1975, Johnson-Laird 1977, JA Fodor 1978, Johnson-Laird 1978, JA Fodor 1979, Woods 1981, Wilks 1982a). There are many variations, but the gist of procedural semantics as a semantic theory is that the meaning of a sentence is the procedure into which the sentence is compiled, either in the computer or in the mind; the procedure itself can be seen as the intension of the sentence, and the result of the execution as the extension. (Woods himself would not agree with this; he argues that truth-conditionality must also play a role (Woods 1981).)

The notion of a procedure is so basic to computation that procedural semantics seems a very natural approach for AI, and it has been used in many systems, including the well-known LUNAR natural language system (Woods, Kaplan, and Nash-Webber 1972). Since its original incarnation it has been refined considerably and is still today perhaps the predominant approach, despite its problems and its essentially ad hoc nature. However, in its pure form as described above, procedural semantics is not adequate for AI, because the procedures themselves do not have an adequate interpretation and the items they manipulate are uninterpreted symbols. This is not a difficulty if one is just inserting or retrieving database values with little or no interpretation,[23] but if one is interested in maintaining and manipulating a knowledge base, performing inference, solving problems, and the like, procedural semantics suffers from the same problem as decompositional se-

---

[21] It may be possible to circumvent this problem by the use of a Prolog-like database language; such a language would have the same procedural–declarative ambiguity, but would resolve the ambiguity in context:

(i)   :- equal (x, y) .

(ii)   equal (x, y) :- .

[22] In addition, because the interpretation of the sentence itself proceeds bottom-up but not left to right, the resolution of intrasentence reference is problematic; see Hirst 1981a[1]: 36–37.

[23] The construction of natural language interfaces to databases whose contents have little meaning to the interface is, of course, still an important area of research. The best interfaces, such as TEAM (Archbold, Grosz, and Sagalowicz 1981; Grosz 1983; Martin, Appelt, and Pereira 1983), have a vocabulary that lets them talk about database fields with words other than the fields' literal names.

mantics: symbols have been translated into other symbols, but the new symbols are scarcely easier to deal with than the old ones.

2.3.2 Knowledge semantics

The AI knowledge base–centered view of semantics has been called KNOWLEDGE SEMANTICS by Tarnawsky (1982). It is Tarnawsky's view that "the meaning of a sentence depends on the knowledge of the interpreter" (1982: ii) and includes the propositions, possibly infinite in number,[24] entailed by the sentence with respect to that knowledge. Tarnawsky formalized a semantic theory in which a knowledge base played a central role. In his approach, semantic interpretation takes as its input surface structures enriched with Chomskyan traces (*e.g.*, Chomsky 1975) and with anaphoric references resolved. Transformational rules then map a surface structure to a statement in higher-order predicate logic, which is added to the knowledge base.[25]

To the extent that each assumes a database in which the system's knowledge is stored, there is an obvious similarity between knowledge semantics and procedural semantics. There are two major differences between the two. First, in knowledge semantics it is the statement added to the knowledge base and the consequences of its addition, rather than the request to add it, that is taken to be the meaning of the sentence.[26] The second is in the attitude toward that knowledge base. Procedural semantics places no semantic burden on the content of the knowledge base; rather, the claim is that the meaning of a sentence inheres in the database manipulation procedures into which it is translated. Knowledge semantics, on the other hand, construes the content of the database, and the inferences generated by the addition of a new item, as the entities in which meaning inheres. The problem of differing representations for declarative and interrogative forms does not arise in knowledge semantics, as the process that translates sentences into knowledge base entries is reasonably compositional—compositional at the SYMBOL-MANIPULATION level, that is; knowledge semantics does not, however, make the MEANING of the whole a systematic function of the meaning of the parts, because it ascribes no meaning to the parts. This is because the knowledge base provides a semantic model for sentences but not for the components of the sentences. For example (Tarnawsky 1982: 159–160):

---

[24] In AI, of course, the number of inferences that result from the addition of a sentence to the knowledge base is finite, and, further, systems carefully restrict the inferences that may be made. Just what should be inferred is still a matter of controversy, however; see Charniak 1976[1].

[25] Thus, again, the entire sentence must be present before semantic interpretation commences.

[26] Interestingly, questions are not taken as requests to retrieve information from the knowledge base. Rather, it is simply predicated that the sentence is interrogative; that a reply might be appropriate is a possible, but not necessary, entailment of the predication (Tarnawsky 1982: 226–230). This reflects the fact that not all questions are really requests for information.

(2-29)   The man ate the kutya.

```
ate (the (man), the (kutya))
```

The semantic interpretation is composed of the same words as the input sentence; it has been restructured, but the symbols themselves have not in any sense been interpreted. The knowledge base may or may not know what kutya is, that is it may or may not contain other assertions about kutya, but it will nowhere contain anything that represents kutya per se. Likewise, constituents such as prepositional phrases cannot be represented, for if the meaning of a sentence includes the inferences it entails in the knowledge base, then what could be the meaning, the inferences entailed, from a fragment such as *with a knife*, even if mapped by the system into a representation such as `with (a (knife))`? There is no semantic object per se in the system that represents *with a knife* and that can combine compositionally with that of a constituent such as *John cut*. Tarnawsky claims (personal communication) that the system could be extended to handle subsentence-level constituents, but I am skeptical of this claim.

Because symbols have no direct interpretation in the knowledge base, the burden of resolving coreferential expressions is placed upon the inference mechanism. Consider, for example, the style often used in news reports:

(2-30)   MONTREAL—Hard-line separatist Guy Bertrand is pulling out all the stops in his bid to topple his opponents and become the new leader of the Parti Québécois.

    The fiery Quebec City lawyer yesterday unveiled a detailed plan of his vision of an independent Quebec that would start with close economic ties to the United States and a new currency for Quebec—the U.S. dollar.[27]

If this text is to be understood, then the second sentence must be recognized as an expansion of the first, with coreference relations between *Guy Bertrand* and *the fiery Quebec City lawyer*, and between *pulling out all the stops ...* and *unveil[ing] a detailed plan ....* This may be done by profligate inference. Any time something is predicated true of *the fiery Quebec City lawyer*, it is inferred to be true of *Guy Bertrand*, of *Mr Bertrand*, of *the dark horse of the PQ leadership race*, and so on. But an inference must be generated for each of the large if not infinite number of different ways an entity in the predicate can be described, an effect that is multiplicative if there is more than one entity in the predicate. This was not a concern for Tarnawsky, who was interested in creating a competence theory, but has obvious problems in any direct computer implementation.[28]

Knowledge semantics is also weak in dealing with case relationships, and makes an artificial distinction between cases flagged by syntactic position and those flagged by a preposition *(section 1.1.2)*. Consider these examples:[29]

---

[27] *The Globe and Mail*, 14 August 1985.

[28] See also section 8.2.2 for another diatribe against uninterpreted symbols.

[29] The first is based on Tarnawsky's structure for *The man loves the girl* (1982: 172); the second is given by Tarnawsky (1982: 183).

(2-31) John hit the nail.
```
hit (John, the (nail))
```

(2-32) John hit the nail with a hammer.
```
with (hit) (John, the (nail), a (hammer))
```

The case flag *with* seems to become a function that operates on the predicate `hit` to change its expected argument structure. Syntactic position seems to be represented by argument position, although syntactic position does not in English unambiguously determine the case it flags; *e.g.*, the system will erroneously ascribe *The hammer hit the nail* a structure similar to (2-31). Tarnawsky (personal communication) believes case to be purely a surface or syntactic phenomenon, and that inference in the knowledge base, rather than case structure in the input predicate, is what counts. Again, this position may be acceptable for a competence theory, but does not seem tenable in a computer implementation.

2.3.3 Object-oriented semantics

We saw in the previous section that Tarnawsky's theory uses higher-order predicate logic as a representation, and thus represents sentences but not the entities to which they refer. That is, the logical statements of the knowledge base may be regarded as interpreted, in that there is a process that generates valid inferences from them, but the components of the statements are still uninterpreted symbols.

We can solve this problem by using a suitable knowledge structure, such as semantic nets or frames *(see sections 1.2 and 1.3.1)*, for our representation. The uninterpreted symbols of the logical statements can then be replaced by references to the appropriate piece of the knowledge structure—let's assume it will be a frame. For example, we replace the string `kutya` in the present representation with a pointer to the frame that represents **kutya**. A lexicon maps words and phrases to their frame representations; synonyms are mapped to the same representation. The pointer for the kutya frame may happen to be the string `kutya`, but this is coincidental; the semantics of this pointer are quite different from those of the similar string in knowledge semantics. If the word *kutya* is represented by a pointer to the **kutya** frame, the frame then provides an interpretation for it and permits access to whatever is known about kutya. Similarly, the frame system gives a method for determining a unique referent for a definite reference. Thus *Nadia, the teacher,* and *my aunt's brother's chaquette* can all be mapped to, and thus interpreted by, the same frame.

A suitable knowledge-structure system thus provides a firmer basis for semantic interpretation than procedural semantics and knowledge semantics do. In particular, it provides a deeper level of interpretation and a more adequate account of reference. It is this approach that I will develop in chapter 3.

2.4 Psycholinguistic research on semantic interpretation

I will touch only briefly upon psycholinguistic research on semantic interpretation. Matters of psychological reality are not immediately relevant to most of the issues discussed in this chapter, and, unlike lexical disambiguation *(section 4.3)*, there are as yet few psycholinguistic data to support an AI approach to semantic interpretation motivated by psychological reality.

However, one aspect of semantic interpretation in which psychological data are relevant is the relationship between syntax and semantics. Are they psychologically separate processes? If so, what is the nature of their interaction?

As we have already observed *(section 2.1)*, it is intuitively obvious that people, unlike LUNAR *(section 2.3.1)* or knowledge semantics *(section 2.3.2)*, do not delay interpreting a sentence until after they have finished parsing it. Rather, semantic interpretation seems to run either in tandem with or closely behind the word-by-word input of the sentence, and semantic and pragmatic information from the earlier parts of the sentence is used to help interpret the later parts (Marslen-Wilson and Tyler 1980). The general approach is "do it as early as possible". Experiments by Marslen-Wilson and Tyler (1980; Tyler and Marslen-Wilson 1982) suggest the reality of separate lexical, syntactic and semantic, and pragmatic knowledge, though the reality of separate processes to use each knowledge source does not necessarily follow *(cf.* footnote 4 of chapter 1).[30] Marslen-Wilson and Tyler suggest a model with BOTTOM-UP PRIORITY, that is, a model in which the lower levels of knowledge have priority over the higher levels. "The system allows for top-down effects in the loose sense that contextual information affects the recognition process. But it does not allow for top-down effects in the more precise sense of the term," in which likely inputs are pre-selected even before the sensory data have been received (Marslen-Wilson and Tyler 1980:62). In a similar vein, Stanovich (1980, 1984) has argued that purely top-down or bottom-up models cannot explain experimental data on individual differences in reading skills.

The high degree of uncertainty in present psycholinguistic results makes it premature to base AI models of semantic interpretation on psychological data. However, it is clear that an AI semantic interpreter should, at least, follow the principles of "do it as early as possible" and bottom-up priority.

> I always get buggered by the bottom-up approach.
> —Rogatien "Gatemouth" Cumberbatch[31]

---

[30] See Forster 1979 for evidence for the autonomy of lexical, syntactic, and semantic processing. Bever (1970) and Reimold (1976) suggest a different division of serial autonomous processes.

[31] While presenting a paper at the first national conference of the Canadian Society for the Computational Studies of Intelligence / Société canadienne pour l'étude de l'intelligence par ordinateur, Vancouver, 26 August 1976.

2.5 Qualities desirable in a semantic interpreter

With the discussion of the previous sections in mind, we now review exactly what it is that we desire in our own semantic interpreter (*cf. section 2.1*).

1. Compositionality. Compositionality is clearly a desideratum. We want each syntactically well-formed component of a sentence to correspond to a semantic object, and we want that object to retain its identity even when it forms part of a larger semantic object.

2. Semantic objects. We saw in section 2.3.3 the advantages of a knowledge-structure representation. If we adopt such a representation—in particular, a frame representation *(see sections 1.2 and 1.3.1)*—we can then take the elements of the system—frames, slots, statements, etc.—as our semantic objects.

3. Not ad hoc. One of the goals of this work is to reduce ad hoc–ness in semantic interpretation, so the next requirement is that the system be elegant and without the unnecessary power in which such messiness can purulate. The semantic rules or formalism should be able to manipulate semantic objects and build new ones, but the rules should not be able to mangle the semantic objects (jeopardizing compositionality), and each should be general and well-motivated. The rules must also be able to take into account the contribution of a sentence's syntactic structure to its meaning.

4. Feedback for the parser. We would like the interpreter to work in parallel with the parser, in order to be able to give it the feedback necessary for structural disambiguation, and we require that the representation of the partially interpreted sentence always be a well-formed semantic object in order that it be used in this way.

5. Lexical ambiguity. It must be possible for ambiguous words to be assigned a unique sense in the representation, and for this to happen as soon after the occurrence of the word as possible.

6. Semantic complexities. The semantic interpreter should be able to deal with all the complexities of semantics that Montague and others have dealt with. These include such things as intension, opaque contexts, generics, complex quantification, and so on.

In Chapter 3, I will describe Absity, a semantic interpreter constructed with these desiderata in mind. It will fulfill the first five of them, and provide a basis for future work on the sixth.

> Like everybody who is not in love, he imagined that one chose the person whom one loved after endless deliberations ... on the strength of various qualities and advantages.
> —Marcel Proust[32]

---

[32]*Remembrance of things past.* 1913.

3   The Absity semantic interpreter

A great interpreter ought not to need interpretation.
—John Morley[1]

3.1 Introduction

In this chapter, I describe the Absity semantic interpreter.[2] Absity meets five of the six requirements for an interpreter listed in section 2.5, and provides a foundation for further research in meeting the remaining requirement.

Absity is part of the artificial intelligence research project at Brown University that was described in section 1.3. It uses one of the project's parsers, Paragram *(see section 1.3.1)*, and the project's frame representation language, Frail *(section 1.3.2)*. The implementation to be described is therefore necessarily dependent upon the nature of these other components, as are many aspects of Absity's design. Nevertheless, in keeping with the goals of this work, the design has been kept as independent as possible of the representation formalism and the parser. The main ideas in Absity should be usable with other representations that have a suitable notion of semantic object and also, in particular, with other parsers, transformational or otherwise.

The organization of this chapter is as follows. In the first half, Absity is gradually built up, by explaining alternately a strategy and then its use in Absity. I then give some examples and some implementation details. In the second half, Absity is put on trial, and its strengths and weaknesses are evaluated.

3.2 Two strategies: Strong typing and tandem processing

In the design of Absity, we will make use of two features of Montague's formalism *(see section 2.2.2)*: a strong typing of semantic objects, and running syntax and semantics not just in parallel but in tandem. These strategies will allow us to simplify the system of semantic rules.

---

[1] MORLEY, John [Viscount Morley of Blackburn]. *Emerson*. New York: Macmillan, 1884.

[2] The name is short for "A Better Semantic Interpreter Than Yours".

By a typing of objects, you will recall, we meant that there are a number of different kinds of object, and each object is of one kind or another—that is, every object has a type. Further, there are some basic, or primitive, types of object, and other types of object are constructed from them; from these, yet other types of object may be constructed, and so on recursively. For example, let X and Y be object types. Then any new object constructed from an object of type X and one of type Y would be of a new type (call it $X+Y$), as would all objects so constructed. It need not be the case that any two types can combine to form another; there may be restrictions on what can combine with what. Clearly, conventional syntactic categories form an object typing like this. Montague also imposed a similar typing upon semantic objects in his formalism, and, in particular, a typing that was in one-to-one correspondence with the typing of the syntactic objects. So, all elements of any given syntactic type are interpreted as corresponding to objects of the same semantic type, and if two syntactic types combined to form a third, then the corresponding semantic types would combine to form the semantic type corresponding to the third. We also will adopt this procedure.

This makes the tandem operation of syntactic and semantic processing very easy. We can now, like Montague, also put our syntactic and semantic construction rules in one-to-one correspondence, so that when the parser constructs a new constituent with some particular syntactic rule, the corresponding semantic rule can be invoked to make the object that will serve as that constituent's representation, in the manner described above. Note, however, that we cannot simply have one semantic rule for EACH syntactic rule, as Montague did. Montague's syntax was very simple, and each of its rules was in fact a CONSTRUCTION RULE. But we cannot assume that this property is true of parsers in general—indeed, it couldn't be true of any but the simplest parser. We therefore need to determine which of the parser's rules or actions are construction rules and therefore require a corresponding semantic construction rule. In the grammar of the Paragram parser, the set of construction rules turns out to be exactly the set of base rules. This should not be surprising; in many transformational theories of grammar, including at least one of Chomsky's (1965: 132), base rules are those that determine the deep structure and the sentence's meaning, while transformations can only make changes to the syntactic structure that do not affect the meaning.[3]

By adopting these two strategies, we have implicitly satisfied the fourth of the requirements in section 2.5, that semantic processing be able to provide feedback to the parser. By having the semantic interpreter proceed in parallel with the parser and by ensuring that the representation of a partially interpreted sentence is always a well-formed semantic object, we ensure that the fullest possible amount of semantic information is always available for the parser to use.

---

[3] Similarly, in her synthesis of transformational syntax with Montague semantics, Partee (1973, 1975) observes that the semantic rule corresponding to many transformations will simply be the identity mapping.

Table 3.1. *Types in the Frail frame language*

BASIC TYPES

Frame
```
(penguin ?x), (love ?x)
```

Slot
```
color, agent
```

Frame determiner
```
(the ?x), (a ?x)
```

OTHER TYPES

Slot–filler pair = slot + frame statement
```
(color=red), (agent=(the ?x (fish ?x)))
```

Frame descriptor = frame + slot–filler pair*
```
(penguin ?x (owner=Nadia)),
(love ?x (agent=Ross) (patient=Nadia)),
(dog ?x)
```

Frame statement or instance
          = frame determiner + frame descriptor
```
(the ?x (penguin ?x (owner=Nadia))),
(a ?x (love ?x (agent=Ross)
            (patient=Nadia))),
(the ?x (dog ?x)),
penguin87 [an instance]
```

3.3 The typing system of Absity

In the previous section, we decided upon the use of a strong typing on the semantic objects. I now introduce such a typing on the elements of the Frail language, and a correspondence between the typing and the lexical categories of English.

The basic elements of Frail are shown in table 3.1, with examples of each. The three basic types are (GENERIC) FRAME, SLOT, and FRAME DETERMINER FUNCTION.[4] The notation for a frame is a list with the frame name and a free variable; the variable is denoted by a question-mark prefix. Thus (penguin ?x) is the penguin frame (which may or may not have something to do with penguins, depending on whether the frame name, which is only an arbitrary symbol, has mnemonic significance for the human observer). A slot is denoted simply by its symbolic name—*e.g.*, agent. The notation for a frame determiner is a list with the function name and a free variable—for example, (the ?x). Do not let the notational sim-

---

[4]If you don't find these self-explanatory, see sections 1.2 and 1.3.1.

ilarity of frames and frame determiners confound you; the two are very different kinds of object—a frame is a data structure, and a frame determiner is a function.

The types that are built from these basic types are SLOT–FILLER PAIR, FRAME DESCRIPTOR, and INSTANCE or FRAME STATEMENT. A slot–filler pair (sometimes *sf-pair* for short) consists of the name of a slot and a value to fill that slot.[5] The value will be a frame statement or instance (to be defined in a moment). The notation for a slot–filler pair is a list of the slot and the value, with an equals sign between them: `(color=red)`.

A frame descriptor is a complete description of a generic frame. It can be used by frame determiner functions when searching the knowledge base for a frame to match that description, and when creating a new instance of a frame of that description. A frame descriptor is composed of a frame with zero or more slot–filler pairs added; thus the frame `(penguin ?x)` is also a frame descriptor, and so is `(penguin ?x (color=red))`. Note that the variable in the frame is still unbound.

A frame statement is a complete knowledge-base access statement in Frail. It is formed by giving a frame descriptor as an argument to a frame determiner function; for example, `(the ?x)` plus `(penguin ?x (color=red))` gives (3-1):

(3-1)   `(the ?y (penguin ?y (color=red)))`

When the two are combined, the free variable in the frame descriptor is bound to the variable in the frame determiner, for which a unique new name is automatically generated. (For simplicity of exposition, I will assume in most of the discussion that variable names are magically correct from the start.) A frame statement can be EVALUATED by Frail, and the result is a FRAME INSTANCE—the unique symbolic name of the particular instantiation of the frame described by the frame descriptor that the frame determiner function caused to be inserted into or retrieved from the knowledge base. For example, the result of evaluating (3-1) might be the instance `penguin87`, one of several instances of the `penguin` frame that the system happens to know about.[6] Because a frame statement can always be turned into an instance by evaluation, the type system of Absity does not distinguish the two, and one may appear wherever the other is allowed.

The correspondence between these semantic types and the syntactic categories of English is shown in table 3.2. This correspondence satisfies the requirements imposed by our application of rules in tandem. For example, a preposition corre-

---

[5] For those not up on typographic subtleties: A slot-filler (spelled with a hyphen) is that which fills a slot; a slot–filler (spelled with an en dash) is the combination of a slot and a slot-filler.

[6] For mnemonic purposes, instances created by Absity as it operates are given names formed by adding digits to the end of the frame name. Instances predefined in the knowledge base, on the other hand, may have been given names even more descriptive. Thus `red` is an instance of the `visible-color` frame, and in other circumstances might have been called, say, `visible-color34`.

Table 3.2. *Type correspondences in Absity*

SYNTACTIC TYPE	SEMANTIC TYPE
Sentence	Frame statement, instance
Sentence body	Frame descriptor
Proper noun phrase	Frame statement, instance
Pronoun	Frame statement, instance
Common noun	Frame
Adjective	Slot–filler pair
Determiner	Frame determiner
Noun phrase	Frame statement, instance
Preposition	Slot name
Prepositional phrase	Slot–filler pair
Subordinate conjunction	Slot name
Subordinate clause	Slot–filler pair
Verb	(Action) frame
Adverb	Slot–filler pair
Auxiliary	Slot–filler pair
Verb phrase	Frame descriptor
Clause end	Frame determiner

sponds to a slot, a noun phrase to a frame statement, and their product, a prepositional phrase, corresponds to a slot–filler pair, as required.

Clearly, table 3.2 makes some very strong claims about the nature of representation systems and language—that a noun in some sense IS a frame, a preposition IS a slot, and so on. The starting point for these claims is Charniak's paper "The case–slot identity theory" (1981c), which argues for the plausibility (and meaningfulness) of the theory that the senses of a verb may be identified with the generic frames of a frame representation, their cases with the slots of the frames, and the noun phrases that fill cases with things that can fill frame slots.[7] Many of the type correspondences of table 3.2 follow immediately from this. It is already asserted that a verb is a frame; if a case is a slot, then a case-flagging preposition must be a slot name; a case-filling noun phrase must be a frame instance; and a prepositional phrase must be a slot–filler pair, as must an adverb. Sentences acting as

---

[7] If you are unfamiliar with case theory, see section 1.1.2.

noun phrases can also fill cases, as in (3-2):

(3-2)   Ross knew <u>that Nadia sought revenge for the trout incident</u>.

so they too must be frame instances—in particular, a sentence will be an instance of the frame that represents the verb of the sentence. Similarly, subordinate conjunct-ions—those such as *because* and *when* that conjoin subordinate clauses with main clauses—can be slots, so that they can combine with sentences to make subordinate clauses slot–filler pairs.[8]

The other types mostly follow as a corollary of the above. If a noun phrase is an instance, then the head noun must be a frame; noun modifiers—adjectives and relative clauses—must be things that qualify a frame; and the noun phrase's deter-miner must be something to instantiate a frame, *i.e.*, a frame determiner function. It seems reasonable that the type of a descriptive adjective may be the simplest kind of qualifier, namely a slot–filler pair; a prepositional phrase that qualifies a noun may also be a slot–filler pair, just like other PPs. A relative clause, however, must be of the same type as other sentences, an instance, or else our strong typ-ing is ruined. This is not a problem, however, if we allow the combination of an instance with another instance to which it refers. For example, this noun phrase:

(3-3)   the grey cat that Ross loves

becomes these two instances, one for the matrix NP and one for the relative clause:

(3-4)   `(the ?x (cat ?x (color=grey)))`
         and
         `(a ?y (love ?y (agent=Ross) (patient=WH)))`

where `WH` represents the relative pronoun *that*, a pointer to the first frame instance. These may then be combined into this Frail representation for the complete NP:

(3-5)   `(the ?x (cat ?x (color=grey)`
         `            (a ?y (love ?y (agent=Ross)`
         `                           (patient=?x)))))`

which asserts that the `cat` sought has two properties: that its `color` is `grey`, and that there is a `love` frame whose `agent` is `Ross` in which it participates as `patient`.

Proper noun phrases, such as *Dr Henry Kissinger*, correspond directly to an instance and therefore need no frame determiner. The same is true of pronouns. On the other hand, all common noun phrases will need a determiner, to turn a frame descriptor into an instance. We therefore make the reasonable assumption that all common NPs do have a determiner, even though it may be null; that is, the null determiner has an associated type and semantics. To see that this is reasonable, we need only consider these sentences (where ∅ marks a null determiner):

(3-6)   Ross likes the cats.

---

[8]I do not treat COORDINATE conjunctions, such as *and* and *or*, in Absity.

(3-7)   Ross likes $\varnothing$ cats.

(3-8)   Ross likes all cats.

As we can see, $\varnothing$ in English often has much the same meaning as *all*. Now, strong typing requires $\varnothing$ *cats* to have the same type as the corresponding NP of the other sentences, a frame instance. But if $\varnothing$ contributed nothing, then the word *cats* would also be a frame instance, identical in all three sentences, implying that *the* and *all* also contribute nothing, an unacceptable conclusion. In the next section I will show how null words can be handled in Absity.

Verb qualifiers, both auxiliaries and adverbs, can be slot–filler pairs on the frame of the verb; their behavior is just like that of adjectives with nouns. A verb phrase is thus a frame descriptor, so we need to find a frame determiner somewhere to turn it into an instance when its construction is complete.[9] A convenient way to do this is to construe the end of the VP itself as corresponding to the frame determiner; that is, the clause end is to be to a verb phrase what a determiner is to a noun phrase. How this may be done will be shown in the next section.

3.4 Another strategy: Turning meaningful syntax into words

In section 3.3, I said that case-flagging prepositions correspond to Frail slots. But cases can also be flagged by syntactic position—by the fact of the filler being in the subject, object, or indirect object position of the sentence. Clearly, Absity needs to have semantic objects—slots—that correspond to these syntactic case flags. Up till now, however, we have tacitly assumed that semantic objects corresponded only to syntactic objects;[10] after all, most of a sentence's meaning comes from the words of the sentence and their grouping into syntactic components, and it seems natural, therefore, to build the meaning of a sentence by taking the individual word meanings and assembling them according to the dictates of syntactic structure. Including syntactic position seems to work against the goal of compositionality— the meaning of the whole would be more than a function of the meaning of the parts. Further, it seems to require us to complicate the semantic rules so that they can deal with the contribution of syntactic position, and thus appears to threaten the strong typing and tandem processing.

There is, however, an easy way around the problem—PRETEND that syntactic positions are words just like the real words of the sentence. In fact, we will carry out the pretense to the extent that we will require the parser to INSERT these pretend words into the sentence, and Absity to then treat them as if they had been in there all along. We will use three such words: *SUBJ*, *OBJ*, and *INDOBJ*, corresponding to

---

[9]I have implicitly equated verb phrases with clause bodies in this statement; the justification for this will become clear in the next section.

[10]The fact of being in subject position is not a syntactic object in the sense that a prepositional phrase is.

the syntactic positions of subject, object, and indirect object. Further, since they are case flags, we will deem our new words to be prepositions; we will sometimes call them PSEUDO-PREPOSITIONS to distinguish them from "natural" prepositions.

So, for example, a sentence like (3-9):

(3-9) Nadia gave Ross a pewter centipede for his birthday, because she knew that he didn't have one already.

will become, and will be parsed as, (3-10):

(3-10) SUBJ Nadia gave INDOBJ Ross OBJ a pewter centipede for his birthday, because SUBJ she knew OBJ that SUBJ he didn't have OBJ one already.

The insertion of pseudo-prepositions requires us to modify our syntax for a simple sentence slightly. Previously, the base rules of the Paragram parser included these conventional rules:

(3-11)   S → NP AUX VP
           VP → V [NP] [NP] PP*

The NPs in these rules are, of course, the subject, object, and indirect object. The new rules are these:[11]

(3-12)   S → PP AUX VP
           VP → V PP*

In the case of Paragram, the base rules of the grammar may be amended directly as shown, and it is straightforward to modify the transformational rules so that they insert pseudo-prepositions at the appropriate places.

The principle of inserting pretend words can also be used in two other cases. The first is the need to treat null determiners as "real". For this, we can just get the parser to insert the PSEUDO-DETERMINER *NULLDET* into any common noun phrase that needs it. Similarly, the VP-DETERMINER *CLEND* (for *clause-end*) can be added by the parser; the sentence punctuation itself serves as a clause-end marker for a major sentence.[12] Collectively, we call our new lexemes PSEUDO-WORDS.

---

[11]We retain the notion of a VP in the syntactic structure in order to handle verb complements and predicates.

[12]Paragram and Parsifal (Marcus 1980) also treat punctuation marks as syntactic objects, and so does Hausser (1984) in his extension of Montague semantics, so this approach is not unprecedented or unorthodox.

He hath found the meaning.
—William Shakespeare[13]

3.5 The semantic rules of Absity

The semantic rules of Absity follow immediately from the results of the preceding sections. Tandem processing means that each rule will simply combine two or more semantic objects to make a new one. What the objects are will be given by the corresponding syntactic rule, their types will be as given by table 3.2, and they will be combined as defined in table 3.1.

Some examples will make our semantic interpreter clearer. First, let's consider a simple noun phrase, *the book*. From table 3.2, the semantic type for the determiner *the* is a frame determiner function, in this case `(the ?x)`, and the type for the noun *book* is a kind of frame, here `(book ?x)`. These are combined in the canonical way shown in table 3.1—the frame name is added as an argument to the frame determiner function—and the result, `(the ?x (book ?x))`, is a Frail frame statement (which evaluates to an instance) that represents the unique book referred to.[14]

Next, consider *the red book*. A descriptive adjective corresponds to a slot–filler pair; so, for example, *red* is represented by `(color=red)`, where `color` is the name of a slot and `red` is a frame instance, the name of a frame. A slot–filler pair can be added as an argument to a frame, so *the red book* would have the semantic interpretation `(the ?x (book ?x (color=red)))`.

Now let's consider a complete sentence:

(3-13)   Nadia bought the book from a store in the mall.

Table 3.3 shows the representation for each component of the sentence; note that in the table the basic noun phrases have already been formed in the manner described above. Also, we have inserted the pseudo-prepositional subject and object markers *SUBJ* and *OBJ*, and represent the clause end with a period. For simplicity, we assume that each word is unambiguous (disambiguation procedures are discussed in chapter 5); we also ignore the tense of the verb. Table 3.4 shows the next four stages in the interpretation. First, noun phrases and their prepositions are combined into prepositional phrases; their semantic objects form slot–filler pairs. Then, second, the prepositional phrase *in the mall* can be attached to *a store* (since a noun phrase, being a frame, can have a slot–filler pair added to it), and the prepositional phrase *from a store in the mall* is formed. The third stage shown in the table is the attachment of the slot–filler pairs for the three top-level prepositional phrases to the frame representing the verb. Finally, the period, which is translated as a frame

---

[13]SHAKESPEARE, William. *Pericles, Prince of Tyre*. 1608. I, i, 143.

[14]Recall that it is the responsibility of Frail to determine, with the help of the discourse focus, which one of the books that it may know about is the correct one in context *(sections 1.3.1 and 3.6)*.

Table 3.3. *Absity example*

WORD OR PHRASE	SEMANTIC OBJECT
SUBJ	`agent`
Nadia	`(the ?x (person ?x` `   (propername="Nadia")))`
bought	`(buy ?x)`
OBJ	`patient`
the book	`(the ?y (book ?y))`
from	`source`
a store	`(a ?z (store ?z))`
in	`location`
the mall	`(the ?w (mall ?w))`
. [period]	`(a ?u)`

determiner function, causes instantiation of the `buy` frame, and the translation is complete.

The next examples show how Absity translates *yes/no* and *wh-* questions. We will use interrogative forms of the previous example:

(3-14)   Did Nadia buy the book from a store in the mall?

(3-15)   What did Nadia buy from a store in the mall?

Sentence (3-14) has almost the same parse as the previous example, and hence almost the same translation. The only difference is that the frame determiner for the clause is now `(question ?x)`, the translation of *?*, instead of `(a ?x)`; thus the translation is (3-16):

```
(3-16)    (question ?u
             (buy ?u
                (agent=(the ?x (person ?x
                   (propername="Nadia"))))
                (patient=(the ?y (book ?y)))
                (source=(a ?z (store ?z
                   (location=(the ?w (mall ?w)))))))))
```

In a complete NLU system, it would be the responsibility of the language generator to take the result of this Frail call, which will be either `nil` or the matching instance or instances, and turn it into a suitable English reply, such as *No, she didn't.*[15]

---

[15] If the answer is negative, a helpful system might then proceed to look for an instance that is a near

Table 3.4. *Absity example (continued)*

SUBJ Nadia
```
(agent=(the ?x
  (person ?x (propername="Nadia"))))
```
OBJ the book
```
(patient=(the ?y (book ?y)))
```
in the mall
```
(location=(the ?w (mall ?w)))
```

---

a store in the mall
```
(a ?z (store ?z
  (location=(the ?w (mall ?w)))))
```
from a store in the mall
```
(source=(a ?z (store ?z
  (location=(the ?w (mall ?w))))))
```

Nadia bought the book from a store in the mall
```
(buy ?u
  (agent=(the ?x (person ?x
    (propername="Nadia"))))
  (patient=(the ?y (book ?y)))
  (source=(a ?z (store ?z
    (location=(the ?w (mall ?w)))))))
```

Nadia bought the book from a store in the mall.
```
(a ?u
  (buy ?u
    (agent=(the ?x (person ?x
      (propername="Nadia"))))
    (patient=(the ?y (book ?y)))
    (source=(a ?z (store ?z
      (location=(the ?w (mall ?w))))))))
```

---

match, and present that to the user:

(i)   No, she didn't, but Ross did.

(The need to find near matches for a frame also occurs in disambiguation, and is discussed in sections 7.2.4 and 7.3.2.) If the answer is positive, a good reply generator would try to determine the salient part of the matching instance—often that which matched the indefinite (a ?x) in the query—to give a reply of the form:

(ii)   Yes, at Bobby's Booktique.

For the *wh-* question, (3-15), we make use of the fact that (question ?x) returns the bindings of its free variables. The translation will be (3-17):

```
(3-17)    (question ?u
              (buy ?u
                  (agent=(the ?x (person ?x
                      (propername="Nadia"))))
                  (patient=?WH)
                  (source=(a ?z (store ?z
                      (location=(the ?w (mall ?w)))))))))
```

Notice that *what* has been translated as the free variable ?WH. As before, the call will return either nil or an instance list, but in the latter case the list will include the bindings found for ?WH, *i.e.*, the book that Nadia bought. The reply generator would use the bindings to compose a suitable answer.

These examples have assumed that the parser has provided all the right information whenever it was needed. This assumption, however, is unrealistic; we must allow for the fact that many parsers (all parsers?), including Paragram, will not necessarily do the syntactic operations in the "correct" order for Absity. Consider, for example, the noun phrase *the cute rabbit*, to be parsed by this Paragram base rule:

(3-18)   NP → DET ADJ N

The lexicon lists the semantic objects corresponding to the three words of the NP as follows:

(3-19)   the = (the ?x)   *(frame determiner)*
              cute = (appearance=cute)   *(slot–filler pair)*
             rabbit = (rabbit ?x)   *(frame name)*

Now, strictly speaking, our approach requires that we combine these three in one operation, the result being a frame statement:

(3-20)   (the ?x (rabbit ?x (appearance=cute)))

In fact, Paragram will not execute (3-18) as a unitary operation, but will proceed left to right, first pulling in the determiner, then the adjective, and then the noun; intermediate structures will be created in the process and transformational rules (without semantic counterparts) may possibly apply.

We therefore must add some new semantic types to Absity, types that will only be used "internally", whose necessity will depend upon the parser. For example, the partial noun phrase *the cute* will have the type:

(3-21)   *frame-statement/frame-name*

which can be thought of as "a thing that will become a frame statement when combined with a frame name". (The notation is intended to suggest that of generalized phrase structure grammars (Gazdar 1982) or categorial grammars, in which *A=B* denotes an *A* that is missing its *B*.) The rule for the creation of this type would be this:

(3-22)   *frame-statement/frame-name = frame-determiner + sf-pair*

The exact representation of these SLASH TYPES is unimportant, and a list of components is almost enough; thus *the cute* could be represented by (3-23):

(3-23)   `[(the ?x) (appearance=cute)]`

This isn't quite adequate, because there could be several sf-pairs, for several adjectives, as in *the cute brown*; thus we really need a list of lists:

(3-24)   `[(the ?x) [(appearance=cute) (color=brown)]]`

Note that this also implies another type formation rule, saying that we can keep adding new sf-pairs to a frame-statement/frame-name:

(3-25)   *frame-statement/frame-name = frame-statement/frame-name + sf-pair*

Other slash types may be created as a given parser necessitates it.

> A lewd interpreter? But come, I'll tell thee all my whole device.
> —William Shakespeare[16]

3.6 Implementation details

The careful reader will have noticed that although there has been no direct contradiction, the Frail expressions that I have shown above have been rather different in form from those that I showed in section 1.3.1. In fact, what I have shown above is not really Frail at all, but a meta-notation for Frail that is translated into real Frail by a simple translator. There are two reasons for doing this:

- Frame determiners, as I said in section 1.3.1, are not part of Frail, but sit on top of it. Most of Absity's Frail calls are actually calls on the frame determiners.

- The syntax of Frail is messy and less compositional than its semantics. The meta-notation smooths over some of the cracks.

Ignoring, for the moment, considerations of focus, we may regard (a ?x) as asserting an instance and (the ?x) as retrieving one. We then have the following equivalences:

(3-26)   `(a ?x (marmot ?x (owner=Nadia)))`
          `[instance:  marmot24`
          `            (marmot`
          `                (owner Nadia))]`[17]

---

[16]SHAKESPEARE, William. *The merchant of Venice.* 1596. III, iv, 80–81.

[17]In fact, this is also a meta-notation, provided in this case by Frail, for its even messier lowest-level representation:

(i)   `(assert '(inst marmot24 marmot))`
       `(assert '(:= '(owner marmot24) Nadia))`

where `marmot24` is a name that has been automatically generated, and:

```
(3-27)   (the ?x (marmot ?x (owner=Nadia)))
         (retrieve
           '(and (marmot ?x)
                 (owner ?x Nadia)))
```

These equivalences are still not exact, since `instance:` returns nothing useful, while `(a ?x)` returns the automatically generated instance name; similarly, `retrieve` returns a binding list such as `((?x marmot24))`, while `(the ?x)` will return just the instance name.

Let's now consider focus. Frame determiners have in the present version a very simple idea of focus: it is simply a list of "current" instances *(see section 1.3.1)*. They operate as follows: The function `(the ?x)` translates its argument, as shown above, and sends the retrieval request to Frail. When the results come back, it checks each binding to see if that instance is in the focus list; it expects to find exactly one that is, and complains if it doesn't. The function `(a ?x)` first performs a retrieval in the same manner as `(the ?x)`. It then compares the bindings with the focus list and asserts a new instance; if some of the bindings were in focus, it restricts the instance to being one of these.[18] The plural frame determiners `(the-pl ?x)` and `(some ?x)` (not yet implemented)[19] are similar. The differences are that `(the-pl ?x)` expects either to find more than one match in focus or to match a set in focus; `(some ?x)` also prefers a set.

To avoid having to have lambda binding and lambda conversion in the system, Absity uses a simpler, back-door method to bind one noun phrase to another.[20] This mechanism is presently used in sentences that require equi-NP-insertion. For example:

(3-28)   An obnoxious multi-national corporation wants to hire Nadia.

Sentence (3-28) is usually assumed to be derived from a form like (3-29):

(3-29)   An obnoxious multi-national corporation$_i$ wants [an obnoxious multi-national corporation$_i$ hire Nadia].

The subscript on the NPs indicates their referential identity, and the equi-NP-deletion rule deletes the second occurrence, giving (3-28). Parsing the sentence requires the reverse operation, equi-NP-insertion, making a copy of the sentence subject to serve as the subject of the embedded sentence. This copy is BOUND to the original, to indicate referential identity of the pair.

---

[18] Since Frail can't do this, the function does it instead, keeping a note of the fact tucked away.

[19] Frail cannot yet handle plural determiners; see point 4 of section 3.8.

[20] DS Warren (1983) points out that first-order representations are not powerful enough for NLU, but higher-order representations seem to be too powerful. This back-door mechanism may be considered a nice compromise between the two. It may, however, prove to be insufficiently powerful for future developments in Absity, and lambdas may have to be introduced.

In Absity, this is done by keeping a table of the interpretations of all the NPs in the sentence. The Frail expression under construction does not contain the actual NP interpretations, but only pointers to entries in the table. Thus, two NPs that are bound to one another are represented by pointers to the same table entry. Pointers are, of course, replaced by the table entry when the surface form of the sentence interpretation is printed.

> Our interpreter does it well.
> —William Shakespeare[21]

3.7 Absity as the fulfillment of our dreams

In section 2.5 I listed in six categories the various qualities desired in a semantic interpreter. It is now time to pass judgment upon Absity with respect to these qualities. We will find that the desiderata are numbered so that Absity meets five of the six.

1. Compositionality. Absity is nothing if not compositional. Its semantic rules do little more than combine objects to make new ones, and have no power to ignore or modify semantic objects. In fact, as we shall see in section 3.8 when discussing its shortcomings, Absity is, if anything, a little too compositional.

2. Semantic objects. The frames of Frail have been suitable semantic objects, as predicted.

3. Not ad hoc. The rules of Absity meet our requirement that they be clean and general and not mangle semantic objects (*cf.* point 1 above). By using pseudo-words, Absity also allows the rules to be sensitive to the contributions to meaning of syntax.

4. Feedback for the parser. Absity is able to provide feedback by running in parallel—a fortiori, in tandem—with the parser, with its partial results always being well-formed semantic objects. I will show in chapter 7 how this property may be used in structural disambiguation.

5. Lexical ambiguity. I will show in chapter 5 how Absity supports a lexical disambiguation procedure.

6. Semantic complexities. This is the requirement that is as yet unfilled by Absity, which, as a new system, has not been developed to the point of perfection. In the next section, I describe some of the complexities of semantics that Absity can't handle and show that the prospects for overcoming these defects are good.

---

[21] SHAKESPEARE, William. *All's well that ends well.* 1602. IV, iii, 209.

3.8 What Absity can't do yet

Although it has the virtues listed in the previous section, Absity still falls short of being The Answer To The Semantics Problem. It does, however, provide a base upon which A More Nearly Perfect Semantic Interpreter can be built, and this is why I refer to it (Hirst 1983a) as a "foundation for semantic interpretation".[22] In this section, I discuss the ways in which Absity is not satisfactory and how its inadequacies may one day be cured.

Sometimes I will put some of the blame for Absity's deficiencies on Frail (and frame representations of the current state of the art in general). Frail, you'll recall from section 1.3.1, is an extensional first-order representation (Charniak, Gavin, and Hendler 1983). As such, it is inadequate for the representation of all of the concepts that natural languages such as English can express, for which a higher-order representation seems necessary (DS Warren 1983). (One such representation is the higher-order modal temporal intensional logic used by Montague (1973), which I mentioned briefly in section 2.2.2.) Absity, therefore, occasionally finds itself embarrassed by not having a suitable representation available to it for certain constructs of English. However, in some cases even if Frail were to be magically improved, it would not be straightforward to amend Absity to take advantage of it.

1. Intensions and opaque contexts. Intensions, obviously, are the first item in the list of things that cannot be represented in a purely extensional formalism.[23] For example:

(3-30)   Nadia talked about unicorns.

This sentence is ambiguous: it has an extensional de re meaning, in which it says that there are some particular unicorns about which Nadia talked:

(3-31)   "I met Belinda and Kennapod, the unicorns that live behind the laundromat, as I was walking home tonight," said Nadia.

and an intensional de dicto meaning, in which it simply says that unicorns were the topic of discussion:

(3-32)   "I wonder whether I shall ever meet a unicorn," Nadia mused.

It cannot be inferred from the de dicto reading that any unicorns exist at all, only that the idea or intension of a unicorn does. This distinction is lost upon Frail, which could only represent the extensional meaning, making the inference that there was a particular set of unicorns of which Nadia spoke. A similar problem occurs with (3-33), a sentence used by Bruin *(see section 1.3)*:

(3-33)   Ross ordered a hamburger.

---

[22]Hence also its earlier name, Cement Semantics.

[23]Although intensions CAN be represented in a first-order system; see McCarthy 1979.

The usual reading of this sentence is intensional; Ross is willing to accept anything that meets his criteria of hamburgerness. He has not ordered any particular hamburger, which would be the extensional reading, illustrated by (3-34):

(3-34)   "Please bring me that hamburger that's up there, the third from the right on the second shelf," said Ross.

Nevertheless, Bruin required that (3-33) be translated extensionally, namely as (3-35):

```
(3-35)    [instance:   order34
                    (order
                      (agent Ross)
                      (patient hamburger61))]
```

This says that there is an instance of a hamburger, namely `hamburger61`, that Ross ordered, as in (3-34). Bruin inferred that the exact same hamburger was the one that was then served and eaten (Wong 1981b:157), but this is obviously an unsatisfactory situation.

The reason for this problem is that although Frail contains intensions, namely generic frames, its deductive section supports only reasoning with instances of frames. That is, there is no way to replace the instance `hamburger61` in (3-35) with the generic `hamburger` frame and still have a legal Frail statement that the reasoning component can manipulate. Frail can reason only about individuals, not abstract descriptions.

There has been little work as yet in AI on intensional representations. As soon as first-order representations are left in favor of representations such as the typed lambda-calculus, major problems, such as a lack of decidability, immediately occur (DS Warren 1983). For preliminary work on the topic see Maida 1982, Maida and Shapiro 1982, DS Warren 1983, and Rapaport 1985; for the detection and representation of intensional ambiguities, see Fawcett 1985 or Fawcett and Hirst 1986; for an opinion on why problems of intensions don't matter very much, see Hobbs 1985.

Since Frail does not provide the necessary support, Absity makes no attempt to handle intensions or opaque contexts. Even if intensions could be represented, however, they would be difficult for Absity, because, ironically, it is TOO compositional: the noun phrase rules always take an NP to refer to an extension, and once it is so construed, none of Absity's higher-level rules have the power to change it.

Exactly how this might be fixed would depend on the particular intensional representation. It is reasonable, however, to assume a representation like Montague's intensional logic (1973) with an operator that converts an intension to an extension at a given index. Absity might then treat all NPs as intensional, but add to each a flag that indicates whether the extension operator should be applied to the NP's representation when it is evaluated by the frame language. This flag could be a pseudo-word, and be "disambiguated" to either the extension operator or the identity operator by the same lexical disambiguation procedures described in chapter

5 for other words. An alternative that might be possible with some representations is to conflate this flag with the determiner of the NP. Thus, for example, the *a* of *a unicorn* would be regarded as an ambiguous word that could map to either an intensional or extensional frame-determiner. Whether this is possible would depend on the relationship between frame determiners and intensionality in the particular representation.

2. Stative and dynamic verbs, and habitual actions. Absity is able to deal with both DYNAMIC and STATIVE verbs, but its approach is not extensible to HABITUAL ACTIONS. A dynamic verb is one that describes an action:

(3-36)   Nadia <u>wrote</u> an angry letter to the company president.

while a stative verb describes a continuing state:

(3-37)   Nadia <u>knows</u> how to get to Boston.[24]

We have already seen that dynamic verbs can be represented by Frail instances:

```
(3-38)    [instance:  write34
                 (write
                      (agent Nadia)
                      (patient letter61)
                      (destination president44)]
```

With statives, however, there is no single instance (in the general sense of the word) of an occurrence of the action. This leads to the temptation not to represent statives with instances (in the Frail sense of the word), but rather to use the logic face of Frail and regard a stative as a continuing relationship between its AGENT and its PATIENT:

```
(3-39)    (know Nadia Boston-travel-method61)
```

Giving in to this temptation, however, presents an immediate problem of non-compositionality, and in fact the temptation is resistible, for instances are in fact quite adequate for representing statives:

```
(3-40)    [instance:  know34
                 (know
                      (agent Nadia)
                      (patient Boston-travel-method61)]
```

---

[24] An easy way to distinguish the two is that stative verbs cannot take the progressive aspect (Quirk, Greenbaum, Leech, and Svartvik 1972: 94):

(i)   Nadia <u>is writing</u> an angry letter to the company president.

(ii)   *Nadia <u>is knowing</u> how to get to Boston.

As long as stative verbs are defined as such in Frail, with the appropriate axioms, we can use the same representation for both dynamic and stative verbs and maintain compositionality. Moreover, this is as it should be: a semantic interpreter should not have to worry itself about stativeness, since it is a feature of the meaning of the verb rather than of the word's use. Absity should therefore be able to handle both dynamic and stative verbs identically and let Frail act on each type accordingly. This is the approach that I have adopted.[25]

However, if we accept this analysis, we still have the problem of what to do with sentences that express habitual actions. Habitual actions may be thought of as the generic form of dynamic verbs, but are like statives in that they express a continuing relationship:

(3-41)   Squirrels eat acorns.

(3-42)   Squirrels pursue Nadia.

(3-43)   IBM makes computers.

(3-44)   Nadia visits Ross (daily).

Note that both the subject and the object of a verb expressing an habitual action may be either extensional or intensional; the examples above show all four possible combinations. I have already discussed problems of intension, so let's concentrate on (3-44), in which both NPs are extensional. On the one hand, it is clearly wrong to represent (3-44) as an instance, since it describes many individual acts of visiting; but on the other hand, it seems equally funny to say that Ross and Nadia stand in a relationship of visiting:

(3-45)   #(visits Nadia Ross)

as this suggests that it is true at all points in time that Nadia is visiting Ross—an implication that is false even though (3-44) itself may be true at all points in time.

Because of these problems, we do not extend Absity's treatment of statives to habitual actions. For Absity to be able to handle habitual actions, we will need a suitable representation for them in Frail, and, in particular, a representation consistent with Absity's approach to compositionality. One possibility is a flag, similar to the one posited above for intensions, that is disambiguated appropriately. We will also need a way to decide whether a particular occurrence of a dynamic verb is habitual or not, so that this flag may be set.[26]

3. Predication and identity. In English, the verb *be*, in addition to being an auxiliary, has three primary senses: the PREDICATIVE *be*, which asserts a property; the IDENTITY *be*, which asserts the extensional identity of two intensions; and the

---

[25] Stativeness axioms have not yet been implemented in Frail, however.

[26] In English, it is probably safe to assume that an occurrence of a dynamic verb in the simple present tense represents an habitual action unless there is evidence to the contrary; *cf.* Quirk, Greenbaum, Leech, and Svartvik 1972: 85.

DEFINITIONAL *be*, which asserts the identity of two intensions. The predicative *be* generally takes an adjective phrase (which may reduce to a prepositional phrase) describing the property that the referent of the subject is being said to have:

(3-46)   Ross is exhausted.

(3-47)   Everyone is eager to see what God hath wrought.

(3-48)   Of all the trees in England,
      Her sweet three corners in,
    Only the Ash, the bonnie Ash
      Burns fierce while it is green.[27]

(3-49)   Hi! handsome hunting man
    Fire your little gun.
    Bang! Now the animal
    Is dead and dumb and done.
    Nevermore to peep again, creep again, leap again,
    Eat or sleep or drink again, oh, what fun![28]

(3-50)   To the Puritan all things are impure.[29]

The *be* of identity takes a noun phrase and asserts its extensional identity with the subject NP:

(3-51)   Ambition, in a private man a vice,
    Is, in a prince, the virtue.[30]

(3-52)   Custom, then, is the great guide of human life.[31]

(3-53)   Brothers and sisters I have none,
    But this man's father is my father's son.

The *be* of definition takes a noun phrase, and asserts its intensional identity with the subject NP; that is, it defines the subject:

(3-54)   A classic is something that everybody wants to have read and nobody wants to read.[32]

---

[27] DE LA MARE, Walter John. "Trees". *The complete poems of Walter de la Mare*. London: Faber and Faber, 1969. 180. [*Peacock pie: A book of rhymes.* 1913.] Reprinted by permission of the Literary Trustees of Walter de la Mare and the Society of Authors as their representative.

[28] DE LA MARE, Walter John. "Hi!". *The complete poems of Walter de la Mare*. London: Faber and Faber, 1969. 268. [*Poems for children.* 1930.] Reprinted by permission of the Literary Trustees of Walter de la Mare and the Society of Authors as their representative.

[29] LAWRENCE, David Herbert. *Etruscan places*. New York: Viking Press. 1932.

[30] MASSINGER, Philip. *The bashful lover.* 1636. I, ii.

[31] HUME, David. *An enquiry concerning human understanding.* 1748.

[32] TWAIN, Mark. Attributed.

(3-55)   A cynic is a man who knows the price of everything and the value of nothing.[33]

It was one of the features of Montague's PTQ formalism that it was able to handle both the *be* of identity and the predicative *be* with the same representation for each and with the same mechanisms as used for other verbs.

In frame terms, the *be* of identity asserts that two frame instances previously believed to be different are actually the same. For example, (3-53) says that `person245`, which represents **this man's father**, and `person112`, which represents **my father's son**, should be identified with one another, and anything known to be true of one is therefore now known to be true of the other. The *be* of definition similarly asserts that two generic frames are identical. The predicative *be* asserts the value of a slot in an instance or generic frame. Thus, if *exhausted* translates as `(tiredness=high)` and *Ross* as `Ross`, then (3-46) says that the `tiredness` slot of `Ross` contains the value `high`.

Frail has no innate mechanism for asserting the identity of two instances or two generic frames, and thus cannot at present handle the *be*s of identity and definition. It would be possible, however, to add a mechanism triggered by assertions of the form of, say, (3-56) and (3-57), that toured the knowledge base making the appropriate adjustments:

(3-56)   Nadia is the captain of the football team.
          `(same-instance Nadia captain21)`

(3-57)   A stool is a chair with no back.
          `(definition stool (chair (back=nil)))`[34]

Frail is able to handle the predicative *be*, though non-compositionally and with an awkward syntax. For example, the translation of (3-58) would be as shown:

(3-58)   The block is red.
          `(assert '(:= '(color block23) red))`

---

[33]WILDE, Oscar Fingal O'Flahertie Wills. *Lady Windermere's fan*. 1892.

[34]If the `stool` frame has not been defined previously, then this statement can just reduce to a basic frame definition:

(i)   `[frame:   stool`
         `    isa:   chair`
         `  slots:   (back=nil)]`

However, if the statement is intended to provide new information about a predefined frame, then Frail's very strict view of the ISA hierarchy *(see sections 1.2 and 1.3.1)* may result in a conflict between the old and new definition. In the present example, if the frames `stool` and `chair` had already been defined as siblings in the hierarchy with, say, `seat` as their parent, then the attempt to redefine `stool` would cause Frail to fail. On the other hand, if `stool` had been placed below `chair` in the hierarchy, there would be no problem.

   Another problem, which may occur if `stool` is undefined in Frail when the sentence occurs, is that the word *stool* is also undefined in the lexicon. Neither Paragram nor Absity can yet handle such a situation with suitable grace.

This assigns the instance `red` to the `color` slot of `block23`. A generic predication has a slightly different syntax:

(3-59)   The ash is green.
        `(assert '(:= '(color (ash)) green))`

Clearly, compositionality will be a serious problem in adding *be* to Absity, as the sentence itself will not correspond to an instance. A partial solution may be achieved by recognizing that the syntax of predications is different from that of other sentences that we have looked at above. Thus, we might add this rule to the base grammar:

(3-60)   S → NP BE ADJ

where BE is a new syntactic category for *be*.[35] Let us then introduce two new semantic types: a PREDICATOR, which will be a basic type corresponding to the category BE, and a PREDICATION, formed from a predicator, an instance (the type of NPs), and a slot–filler pair (the type of adjectives). Thus, we could have the following translation:

(3-61)   The block is red.
        `(slot-value (the ?x (block x)) (color=red))`

where `slot-value` is the predicator that is the translation of *be* and turns its arguments into the form required by Frail, as shown in (3-58) above. When intensions are added to Absity, as discussed earlier, (3-59) may be handled in a similar manner.

It should be pointed out that this solution is still problematic, because sentences now have two different semantic types: instances and predications. As long as we are dealing only with simple sentences like the examples above, we can turn a blind eye to the problem. However, when a predication is used as a subsentence, type conflicts will arise; compare:

(3-62)   Ross knows that Nadia fed Daryel.
        `(a ?x`
        `    (know ?x`
        `        (agent=Ross)`
        `        (patient=(a ?y (feed ?y`
        `                            (agent=Nadia)`
        `                            (patient=Daryel))))))`

(3-63)   Ross knows that the block is red.
        `(a ?x`
        `    (know ?x`
        `        (agent=Ross)`

---

[35]The category BE will also include a few other words that act similarly, such as *become*, *wax*, and *turn*. These words tend to imply change as well as predication, and I will not discuss this additional complexity; see Somers 1983:258.

```
                    (patient=(slot-value (the ?x (block x))
                                         (color=red))))))
```

The translation of (3-63) is obviously unsatisfactory, and some method by which a predication can at least masquerade as an instance is needed.

We can extend the method we used for predicative *be*s to identity *be*s. These will require this new base rule:

(3-64)   S → NP BE2 NP

BE2 is another new syntactic category that also contains *be*. Its type will be FRAME EQUIVALENCER, and together with two instances, one from each NP, it will form a FRAME EQUIVALENCE STATEMENT that will correspond to the sentence. For example:

(3-65)   This man's father is my father's son.
```
          (same-instance (the ?x (father ?x ...))
                         (the ?y (son ?y ...)))
```

Here, `same-instance` is the translation of *be* when its syntactic category is BE2. When intensions are added to Absity, this rule should be able to handle the definitional *be* as well. It will then, however, be necessary to decide whether *be* translates to `same-instance` or `definition`; this could be done by the word disambiguation procedures that I will describe in chapter 5.[36] Note that the rule has the same difficulties with embedded sentences that the rule for predicative *be*s has.

4. Complex quantifiers. Frail has no method at present to represent sets or their cardinality. One can in Frail retrieve a set of instances with a given property, but all one gets is a list of bindings. For example, to find **the students whose fathers like cheese**, one could ask Frail for the following:

(3-66)   (retrieve
          '(and (student ?x)
                (likes (father ?x) cheese)))

The result, however, is simply a list of the various bindings of ?x that satisfied the request:

(3-67)   ((?x Ross) (?x Nadia) (?x Kennapod))

There is no facility for representing a collection of instances as a Frail object, nor for representing a set intensionally by specifying a generic frame that describes its members, nor for representing the cardinality of a set. Thus Frail cannot represent as a semantic object any of the following NPs:

(3-68)   the students whose fathers like cheese

(3-69)   the integers

---

[36] See also Mallery 1985.

(3-70)   seven red blocks

(3-71)   all but five of Nadia's marmots

Thus complex determiners such as *all but five of the* can be neither parsed by Paragram nor represented by Frail; Absity therefore has no qualms about ignoring them too. Simple plurals pose no problem for Absity, except that Frail doesn't know what to do with them.

Sentences with QUANTIFIERS whose scope is wider than the noun phrase in which they occur cannot yet be handled by Absity:

(3-72)   Every boy gave every girl three peaches.

Sentence (3-72) implies that there was not one giving event but rather a number of them, equal to the product of the number of boys and the number of girls. The over-compositionality of Absity is the main problem here: the universal quantifi-cations have to be pulled out of the noun phrases so that their scopes are correct, but Absity is not amenable to that. In addition, the representation of such sentences in Frail is problematic; if we solved the previous problem, we could then gener-ate a representation with a frame determiner that found all instances of boys and girls and asserted a give instance for each pair. But if there were many pairs, this would be both inefficient and counter-intuitive; rather, it would be preferable to assert the fact that there were these givings, and use it later to infer, for example, that Ross gave Nadia three peaches if that fact is needed. Possible solutions in-clude the use of a representation that is vague with respect to scoping, as suggested by Hobbs (1983), and the use of QUANTIFIER STORAGE (Cooper 1983).

5. Inherent vagueness. Often language is INHERENTLY VAGUE, and it is left to the interpreter to supply that which is unsaid. Two particularly important instances of this are the words *have* and *with*, many uses of which are extremely vague. Consider:

(3-73)   Ross has green eyes / a cold / a sinister laugh / intelligence / a book under his arm / ...

(3-74)   the girl with green eyes / a cold / a sinister laugh / intelligence / a book under her arm / ...

At present, Absity relies on being able to determine the precise meaning of a word from its context. In the case of words like *have* and *with*, however, it seems wrong to say that they are ambiguous words with a large number of precise meanings; rather, they seem to be inherently vague, with their intent to be figured out from the nature of the entities they relate.

I believe that this could be handled properly with the present Absity and Frail by adding a mechanism that takes a vague sentence in the Frail representation and uses the definitions of the objects to resolve the vagueness.[37] In anticipation of

---

[37] Such a mechanism is described very briefly by Steinacker and Trost (1983).

such a mechanism, Absity simply translates all verb occurrences of *have* as have, and all NP-attached uses of *with* as attr (an abbreviation for *attribute*).

6. Time and space. The representation of time is an extremely difficult problem. While Frail can represent points in time and time intervals as frame instances, it does not support any form of temporal logic. Similarly, its ability to handle spatial location is very limited. Absity can handle the simple representations of time and space that Frail permits, and it is to be hoped that as better representations are developed, they will be suitably compositional and amenable to Absity's approach.

7. Moral and contingent obligation. As is all too typical of computer systems, Frail cannot even conceive of contingent obligation, let alone moral imperatives:

(3-75)   Nadia <u>ought</u> to prevent Ross from driving until he sobers up a bit.

(3-76)   You <u>ought not</u> to read Hirst's book if you are under 18.

(3-77)   The wheelhouse vacuum chamber pump bearings <u>should</u> be oiled daily.

(3-78)   Persons desiring an I–94 form <u>must</u> complete an IAP–66 form.

Again, it is to be hoped that as better representations are developed, they will be suitably compositional and amenable to Absity's approach.[38]

8. Negation and conjunction. Frail permits the assertion that a particular instance does not exist. Thus (3-79):

(3-79)   Ross didn't kiss Nadia.

could be represented as (3-80):

(3-80)   (not (and (instance ?x kiss)
                     (:= (agent ?x) Ross)
                     (:= (patient ?x) Nadia)))

---

[38] In fact, Frail is able to represent contingencies in a manner suitable for use by Bruin's NASL problem solver (Wong 1981a, 1981b) *(see section 1.3)*. Thus, one might have the following translation:

(i)   To get an I–94 form, complete an IAP–66 form.
       (to-do (possess I-94) (complete IAP-66))

The same kind of information may also be represented in a script-like frame:

(ii)   [frame: getting-I-94
          isa: task
        slots: (first-step (complete IAP-66))
                (second-step (receive I-94))
        facts: (before ?first-step ?second-step)]

These representations are designed for manipulation by NASL, but are not suitable as targets for semantic interpretation.

Absity, however, is unable to handle (3-79), or negation in general. To do so, it would need a new frame determiner, `nota`, say, that could provide a suitable meta-notation for (3-80), as described in section 3.6, and a way of getting the negation into the frame determiner.

Absity also makes no attempt to handle the conjunctions *and* and *or* at any constituent level.

9. Noun modifiers. Absity considers all noun modifiers to be slot–filler pairs that qualify their head noun. This implies that the modifier is either an ABSOLUTE or MEASURE adjective (Ali 1985), and that (from Absity's perspective) the relationship between it and the noun is defined solely by the modifier. For example, if *red*, an absolute adjective, translates as `(color=red)`, then the relationship is that the modifier is saying something about the noun frame's `color` slot.[39] Similarly, the measure adjective *tall* translates as `(height=tall)`, though measure adjectives bring the additional problem (for Frail, not Absity) that their final interpretation also depends on the noun; a *tall jockey* is probably not as tall as a *short basketball-player*, for example. (Ali (1985) has constructed a system for the interpretation of such constructs.)

Problems arise with other classes of noun modifiers, such as ROLE adjectives and INTENSIONAL adjectives. A role adjective is one such as *annoyed* in *an annoyed look*, which may be glossed as **a look whose agent is an annoyed person** (Ali 1985; Ali's system could also handle these adjectives). An intensional adjective is one such as *alleged*; an *alleged thief* may not be a thief at all.

In general, the relationship between modifier and head noun is often controlled by both, and is sometimes not one of frame and slot–filler pair at all. For example, a reasonable representation of *computer science* is (3-81):

(3-81)   `(a ?x (science ?x (object-of-study=computer)))`

This implies that the meaning of *computer*, when used as a noun modifier, is `(object-of-study=computer)`. But the same reasoning gives us many other meanings for the same word:

(3-82)   computer maintenance
        `(a ?x (maintain ?x (patient=computer)))`

(3-83)   computer language
        `(a ?x (language ?x (comprehender=computer)))`

(3-84)   computer game
        `(a ?x (game ?x (medium-of-play=computer)))`

It would be wrong simply to regard *computer* as a highly polysemous adjective. In fact, language is extremely productive in its creation of such noun groups (Downing 1977, Levi 1978, B Warren 1978), and it seems that the relationship between

---

[39] If it doesn't have such a slot, then there's trouble; if the adjective or noun is ambiguous, then making sure that the sf-pair fits the frame is a good heuristic for disambiguation; see section 5.3.2.

the head noun and the modifier does not inhere in the modifier, nor even in the head, but rather is constructed by inference on the meanings of both (Bauer 1979). While a frequently used noun group will generally become LEXICALIZED (that is, treated as a single word or "CANNED PHRASE" with its own entry in the mental lexicon), people generally have no trouble creating and comprehending novel forms (Downing 1977).

There is nothing in Absity at present for inferring or interpreting such relationships, and this is obviously a major gap. One interesting possibility for a solution comes from the work of DB McDonald (1982), who used for noun group interpretation a marker passer not dissimilar to the one I use in chapter 5 for lexical disambiguation. It may therefore be possible to employ the marker passer for noun group interpretation in Absity as well. In addition, Finin (1980) described an approach to noun group interpretation, based on a frame system not unlike Frail, that might be adaptable.

10. Non-restrictive noun phrase modifiers. Absity is not able to handle non-restrictive modifiers, whether appositive or not:

(3-85)   Ross, <u>whose balloon had now deflated completely</u>, began to cry.

(3-86)   Ross <u>in a bad mood</u> is a sight to be seen.

Ideally, (3-85) should be translated into two separate Frail statements representing the two sentences from which it is composed:

(3-87)   Ross's balloon had now deflated completely.
          Ross began to cry.

but Absity has as yet no mechanism for this.[40] Sentence (3-86) is problematic because it is unclear exactly how the NP *Ross in a bad mood* should be represented in Frail.

11. Adverbial *wh-* **questions.** Questions with an adverbial *wh-* can be difficult. In section 3.5, we saw that the translation is straightforward if the *wh-* is an NP:

(3-88)   What did Nadia buy from a store in the mall?
```
(question ?u
    (buy ?u
        (agent=(the ?x (person ?x
            (propername="Nadia"))))
        (patient=?WH)
        (source=(a ?z (store ?z
            (location=(the ?w (mall ?w)))))))))
```

We knew that the ?WH was the PATIENT because the syntax of the sentence indicated that the pseudo-preposition *OBJ* was its case flag. However, adverbial *wh*-s contain their own case flag, and it is not always unambiguous:

---

[40]In anticipation of such a mechanism, however, section 7.3.2 discusses structural ambiguity resolution for such cases.

(3-89)   Where did Nadia kiss Ross?

It would be wrong simply to translate *where* as `(location=?WH)`, because there are two different LOCATION slots for *kiss*: one a true case slot, the other a verb modifier. This is demonstrated by the two possible kinds of answer to (3-89):

(3-90)   On the cheek.

(3-91)   Behind the gym.

Thus the translation of *where* is not always unambiguous, even when the sentence verb is known; moreover, it is probably NOT amenable to the local disambiguation techniques of chapter 5, because context and discourse pragmatics are necessarily involved in determining exactly what is being asked *(cf. section 5.3.6)*.[41]

12. Words with apparently non-compositional effects. There are many words whose semantic characterization is problematic in any compositional semantics. These are words, usually adverbs, that serve to change the meaning of their matrix sentence (or constituent) in some way. Examples:

(3-92)   Ross has been rummaging through Nadia's wastebasket <u>again</u>.

(3-93)   Ross <u>even</u> suggested that Nadia spend the weekend at his apartment.

(3-94)   Ross hasn't <u>actually</u> made it with Nadia <u>yet</u>.

(3-95)   He hasn't touched her, <u>let alone</u> kissed her.

These sentences are simple enough to represent if the underlined words are omitted (or replaced by *or*, in the case of (3-95)). But it is by no means clear how the full sentences, let alone the underlined words, should be represented if the meanings of the full sentences are to be formed compositionally from the representations of the simple forms and those of the underlined words.

It is tempting, and not without motivation, to sweep these words under the rug of discourse pragmatics, along with other matters discussed in point 13 below; that is, to say that they have no semantics per se and Absity can simply ignore them. For example, in (3-92), the word *again* seems to mean "and this is a new occurrence of such an event, not any of the ones that I believe you've heard of before"—that is, it is a meta-level comment on the knowledge of the participants of the discourse. Similarly, in (3-94), we can gloss *actually* as "despite indications or beliefs to the contrary that you may have", and *yet* as an intensifier of the verb tense, with the conversational implicature (Grice 1975; Levinson 1983) that the situation described may not remain true.

This is not an entirely satisfactory situation, however. If Absity ignores these words, then we must posit some other process that deals with them, a process that must necessarily use the syntactic and semantic representations created by Paragram and Absity. The questions of methods of interaction and possible changes

---

[41] In any case, Paragram can't parse adverbial *wh-s* yet.

to Absity then arise. Moreover, if Absity's structures are to be used in machine translation between natural languages, then they are now lacking important information that must be carried over to the output; it is distressing and counterintuitive to have to posit a second representation in which such information is carried separately from the meaning itself and then somehow re-integrated with it.

My intuition is that if these words are to be handled at the semantic level, then they should be represented not as passive objects for composition, but rather (more in the original Montague style) as functions that take a semantic object (for a sentence or other constituent) and produce a suitable modification of it. It may be possible to do this without too much violence to the principles of Absity.

13. Topic, tenor, and subtleties of discourse. We have already *(section 1.1.1)* discussed the exclusion of matters of discourse from Absity, but it is worth mentioning briefly here some of the things we have lost. In particular, Absity ignores the shades of meaning conveyed by surface form and choice of words. For example, topicalization is ignored; (3-96) and (3-97) would receive exactly the same representation in Frail:

(3-96)   Egg creams, I like.

(3-97)   I like egg creams.

Irony is also lost on Absity; compare:

(3-98)   While I was holding the baby, it wet itself.

(3-99)   While I was holding the baby, the little darling wet itself.

Presumably, any anaphora mechanism working with Absity would resolve both *it* and the epithet (Hirst 1981a[1]: 13) *the little darling* as **the baby** and simply plug in the appropriate frame statement (the ?x (baby ?x)) in each case. As with the matter discussed in the previous point, this sort of discourse subtlety must also be preserved in machine translation.

3.9 Conclusion

I have presented Absity, a semantic interpreter that works with the Paragram parser and the Frail frame system. Absity is clean and compositional, works in tandem with the parser, and provides feedback for structural disambiguation. Absity is still limited by the abilities of Frail and by its own over-compositionality, but should provide a firm foundation for further development of semantic interpretation. Table 3.5 shows some of the sentences that Absity can handle, and some that it can't. (Some of the examples assume the disambiguation mechanisms of chapters 5 and 7.)

Table 3.5. *What Absity can and can't do*

SENTENCES THAT CAN BE INTERPRETED

Nadia gave Ross a marmot for his birthday.
The fish that Ross loved loved the fish that Nadia loved.
Ross promised to study astrology.
Nadia wanted the penguin to catch some fish.
What did Ross eat for breakfast?
Did a computer destroy the world?
Ross knows that Nadia assembled the plane.
A seagull landed on the beach.
What does Nadia want from Ross?
An obnoxious multi-national corporation wants to hire Nadia.

SENTENCES THAT CAN'T BE INTERPRETED

Nadia resembles a pika. *(de dicto reading)*
Ross sleeps on the floor. *(habitual reading)*
Ross is exhausted.
The mysterious stranger was Nadia.
All but five of the students whose fathers like cheese gave three peaches
    to many of the tourists.
Ross ought to swim home tomorrow.
Nadia didn't see that Ross was creeping round the corner.
Computer games are devastating the youth of the nation.
Ross in a bad mood should be avoided.
Where did Ross buy the unicycle?
Ross hasn't actually made it with Nadia yet.

Part II

Lexical Disambiguation

4 Lexical disambiguation

There's no need to think, dear. Just do what's in the script, and it'll all come
out right.
—Alfred Hitchcock[1]

4.1 What is necessary for lexical disambiguation?

The problem of determining the correct sense of a lexically ambiguous word in
context has often been seen as one primarily of context recognition, a word being
disambiguated to the unique meaning appropriate to the frame or script representing the known or newly-established context. For example, in the well-known SAM
program (Cullingford 1978, Schank and the Yale AI Project 1975, Schank and
Abelson 1977), each script has associated with it a set of word meanings appropriate to that script; in the restaurant script, there will be unique meanings given
for such words as *waiter* and *serve*, and when (4-1) is processed:

(4-1)   The waiter served the lasagna.

the fact that *serve* has quite a different meaning in the tennis script will not even
be noticed (Schank and Abelson 1977: 183). (Certain words naming well-known
people and things, such as *Manhattan*, are always present (Cullingford 1978: 13).)[2]

In its most simple-minded form, the script approach can easily fail:

(4-2)   The lawyer stopped at the bar for a drink.

---

[1] Probably apocryphal.

[2] The script approach is in some ways reminiscent of early statistical approaches. In 1965, Madhu and
Lytle proposed that in machine translation of scientific papers, it was generally sufficient for resolution
of lexical ambiguity to know the likelihood of usage of each sense in the particular subfield of science
that the paper was concerned with. The particular subfield of a paper was determined by looking at
the subfield associations of the unambiguous words in it. Data for the probability of use in a particular
sense in each subfield was obtained from textual analysis. A Bayesian formula then gave the probability
of a given sense of a particular word in a particular context. 90% accuracy was claimed.

If only the lawyering script is active, then *bar* as **an establishment purveying alcoholic beverages by the glass** will be unavailable, and its legal sense will be incorrectly chosen. If resolution is delayed until the word *drink* has had a chance to bring in a more suitable script, then there will be the problem of deciding which script to choose the sense from;[3] as Charniak (1984) points out, it is reasonable to expect in practice to have fifty or more scripts simultaneously active, each with its own lexicon, necessitating extensive search and choice among alternatives. Thus the main advantage of the script approach, having disambiguation "fall out" of context recognition, is lost.[4]

Further, even in a single script, a word, especially a polysemous one, may still be ambiguous. In the lawyering script, the word *bar* could mean **the physical bar of a courtroom** or **the legal profession**.[5] Moreover, choosing which script to invoke in the first place may require deciding the meaning of an ambiguous word, such as *play* in these sentences:

(4-3)   Ross played with his toys. *(script = recreation)*

(4-4)   Ross played his guitar. *(script = music-making)*

Note that the word *guitar* is by itself insufficient to invoke the music-making script. Compare:

(4-5)   The baby played with the guitar. *(script = recreation)*

In general, word sense can depend not only upon global context, but also (or only) upon local cues, such as the meaning of nearby words. In (4-6):

(4-6)   Nadia's car is a lemon-colored Subaru.

the **badly-made-car** meaning of *lemon* can be rejected in favor of the **citrus-fruit** meaning, without any consideration of global context; all one has to do is look at the word with which it has been hyphenated, knowing that color is salient and constant for only one of *lemon*'s two meanings. Often, all that seems necessary for disambiguation is that there be a "semantic association" between one sense of the ambiguous word and nearby words (Quillian 1962, 1969):

(4-7)   The dog's <u>bark</u> woke me up. *(bark ≠ **surface of tree**)*

---

[3] Schank and Abelson (1977: 183) claim that SAM would choose the non-script meaning of a word when the situation forces it, as with *serve* in sentence (i):

(i)   The waiter served in the army.

but they are rather vague on how this happens.

[4] An additional argument against using context as the main source of information is the evidence that better readers depend LESS on context for word recognition than poor readers (West and Stanovich 1978; Stanovich, West, and Feeman 1981; West, Stanovich, Feeman, and Cunningham 1983; Stanovich, Cunningham, and Feeman 1984; Stanovich 1984; Nathan 1984).

[5] In fact, *Webster's ninth new collegiate dictionary* (Webster 1983) distinguishes seven different law-related senses of *bar*.

As Hayes (1977a: 43) puts it, "an association between a sense of an ambiguous word and the context surrounding a use of that word is strong evidence that the interpretation of that word should come through that sense". The nearby disambiguating words may themselves be ambiguous; a well-known example (Small 1980) is *deep pit*. The word *deep* can mean **profound** or **extending far down** and *pit* can be **fruit stone** or **hole in the ground**; however, only one meaning of each fits with the other, so they are mutually disambiguating.

Knowledge about case slot flags and restrictions on case slot fillers is also a good source of disambiguating information. For example, (4-3) and (4-4) can be disambiguated easily if one knows that the **music-making** sense requires its PATIENT to be flagged by *OBJ*, while the **recreation** sense flags it with *with*. The **game-playing** sense also flags its PATIENT with *OBJ*, but can be distinguished from **music-making** by the fact that the former requires the PATIENT to be a game, while the latter requires a musical instrument.[6]

I noted in section 1.1.2 that the problem of deciding which case slot is flagged by a particular preposition or syntactic position is very similar to lexical disambiguation. The strategy of inserting pseudo-prepositions to represent case-flagging syntactic positions *(section 3.4)* makes the problems even more similar by making all case flags lexemes. The *play* examples suggest that verbs and case flags can be mutually disambiguating, just like the words in the *deep pit* example; though each may individually have many meanings, there will only be one combination of meanings that fits together (if the sentence is truly unambiguous).

Syntax can also supply disambiguating information. For example, the word *keep*, meaning **continue to do**, **continue to be**, or **maintain**, can be disambiguated by seeing whether its object is a gerund, an adjectival phrase, or a noun phrase:

(4-8)   Ross kept staring at Nadia's décolletage.

(4-9)   Nadia kept calm and made a cutting remark.

(4-10)   Ross wrote of his embarrassment in the diary that he kept.

Sometimes, however, high-level inference, a relatively expensive operation, will be necessary. Compare:

(4-11)   The lawyer stopped at the bar for a drink.

(4-12)   The lawyer stopped at the bar, and turned to face the court.

Note that (4-12) has several sensible meanings: *bar* could be **the railing in a courtroom**, with *court* being the **judiciary assembled** in the courtroom, or it could be a **drinking establishment**, with *court* being a **courthouse** across the street, or a **tennis court**, or some other kind of court. Deciding which is better in a particular instance requires inference on the preceding context. Another example (from Hayes 1977a):

---

[6]This is, of course, a great simplification, made just to establish the point. In fact, *play* is a verb with a particularly complex and interesting case structure, analyzed extensively by Taylor (1975; Taylor and Rosenberg 1975).

(4-13)   Nadia swung the hammer at the nail, and the <u>head</u> flew off.

The word *head* is most naturally interpreted as the **hammer-head**, not the **nail-head** (or Nadia's **person-head**), but figuring this out requires inference about the reasons for which one head or the other might have flown off, with a knowledge of centrifugal force suggesting the head of the hammer. In (4-14):

(4-14)   <u>Gag</u> me with a spoon![7]

the disambiguation of *gag* (meaning either **choke** or **render unable to speak by blocking the mouth**) requires deciding which of its meanings might best be accomplished with a spoon, a non-trivial task.

Necessary for word sense disambiguation, then, are:

- a knowledge of context;

- a mechanism to find associations between nearby words;

- a mechanism to handle syntactic disambiguation cues;

- a mechanism to handle selectional restriction reconciliation negotiations between ambiguous words; and

- inference, as a last resort.

4.2 Lexical disambiguation research in AI

In this section I discuss work in AI on lexical disambiguation that takes into account local disambiguating cues. We will look at four very different approaches: those of Yorick Wilks, Philip Hayes, Branimir Boguraev, and Steven Small.

4.2.1 Wilks: Preference semantics

Wilks's Preference Semantics system (Wilks 1973, 1975b, 1975c, 1975d) was perhaps the first NLU system to be explicitly designed around the need for lexical disambiguation (Boguraev 1979). The system's strategy was based on selectional restrictions, expressed in the form of templates that meanings had to fit. However, the restrictions were not absolute, but rather expressed PREFERENCES only. A word sense that fitted the preferences was always preferred, but if none was available, the system would take what it could get. This permitted some metaphor to be handled in sentences like (4-15) (Wilks 1977, 1982b):

(4-15)   My car drinks gasoline.

---

[7] Vogue expression, 1982–1983. COREY, Mary and WESTERMARK, Victoria. *Fer shurr! How to be a Valley Girl—Totally!* New York: Bantam, November 1982.

(*Drink* prefers an animate subject, but accepts a machine.) Not just verbs but all parts of speech were labeled with their preferences. For example, the adjective *big* was expected to qualify a physical object. Preferences were even used in anaphora resolution, as for the word *it* in (4-16) (Wilks 1975d), which may not refer to the rock because *drink* prefers a liquid object:

(4-16)   I bought the wine, sat on a rock, and drank it.

This approach is consistent with the predictive method of parsing and semantic interpretation used by Riesbeck (1974, 1975; Schank, Goldman, Rieger and Riesbeck 1975; Riesbeck and Schank 1978); in Riesbeck's analyzer, a verb such as *drink* would set up an explicit prediction that the next thing in the sentence would be a liquid.

The shortcomings of this approach lie in the fact that preferences or selectional restrictions are, by themselves, inadequate to deal with all instances of lexical ambiguity, such as those that need global context, association of nearby concepts, or inference for their resolution. Boguraev (1979: 3.23–3.25) points out that Wilks's approach is also unable to deal adequately with polysemous verbs such as in the *keep* examples of section 4.1 ((4-8) to (4-10)), or these different senses of *ask*:

(4-17)   Ross asked Nadia a question. *(ask = **request an answer to***)

(4-18)   Ross asked Nadia to come with him. *(ask = **request [the performance of an action]***)

(4-19)   Ross asked Nadia for the numbat. *(ask = **request to be given***)

The problem, says Boguraev, is that templates simultaneously have to be both general enough to translate the input text to a semantic representation and specific enough to disambiguate words. For a discussion of the shortcomings of using preferences for anaphora resolution, see Hirst 1981a.

4.2.2 Boguraev: Semantic judgments

Boguraev's disambiguation system (1979) was based on Wilks's approach to semantics, but attempted to eliminate many of the shortcomings of the simple preference method by using not just preferences but SEMANTIC JUDGMENTS. His system integrated both lexical and structural disambiguation with semantic interpretation. (Boguraev's methods for structural disambiguation will be discussed in section 6.3.1.)

The system consisted of an ATN parser *(see section 1.3.2)* to which semantic procedures had been added as actions to be performed upon the completion of noun phrases and clauses. These procedures were responsible for both kinds of disambiguation and for building the semantic representation (in a formalism similar to Wilks's). They first applied selectional restrictions, preferences, verb case structures, and the like in an attempt to disambiguate words. Further lexical disambiguation was integrated with structural disambiguation; judgments were made on the SEMANTIC COHERENCE of potential readings, which were rejected if found implausible *(see section 6.3.1)*. If all readings were found implausible, this was signaled to the parser, and it would back up and try a different path. The semantic judgments were made solely on the basis of lexical knowledge; the system did not have any general world knowledge base.

4.2.3 Hayes: Disambiguation with frames and associations

Hayes's work (1976, 1977a, 1977b, 1978) on the CSAW program was perhaps the first to consider multiple sources of knowledge in lexical disambiguation, with an emphasis on finding semantic associations between words.[8] The program also used case structures and selectional restrictions, both absolute and preferential, for disambiguation. CSAW tried to use the most restrictive methods first: case slots, associations, and finally selectional restrictions. The program first parsed its input with an ATN, and then started disambiguating the words that had multiple senses, all of which were considered together, until it converged on a solution. If a choice occurred at any point, the possibilities were considered in parallel; multiple forking was permitted.

Association-finding was facilitated by the knowledge representation that Hayes used: a semantic network upon which a frame system was superimposed. Generally speaking, frame systems and semantic networks are simply notational variants for the same kind of structure, but in Hayes's representation both notations were used. One could think of the knowledge base as a system of frames, each frame being a small piece of semantic net; alternatively, one could think of it as a network divided up into areas, each area a frame. Frames participated in two hierarchies: one for the ISA relation, and one for the PART-OF relation. Noun senses were represented as nodes in the network, and verbs were represented as frames (Hayes 1976: 30).

Associations were then found by looking at this representation. For example, a node was associated with any frame it was in; the node representing a human hand was in the frame representing a person. Since Ross is an instance of a person, a disambiguating association was found in (4-20):

(4-20)   Ross's <u>hand</u> was covered with bandages.

A node was also associated with any frame that was an ancestor or descendant in the ISA hierarchy of the frame it was in, and other associations were specified by rules operating on the ISA and PART-OF hierarchies (Hayes 1976: 126). Such

---

[8] However, Quillian's Teachable Language Comprehender (1969) included a rudimentary form of disambiguation by association. Given (i):

(i)   John shoots the teacher.

if John was known to be a photographer or a gangster, then word association would be used to determine whether *shoot* meant **photograph** or **assault with a firearm**. Quillian first proposed the technique in 1961 (see below, and Quillian 1962).

associations relied on finding a CHAIN OF CONNECTIONS in the knowledge base between a node and a frame.

Hayes found that association is useful mostly for dealing with homonyms, where there are large differences between the senses; it is less successful with polysemous words (Hayes 1976: 30), where an association for more than one sense will tend to be found. Although verbs as well as nouns can be disambiguated by association, Hayes's treatment did not include verbs (1977: 46) because of their extra complexity. (Recall also that verbs tend to be polysemous while nouns tend to be homonymous—see section 1.1.2.)

4.2.4 Small: Word expert parsing

The Word Expert Parser of Steven Small (1980, 1983; Small and Rieger 1982) featured an unconventional architecture in which each word in the lexicon was represented by a procedure, and the parsing, disambiguation, and semantic interpretation of a sentence were performed by a consortium of the procedures that represented the words of the sentence. As the system's name suggests, each procedure could be thought of as an expert on both the syntax and semantics of the word that it represented. Together, these word experts built a semantic representation of the input, performing disambiguation and minimal syntactic analysis on the way. A distributed control environment governed the experts, which ran as deterministic coroutines, letting each have its turn when appropriate.

Each expert for an ambiguous word included a DISCRIMINATION NET for the possible meanings of that word. By asking appropriate questions of context and of its environment (that is, of the experts for nearby words), the expert traversed the net to reach a unique meaning for its word. The expert would report partial results as it became sure of them, and would go to sleep if it needed to await results that other experts hadn't yet determined. When it determined its correct sense, the expert added the result to the conceptual structure that was being built as the representation of the sentence.

Because the system conflated parsing, disambiguation and semantic interpretation, each expert had a lot of work to do, and experts were the sole repository of linguistic knowledge in the system.[9] Word expert procedures were therefore large and complicated and necessarily individually hand-crafted; "the construction of word experts requires patience, dedication, and finesse" (Small 1980: 200). For example, the expert for *throw* is "currently six pages long, but should be ten times that size" (Small and Rieger 1982: 146). This is the biggest drawback of the Word Expert Parser: its rejection of general mechanisms in favor of a very large number of loosely constrained particular ones, loosely related to one another.[10]

---

[9]This is in accord with Small's view that language is too irregular for generalizations to be usefully captured at any level higher than the lexical (Small and Rieger 1982: 90); *cf.* footnote 2 of chapter 1.

[10]To some large degree this is a religious argument. If one accepts Small's view of language, then

4.3 Psycholinguistic research on lexical disambiguation

There has been much psycholinguistic research in the last decade on how people deal with lexical ambiguity and choose the correct word sense. In this section I look at this research, in preparation for developing an AI lexical disambiguation mechanism *(cf. section 1.4)*.

In general, people do not notice occurrences of lexical ambiguity, and seem to disambiguate without any conscious effort.[11] There are exceptions to this, of course. Many jokes rely on the perceiver seeing only one meaning at first, and then noticing the other (Hirst 1988):

(4-21)   [From the television program *The two Ronnies*]
          Ronnie Corbett: In the sketch that follows, I'll be playing a man whose wife leaves him for the garbageman.
          Ronnie Barker: And I'll be playing the garbageman who refuses to take him.[12]

(4-22)   **Julia:**   Why didst thou stoop then?
          Lucetta: To take a paper up that I let fall.
          Julia: And is that paper nothing?
          Lucetta: Nothing concerning me.
          Julia: Then let it lie for those that it concerns.
          Lucetta: Madam, it will not lie where it concerns,
          Unless it have a false interpreter.[13]

while others, puns and double entendres, rely on just the opposite, that both meanings be seen:

(4-23)   One man's Mede is another man's Persian.[14]

(4-24)   There is no <u>seeming</u> mercy in the King.[15] *(seeming = both* **apparent** *and* **fraudulent***)*[16]

---

his approach is both reasonable and necessary, and the Word Expert Parser is a good first attempt at a system based upon this view. My opinion is that this is a rather inconvenient religion, and not one to be adopted lightly. Before one dons a hair shirt, one has to be convinced that God really thinks it necessary.

[11] Nevertheless, Mohanty (1983) has shown that the presentation of a lexically or structurally ambiguous sentence causes a small but significantly greater increase in the rate of a person's heartbeat than an unambiguous sentence does.

[12] DEYKIN, Graham. In VINCENT, Peter (compiler). *The two Ronnies—but first the news*. London: Star, 1977. 36.

[13] SHAKESPEARE, William. *Two gentlemen of Verona*. 1594. I, ii, 69–75.

[14] COHAN, George M. Attributed.

[15] SHAKESPEARE, William. *Henry IV, part I*. 1590. V, ii, 34.

[16] "Worcester is withholding the King's offer of amnesty from Hotspur because he believes it fraudulent, merely a seeming mercy, and this gives his words a negative dramatic irony. They gain also a positive irony from the audience's belief that the King's offer is sincere; Worcester is more right than he knows, since the King's mercy is not seeming but genuine" (Mahood 1957:43).

(See Hirst 1988 for more discussion; see Hillier 1974 for a discussion, with examples, of the ten different types of pun; see Raskin 1985 for a discussion of linguistic ambiguity in humor; see Levine 1965, 1985 for discussions of the use and benefits of other kinds of deliberate linguistic ambiguity in non-Western cultures.)

Shamelessly leaving aside such awkward counterexamples, we can consider how people might disambiguate words. The main problem we look at is the LEXICAL ACCESS question:

- Do people consider (unconsciously) some or all of the possible meanings of an ambiguous word, or do context and/or expectations take them straight to the "correct" meaning?

The competing hypotheses are these:

- The PRIOR CHOICE hypothesis: "Prior context biases the interpretive process before the ambiguity itself is encountered ... perhaps allowing only a single reading ever to be accessed" (Swinney and Hakes 1976:683).

- The ALL-READINGS hypothesis: "Prior context influences the interpretation of an ambiguity only after all readings are accessed; it aids in the selection of an appropriate reading to retain from those accessed, but does not affect the access process itself" (Swinney and Hakes 1976:683).

- The ORDERED SEARCH hypothesis: "The order of search [of senses of an ambiguous word] is determined by frequency of usage, the most frequent being first. The search is self-terminating, so that as soon as an acceptable match occurs, no [other] entries will be checked" (Hogaboam and Perfetti 1975:66).

Another question that immediately arises is the DECISION POINT problem:

- If more than one meaning is accessed, how and when is a choice made?

There are three possibilities: that the choice is virtually immediate; that it does not happen until the end of the clause (or some smaller syntactic unit), with the several meanings remaining around until then; and that it happens as soon as enough information is available, whether this be immediately or later.

The discussion below will deal with the lexical access question rather than the decision point question. This is because research has focused so far almost exclusively on cases where both enough information is present at the time of the word's occurrence for it to be immediately disambiguated and the word is the last of the clause anyway.[17] It has been found, unsurprisingly, that disambiguation is immediate in such cases; in addition, the work of Swinney (1979) and Onifer and Swinney (1981) that I will discuss in section 4.3.4 suggests that this result also holds when there is sufficient information, even if the word is not clause-final. Further, intuition suggests that ambiguities are always resolved by the end of the sentence, with a good guess being made if the information provided is insufficient.

---

[17] A notable exception is the work of Carpenter and Daneman (1981).

The review below will not attempt to cover the large body of literature, but rather a representative sample. Moreover, I will be almost exclusively concerned with homonymous nouns; there seems to have been very little psycholinguistic research on other forms of lexical ambiguity, except for a bit on homonyms that are also noun–verb categorially ambiguous. I first discuss the concept of spreading activation, which will be necessary for the subsequent discussion of the three hypotheses for the lexical access question.

4.3.1 Semantic priming and spreading activation

A phenomenon whose psychological reality is well established is SEMANTIC PRIM-ING: the fact that the mental processing of a particular concept will facilitate processing of other concepts that have a semantic relationship to the first. For example, Meyer and Schvaneveldt (1971) found that subjects could answer the question "Are these strings both English words?" faster if the stimulus was a related pair like *doctor–nurse* than an unrelated pair like *doctor–butter*. Accessing the first word seemed to facilitate access to the second when it was semantically related.

Models of semantic priming are generally based on SPREADING ACTIVATION. It is assumed that the mental representation of concepts is a network of some kind, similar to a semantic network or network of frames, in which semantically related concepts are close to one another. Using a concept in the network causes it to become ACTIVATED; for example, processing a word will cause the word's meaning to become activated. This activation, however, is not limited just to the concept accessed. Rather, activation will spread from the ORIGIN to nearby nodes, causing them to also be activated. When a node is activated, access to it is facilitated. Thus, seeing the word *doctor* activates the **doctor** concept and also nearby, semantically related concepts such as **nurse**. When the word *nurse* is then seen, its corresponding node has been pre-activated, making access to it faster than access to concepts like **butter** that have not been activated.

Spreading activation models generally assume that the more a concept is used, or the more activation that is spread to it, the more highly activated it becomes. For example, Reder (1983) found that priming a concept twice doubled its degree of facilitation. However, activation gets weaker as it spreads until it can spread no further, so that the degree of activation of a concept will be a function of its semantic closeness to the origin. In addition, concepts do not remain activated long; their activation decays with time until they return to their normal state.

One of the earliest models of spreading activation was that of Quillian (1962, 1967, 1968, 1969), who, following early work on semantic networks by Richens (1958) and Masterman (1961), developed a semantic network in which connections between concepts could be found. This work inspired considerable research in cognitive psychology on spreading activation models; for an overview, see Collins and Loftus 1975 and Lorch 1982, or Anderson 1976, 1983.

In the sections below, we will see semantic priming and spreading activation used both as tools for the investigation of lexical disambiguation and as explanations of the disambiguation mechanism itself.

> *Wigan* (n.) — If, when talking to someone you know has only one leg, you're trying to treat them perfectly casually and normally, but find to your horror that your conversation is liberally studded with references to *(a)* Long John Silver, *(b)* Hopalong Cassidy, *(c)* the Hokey Cokey, *(d)* 'putting your foot in it', *(e)* 'the last leg of the UEFA competition', you are said to have committed a *wigan*.
>
> The word is derived from the fact that sub-editors at ITN used to manage to mention the name of either the town Wigan, or Lord Wigg, in every fourth script that Reginald Bosanquet was given to read.
> —Douglas Adams and John Lloyd[18]

4.3.2 *Phoneme monitoring and prior choice activation models*

An answer to the lexical access question might be based on the observation that if the prior choice hypothesis is correct, then ambiguous words should require no longer to process than other words, as their ambiguity will not affect their processing time. This would be predicted by the script approach of Schank and Abelson (1977), a strong form of the prior choice hypothesis in which the invocation of a script gives the system a list of unique word meanings for the present context *(see section 4.1)*. Thus any extra processing time incurred by lexical ambiguity happens when scripts are initially invoked, rather than when individual word occurrences are processed.

The data on the processing times for ambiguous words are somewhat equivocal.[19] Foss (1970) asked subjects to press a button upon hearing a specified phoneme in a sentence; reaction time was found to be greater if the target phoneme was immediately preceded by an ambiguous word, suggesting that lexical processing is slowed down by the ambiguity and that ambiguous words therefore require greater processing. Foss and Jenkins (1973) found that this effect was present even when the sentence provided a context that biased the meaning choice:

(4-25)   The farmer put his <u>straw</u> beside the machine. *(straw ≠ **drinking-straw**)*

The implication is that despite the context, both meanings of the word were retrieved and considered. However, a replication with the phoneme-monitoring task by Swinney and Hakes (1976), in which the bias of the context was extremely

---

[18] ADAMS, Douglas and LLOYD, John. *The meaning of Liff.* London: Pan Books and Faber and Faber, 1983. Reprinted by permission.

[19] The content of this paragraph and the next is based on Foss and Hakes 1978: 120–124. A good overview and critique of the work discussed in the remainder of this section is also given by Simpson (1981).

strong, found no difference between the reaction time for ambiguous and unambiguous words:

(4-26)   Rumor had it that, for years, the government building had been plagued with
         problems. The man was not surprised when he found several spiders, roaches,
         and other <u>bugs</u> in the corner of his room. *(bug ≠ **hidden microphone***)

These data suggest a partial prior choice model based on activation of word senses. When the correct sense for a particular occurrence of a word is sought, only the most active senses are considered. If the preceding context has highly activated one sense, only that sense will ever be seen; if there is no contextual bias, all senses will be seen, and a choice made from them.[20] A mild contextual bias will not activate a single meaning enough to prevent some of the other meanings from being seen.[21] Blank and Foss (1978) similarly found that the phoneme-monitoring task was facilitated by semantically related prior context, even if the word at which the target occurred was not ambiguous.

This model predicts that if, for some reason, the incorrect meaning of an ambiguous word has been highly pre-activated, then that word will be misinterpreted, resulting in a SEMANTIC GARDEN-PATH SENTENCE. This does in fact occur; most people have a great deal of trouble with NEGATIVELY PRIMED sentences such as these:

(4-27)   The astronomer married the star.

(4-28)   The sailor ate the submarine.

(4-29)   The watchmaker removed the tick.

(4-30)   The rabbi who addressed the congregation was hit on the temple.

(4-31)   The catcher filled the pitcher.[22]

---

[20] Note that it is necessary to assume that spreading activation does NOT spread through the mental representation of words themselves, but only through the representation of meanings. Otherwise, activation would spread from one sense of a word through the word itself to another of its senses, pre-activating more than one of its meanings! Lucas (1983, 1984) tested activation of the various senses of ambiguous words just at their onset, and found that only the sense primed by the context was active, so the assumption seems to be a safe one.

[21] This model is similar to Morton's "logogen" model (1969).

[22] Vocabulary for the non–North American reader: A *submarine* is a type of sandwich, and a *catcher* and a *pitcher* are players on a baseball team; readers who prefer cricket to baseball may substitute (i) for (4-31):

(i)   The wicket-keeper wore the bowler.

Example (4-27) is due to John Anderson (Lynne Reder, personal communication), and examples (4-29) to (4-31) are based on ones from Reder 1983; (4-28) and (i) are my own.

Reder (1983) found that comprehension errors increased markedly in negatively primed sentences. For example, in (4-27), people often take *star* to be **astronomical object** instead of **celebrity**, although this violates selectional restrictions on *marry*, and then become confused, or attempt to reinterpret the sentence metaphorically. (There seem to be wide individual differences in the processing of such sentences. This is to be expected to some extent, as people will differ in their mental organization of concepts and hence in the exact boundary effects of spreading activation.)

Note that the partial prior choice model differs significantly from the script model. While it claims that there is often a prior choice, it does not rely solely on context to provide a unique word sense, but also contains a complete (unspecified) disambiguation mechanism for use in mild or neutral contexts where no single sense is more highly activated than the others. Also, it accounts not only for the effect of global context but the effect of local word association as well; scripts, even if they had psychological reality, could not be the only sense pre-selection mechanism.

There are, however, three major criticisms of these results. The first is that none of these experiments controlled for relative sense frequency.[23] The ordered search hypothesis suggests that the word *bug* in (4-26) is disambiguated quickly just because **insect** is the more common meaning; most people would require only one lexical access to get this sense, whereas a context indicating the **hidden microphone** sense would require a second access after the **insect** sense failed. On the other hand, (4-25) would require an average of 1.5 accesses to disambiguate *straw*, as neither of its senses dominates the other, and we would therefore expect that about 50% of the subjects would get it on the first access and 50% would require a second access.[24] Thus the discrepancy between the results of Foss and Jenkins and those of Swinney and Hakes would be explained as artifacts of their experimental materials.[25]

---

[23] Experiments on eye fixations in reading suggest that lexical retrieval time is in general a function of word frequency (Just and Carpenter 1980).

[24] Foss and Jenkins's own data on meaning preferences for *straw* show that in a neutral context (*The merchant put the straw beside the machine*), 48% of subjects chose the **hay** meaning and 52% chose **drinking-straw**.

[25] Also indicating an effect of word frequency are the results of Carpenter and Daneman (1981), who had subjects read aloud texts in which one of the meanings of a heteronym (an ambiguous word whose meanings have different pronunciations) was biased by the previous context. They found that readers not infrequently said the more frequent meaning of the word, even when the bias was otherwise, and did not always correct themselves even when the rest of the sentence made it clear that their choice was wrong.

One cannot generalize from their results, however, as reading aloud may require different strategies from normal sentence comprehension, since there is not the same motivation to process the sentence completely, but instead a desire to say the word as soon as possible after seeing it (though voice trails a word or two behind eye fixation), and simple word recognition without complete comprehension is

The second criticism of the phoneme-monitoring experiments is that they infer the difficulty of processing an ambiguous word from the degree to which it seems to interfere with the phoneme recognition process. However, the target phoneme was always in a word after the ambiguous word, leaving a relatively long temporal gap after the occurrence of the ambiguity. Thus, phoneme-monitoring tasks at best give information about the processing load AFTER lexical access, but provide no clue about lexical access itself (Swinney 1979). In the Foss (1970) and Foss and Jenkins (1973) experiments, the target phoneme usually started the syllable after the ambiguous word, but was sometimes the start of the second syllable following; in Swinney and Hakes's (1976) experiment, the target was as many as three syllables away from the ambiguity ("never more than two words" (Swinney and Hakes 1976:685)). This alone may account for the difference in the results, as Cairns and Kamerman (1975) have shown that a two-word distance between the ambiguity and the target is sufficient to eliminate any latency effect of the ambiguity.

The third criticism is that the length and phonological properties of the words used in the tests could account for most of the effect found. See Newman and Dell 1978 or Swinney 1979:647 for details of this point, which need not concern us further here.

I now turn to work that attempts to overcome these criticisms. In the next section, I look at work that controls for dominant word sense, and in the section after that, at work that avoids the other methodological problems of phoneme monitoring.

4.3.3 The ordered search hypothesis

Hogaboam and Perfetti (1975) tested the ordered search hypothesis with a set of ambiguous words that each had a dominant sense and a secondary sense;[26] for example, the dominant sense of *arms* is **human limbs**, and the secondary sense is **weapons**.[27] Instead of using a phoneme monitoring task, they asked subjects to respond as rapidly as possible when the last word of a sentence could have a meaning other than the one it had in the sentence. Given (4-32):

(4-32)   A good sprinter uses his arms.

a subject would have to respond positively, and then briefly explain the **weapons** sense of *arms*. The ordered search hypothesis predicts that subjects will be faster

---

adequate for giving the pronunciation of most words; *cf.* Shallice, Warrington, and McCarthy 1983.

[26]There is evidence that the most frequent sense is psychologically distinguished. For example, schizophrenia patients often interpret ambiguous words only with their most frequent meaning, even if the result is nonsense (Chapman, Chapman, and Miller 1964; Benjamin and Watt 1969).

[27]These norms were determined by word association tests. Given a stimulus such as *arms*, most subjects would respond with, say, "legs", while few would say "rifles" or "right to keep and bear shall not be infringed".

on this task when the sentence uses the secondary meaning, as the primary meaning will have already been accessed and rejected, and the subject will know the word to be ambiguous. On the other hand, if the dominant meaning is used, the subject will still have to see if a second access is possible, in order to determine whether the word is ambiguous, and reaction time will be slower. Both the prior choice and all-readings hypotheses predict no difference in the two cases. Hogaboam and Perfetti found the result predicted by the ordered search hypothesis. However, as Swinney and Hakes (1976) and Onifer and Swinney (1981) point out, the nature of the task, in which subjects explicitly and consciously listened for ambiguity, may have affected the manner in which they processed the sentences, and thus the results may not reflect normal unconscious lexical access.[28] Simpson (1981) therefore tested the same hypothesis, but used a simple lexical decision task in which an ambiguous word was followed by a second word, either related to its dominant meaning, or to its secondary meaning, or completely unrelated. Supporting the ordered search hypothesis, he found that response time on the second word was faster only when it was related to the dominant meaning of the first word; words whose relationship was to the secondary sense had a reaction time as slow as unrelated words.

However, Simpson repeated his experiment with the addition of context; the ambiguous word was now the final word of a sentence that gave either a strong bias, a weak bias, or no bias to the ambiguous word. In the unbiased case, the results were as before. However, in a strongly biased context, retrieval was facilitated only for words related to the biased sense of the ambiguous word, regardless of whether it was the dominant or secondary sense. In a weakly biased context, a dominant sense facilitated retrieval only of words related to that sense, but a secondary sense facilitated both. Simpson's interpretation of these results is that the dominance of one sense and the effects of context are independent. Without context, dominance prevails, and only the primary sense is initially retrieved. In a strong context, context effects prevail, and only the appropriate sense is retrieved initially. But when the context only weakly chooses the secondary sense, neither context nor dominance prevails, and both senses are retrieved. The activation model can account for these results if we allow two changes: first, that dominant word senses are given a "head start" in the activation race, a lead that can be overcome by strong bias to the secondary meaning but only equaled by weak bias; and second, that if the sense or senses retrieved the first time are found unacceptable, the other senses are then retrieved.

---

[28] An example of how the nature of the task can affect results, even when the subjects are not conscious of ambiguity in the stimuli: Yates (1978) had subjects respond as fast as possible with the truth of statements of the form *An A is a B*, where *A* was a homonym and *B* was either its dominant sense or a very unusual sense: *A bug is an insect*, *A bug is a Volkswagen*. If subjects received trials that used dominant and unusual senses equally often, then semantic priming facilitated access to both senses; if they received trials that mostly used dominant senses, then priming facilitated dominant senses more than it did secondary senses. Note that subjects were not told about the ambiguity in the stimuli, nor about the distribution of dominant and secondary senses that they could expect.

4.3.4 Semantic priming and the all-readings hypothesis

Contrary to Simpson's results, other recent work provides evidence for the all-readings hypothesis. Swinney (1979) used the test materials of the Swinney and Hakes (1976) experiment but substituted a lexical decision task ("Is this string a word?") for phoneme monitoring. To reduce the temporal gap, the string for the lexical decision was presented on a computer terminal exactly as the end of the ambiguous word was heard. He found that the speed of the lexical decision task was increased when the string was a word related to some sense of the ambiguous word, even if the context was strongly biased toward another sense. This was true even for strings related to the secondary sense when the context was biased to the dominant sense (Onifer and Swinney 1981). The implication is that both senses were accessed and primed in all contexts. A similar experiment by Tanenhaus, Leiman, and Seidenberg (hereafter *TLS*) (1979) showed that the effect held even for categorially ambiguous homonyms;[29] for example, a sentence such as (4-33):

(4-33)   They needed a new <u>sink</u>.

facilitated the word *swim*, which is related to the verb *sink* but not to the noun form used in the stimulus.

When the experiment was repeated with the lexical decision task occurring three syllables after the ambiguous word (in the replication by TLS), or 1.5 seconds after it (in the Onifer and Swinney 1981 replication), only strings related to the contextually appropriate meaning of the ambiguous word were facilitated, suggesting that the activation of the inappropriate sense decays, or is actively suppressed (TLS 1979:436), in less than the span of three syllables (or 1.5 seconds). In fact, TLS found that with categorial ambiguities, the facilitation effect had disappeared within only 200 milliseconds; Lucas (1983, 1984) found it still present after 100 and 125 milliseconds with noun–noun ambiguities.[30]

However, a subsequent study cast doubt on the generality of these results. In a series of experiments, Seidenberg, Tanenhaus, Leiman, and Bienkowski *(STLB)* (1982; Seidenberg and Tanenhaus 1980) varied the type of ambiguity—noun homonyms or categorially ambiguous noun–verb homonyms—and the type of context that biased the sense of the ambiguous verbs. The types of context were as follows:

•   Neutral—No contextual cues to resolve ambiguity: *Joe buys the <u>straw</u>.*

---

[29] Instead of a lexical decision task, TLS's experiments used word-naming; the strings were always words, which the subjects had to say out loud, thereby stopping a sound-activated timer.

[30] An initial explanation for the discrepancy between Simpson's results *(see previous section)* and TLS's was that Simpson had used a 120-millisecond gap between the stimulus and target (1981:134); however, Lucas's results cast doubt on this. Nevertheless, these every-millisecond-counts results should be treated with caution. Simpson points out (1981:130) that determining the exact millisecond at which the stimulus ends and timing should commence is made extremely difficult by variations in the characteristics of the final phoneme of the stimulus, the volume of the speaker's voice, and so on.

Table 4.1. *Summary of results of Seidenberg et al (1982)*

TYPE OF CONTEXT	TYPE OF LEXI-CAL AMBIGUITY	OUTCOME
Neutral	Noun–Noun	Multiple access
Syntactic	Noun–Verb	Multiple access
Semantic priming	Noun–Noun	Selective access
Semantic priming	Noun–Verb	Multiple access
Non-priming biased	Noun–Noun	Multiple access

(From Seidenberg, Tanenhaus, Leiman, and Bienkowski 1982.)

- Semantic priming—The context contains a word associated with one sense of the ambiguous word: *The bridge player trumped the spade.*

- Syntactic bias—The syntax of the context selects the noun or verb sense of a categorially ambiguous word: *The congregation rose.*

- Non-priming biased—The context selects one sense of a noun homonym, but does so without containing any word related to that sense: *The man walked on the deck.*

Using the same techniques as the previous experiments, they found that all senses seemed to be activated (for less than 200 milliseconds), EXCEPT in the case of noun homonyms in a semantically primed context, when only the context-related sense was activated;[31] table 4.1 summarizes these results. Thus prior choice occurs only when the context contains a semantically related concept; a context that constrains the sense only by selectional restrictions or the like does not inhibit multiple access. Further, semantically primed contexts do NOT inhibit multiple access in categorially ambiguous words.[32]

---

[31] Lucas (1984) has suggested that there is multiple access in ALL cases, and in apparent exceptions it is simply extremely fast.

[32] In contrast to this finding, Ryder and Walker (1982) found that without context only the most frequent sense of a categorial ambiguity seemed to be activated. It is possible that this was because the ambiguous word was presented for a full second before the probe; STLB's results suggest that this was long enough for a meaning to have been activated and decay again. On the other hand, even though they had a 500-millisecond delay after the ambiguous stimulus, Oden and Spira (1983) obtained results partly supporting STLB: both senses of a categorially ambiguous word were activated, though the one to which the context was biased was activated more. Unfortunately these results must be used with caution, as there were errors in their experimental materials. For example, the words *bounce* and *jump* were used to bias the word *spring* toward the sense **coil**, and the senses of the homophone pair *die* and *dye* were taken to be about equally common, although they clearly are not.

Swinney (1979), Onifer and Swinney (1981), and Simpson (1981), although they used strongly biased contexts, did not control for semantic priming as the source of the bias; some of their sentences contained semantically related words, while others had non-priming bias (Onifer and Swinney 1981: 234):

(4-34)   The team [*prime*] came out of the locker room with fire in their eyes after the coach delivered what was perhaps the best speech of his life.

(4-35)   John sat down to make out checks for the monthly bills, but could not find a single working pen anywhere in the house.

STLB suggest that this may be why Swinney and Onifer and Swinney found apparent multiple access in all cases.[33] Not controlling for this type of bias may also have confounded Simpson's results.

STLB suggest a model in which semantic priming and frequency of use both affect activation, but non-priming bias does not. If one sense is much more pre-activated than the others, it alone is selected; otherwise several or all senses are. Also in this model, categorially ambiguous words are represented separately for each syntactic category; thus semantic priming of one noun sense of a word may cause that sense to be favored over other noun senses, but won't restrict access to any verb senses of the same word.[34]

Subsequent work has sought to clarify the role of word frequency in this model. Simpson and Burgess (1985; Simpson 1984), presenting homographs out of context, measured facilitation at several points after the stimulus, from 16 milliseconds to 750 milliseconds. They found the dominant sense active at all points; the secondary sense became active more slowly, however, being facilitated between 100 and 500 milliseconds, but not at 16 or 750 milliseconds. This suggests that dominant senses have a "head start", but not so as to preclude activation of a secondary sense; in the absence of context, the dominant sense wins, and the activation of the other sense decays.

4.3.5 Conclusion

There are clearly many questions yet to be resolved in the study of human lexical access and disambiguation. However, this much seems clear: in many cases, more than one meaning of an ambiguous word is accessed. Semantic priming and frequency of a particular sense can facilitate lexical access and disambiguation, and

---

[33] They also suggest that the difference may be due to the fact that the priming word, when there was one, was further from the ambiguity in Swinney's and Onifer and Swinney's experiments—four or more words earlier, instead of two or three as in STLB's sentences, with the priming effect already starting to decay. However, if priming has an effect at all, one would expect it to last longer than that, or it would lose much of its functional advantage. A more interesting question is what the effect of a clause boundary between the prime and the ambiguity might be.

[34] See also Stanovich and West 1983b for a model of contextual priming that includes spreading activation.

in some cases may cause one meaning to be accessed to the exclusion of others. In the next chapter, I develop a lexical disambiguation system for use with Absity that has similar properties.

5   Polaroid Words

5.1 Introduction

In the description of Absity in chapter 3, I made the unrealistic assumption that each word and pseudo-word corresponds to the same unique semantic object whenever and wherever it occurs; that is, I assumed there to be no lexical ambiguity and no case flag ambiguity. In this chapter, I will remove this assumption. The goal will be to develop a method for disambiguating words and case flags within the framework of Absity, finding the correct semantic object for an ambiguous lexeme.

Since Absity is "Montague-inspired" *(sections 2.2.2 and 3.2)*, the obvious thing to do first is see how Montague handled lexical ambiguity in his PTQ formalism (Montague 1973) *(see section 2.2.2)*. It turns out, however, that Montague had nothing to say on the matter. His PTQ fragment assumes, as we did in chapter 3 but no longer wish to, that there is a unique semantic object for each lexeme.[1] Nor does Montague explicitly use case flags. The verbs of the fragment are all treated as one-place or two-place functions, and syntactic position in the sentence distinguishes the arguments. Nevertheless, there is an easy opening in the formalism where we may deal with lexical ambiguity: except for a few special words, Montague's formalism does not specify where the translation of a word comes from; rather, there is assumed to be a function g that maps a word α to its translation, or semantic object, $g(\alpha)$, and as long as $g(\alpha)$ (which is usually denoted α') is of the correct semantic type, it doesn't really matter how g does its mapping. This means that if we can "hide" disambiguation inside g, we need make no change to the formalism itself to deal with ambiguity in PTQ.

Moreover, we can do exactly the same thing in Absity. Absity, like the PTQ formalism, does not put any constraints on the lexicon look-up process that associates a word, pseudo-word, or case flag with its corresponding semantic object.

---

[1] Montague allows the extension of the denotation of the object to differ in different possible worlds and points in time. This is not the same as lexical ambiguity, however. While the set of things that are pens, say, may vary over indexes, he makes no provision for allowing more than one set at the same index, with the appropriate set depending upon the context that contains the lexeme.

If this process could disambiguate each lexeme before returning the semantic object to Absity, then no change would have to be made to Absity itself to deal with ambiguity; disambiguation would be completely transparent to it.

There is, however, an immediate catch in this scheme: often a word cannot be disambiguated until well after its occurrence, whereas Absity wants its semantic object as soon as the word appears. But this is easily fixed. What we shall do is give Absity a FAKE semantic object, with the promise that in due course it shall be replaced by the real thing. The fake can be labeled with everything that Absity needs to know about the object, that is, with the word itself and its semantic type (which is readily determined). Absity can build its semantic structure with the fake, and when the real object is available, it can just be slipped in where the fake is. We will do this thus: the fakes that we shall give Absity will be self-developing Polaroid[2] photographs of the semantic object, and the promise shall be that by the time the sentence is complete, the photograph will be a fully developed picture of the desired semantic object. And even as the picture develops, Absity will be able to manipulate the photograph, build it into a structure, and indeed do everything with it that it could do with a fully developed photograph, except look at the final picture. Moreover, like real Polaroid photographs, these will have the property that as development takes place, the partly developed picture will be viewable and usable in its degraded form. That is, just as one can look at a partly developed Polaroid picture and determine whether it is a picture of a person or a mountain range, but perhaps not which person or which mountain range, so it will be possible to look at our POLAROID WORDS and get a partial idea of what the semantic objects they show look like.[3]

I will describe the operation of Polaroid Words in section 5.3. Before then, in section 5.2, I will discuss marker passing, a mechanism that Polaroid Words will use for finding associations between words.[4] In section 5.4, I discuss some of the ways in which Polaroid Words are not yet adequate. I then compare our use of lexical and world knowledge with that of linguistic theory (section 5.5), and discuss the extent to which Polaroid Words are a psychological model (section 5.6). I assume throughout this chapter that the sentence is not structurally ambiguous. In chapter 7, I will show how Polaroid Words work when the correct parse of the sentence cannot be immediately determined.

5.2 Marker passing

In chapter 4, we saw the importance of semantic associations between words in

---

[2]*Polaroid* is a trademark of the Polaroid Corporation for its range of photographic and other products. It is used here to emphasize the metaphor of a self-developing semantic object, and the system described herein carries no association with, or endorsement by, the Polaroid Corporation.

[3]This point will also be important in chapter 7, when I describe the Semantic Enquiry Desk.

[4]These sections differ in some details from the description of an earlier design in Hirst and Charniak 1982.

lexical disambiguation. Section 4.1 showed that an association between one sense of an ambiguous word and other words in the sentence or context can be an important disambiguation cue. Psycholinguistic research on lexical disambiguation showed that semantic priming—that is, the previous occurrence of an associated word—speeds up people's disambiguation *(section 4.3.1)* and may lead the retrieval process straight to the correct meaning.[5]

The lexical disambiguation program for Absity therefore needs a mechanism that will allow it to find semantic associations. One such mechanism was that of Hayes's CSAW system *(section 4.2.3)*, which imposed upon a semantic network a frame system with ISA and PART-OF hierarchies in order to detect associations. Our mechanism will be similar but more general; we will use MARKER PASSING in the Frail knowledge base.

Marker passing can be thought of as passing tags or markers along the arcs of the knowledge base, from frame to frame, from slot to filler, under the rules to be discussed below *(section 5.2.3)*. It is a discrete computational analogue of the SPREADING ACTIVATION models that we saw in section 4.3. The network of frames corresponds to the mental conceptual and lexical network, with the fact of a connection's existence implying a semantic relationship of some kind between its two nodes. Passing a marker from one node to another corresponds to activating the receiving node. If marker passing is breadth-first from the starting point (new markers being created if a node wishes to pass to two or more other nodes simultaneously), then marker passing will "spread" much as spreading activation does.

Marker passing was first used in AI by Quillian (1968, 1969), who used it to find connections between concepts in a semantic network. Marker passing is, of course, expensive when the net is interestingly large. Fahlman (1979), who used it for deduction in his NETL system, proposed super-parallel hardware for marker passing. Although our scheme is much simpler than Fahlman's, we too assume that hardware of the future will, like people of the present, be able to derive connections between concepts in parallel, and that the serial implementation to be described below is only an interim measure.

5.2.1 Marker passing in Frail

The frame language Frail *(see section 1.3.1)* contains a built-in marker passer (*MP* for short) that operates upon the Frail knowledge base (Charniak, Gavin, and Hendler 1983).[6] The MP is called with the name of a node (a frame, slot, or instance) as its argument, to use as a starting point. From this origin, it marks all

---

[5]Or perhaps straight to an incorrect meaning, if the semantic prime is misleading; see sections 4.3.1 and 5.6.1.

[6]Research is proceeding at Brown in other applications for marker passing besides those discussed here. These include context recognition and discovering causal connections (Charniak 1981b, 1982) and problem solving (Hendler 1985, 1986a).

nodes in the knowledge base that participate in assertions that also contain the origin; these can include slots, slot restrictions and ISA relationships. For example, suppose the origin is to be the frame that describes airplanes:

```
(5-1)     [frame:  airplane
              isa:  vehicle
            slots:  (owner (airline))
                    (type (airplane-type))
                    ... ]
```

Markers would be placed on `vehicle`, `owner`, `airline`, `type`, `airplane-type`, and so on. Markers take the form of a list of node names interleaved with the assertion that permitted the marker to be placed. In our example, the marker put on `owner` would be (5-2):

```
(5-2)     (airplane
              (slot owner airplane)
          owner)
```

which simply says that a marker went from `airplane` to `owner` because the latter is a slot of the former. The mark on `airline` would be (5-3):

```
(5-3)     (airplane
              (restriction (owner (airplane)) (airline))
          airline)
```

which says that a marker went from `airplane` to `airline` because the latter is what the contents of the `owner` slot of the former must be.

Once all the nodes reachable in one step from the origin are marked, each node reachable from these nodes—that is, each node two steps from the origin—is marked. These nodes are marked in the same way. For example, if an ISA link connects `airline` and `corporation`, then the mark on `corporation` would be (5-4):

```
(5-4)     (airplane
              (restriction (owner (airplane)) (airline))
          airline
              (isa airline corporation)
          corporation)
```

Thus marker passing proceeds, fanning out from the origin until all nodes whose distance is *n* or less from the origin have been marked, where *n* defaults to 5 if the programmer doesn't specify otherwise.[7]

If at any time during marker passing the MP comes upon a node already marked by a previous call, then a PATH (or CHAIN) has been found between the origin node of the present call and that of a previous call. The MP uses the pre-existing mark

---

[7] The astute reader will recognize 5 as being in the range 7±2; see my remarks in section 5.6.3 about "magic numbers" in marker passing.

on the node to construct the full origin-to-origin path. Suppose that in the example above, the `corporation` node had been found to have the following mark, indicating a connection to it from `president`:

```
(5-5)    (corporation
               (slot president corporation)
         president)
```

The MP can then note that the following path has been found between `airplane` and `president`:

```
(5-6)    (airplane
               (restriction (owner (airplane))) (airline))
         airline
               (isa airline corporation)
         corporation
               (slot president corporation)
         president)
```

It is also possible that the origin itself has been marked by a previous call to the MP, resulting in an instantly discovered path. I call such paths IMMEDIATE PATHS to distinguish them from CONSTRUCTED PATHS, such as that of the example above in which the intersection occurs at a third node.

When marking is finished, the MP returns a list of all the paths (if any) that it found. The user may, at any time, clean the markers from all nodes in the knowledge base.

5.2.2 Lexical disambiguation with marker passing

In this section, I give a very simple example of lexical disambiguation with the Frail marker passer that was discussed in the previous section. In later sections, I will refine and extend these disambiguation mechanisms considerably.

The marker passer operates independently of Absity and in parallel with it. That is, following only basic morphological analysis, the input sentence goes to both the Paragram parser and the MP, both of which separately grind away on each word as it comes in. Suppose the input is (5-7), an example chosen especially because it contains several ambiguous words that can be resolved purely by association cues:

(5-7)   Nadia's plane taxied to the terminal.

The words *plane*, *taxi*, and *terminal* are all ambiguous. Note that the ambiguity of *taxi* is categorial: it can be a noun meaning **vehicle with driver for hire**, or a verb meaning (of an airplane) **to travel at low speed on the ground**. Since the MP has no access to syntactic information, it looks at all meanings for each word, regardless of part of speech; marker chains from syntactically inappropriate origins will be ignored by other processes.

As the words come in from left to right, the MP passes markers from the frames representing each known meaning of each open-class word in the sentence (including unambiguous ones such as *Nadia*). In (5-7), immediate paths would be found between the frames `airplane` and `airport-building`, which were starting points for *plane* and *terminal*, and between `airplane` and `aircraft-ground-travel` (*plane* and *taxi*), indicating that the corresponding meanings of *plane*, *terminal*, and *taxi* should be chosen. (A path will also be found between `airport-building` and `aircraft-ground-travel`, but this adds no new information.) Markers will also be passed from the frames representing the other meanings of *plane*, *taxi*, and *terminal*, namely `wood-smoother`, `taxi-cab`, and `computer-terminal`, but these paths will go off into the wilderness and never connect with any of the other paths.[8]

5.2.3 Constraining marker passing

Since marker passing is a blind and mindless process, it is clear that many paths in the knowledge base will be marked besides the ones that provide useful disambiguating information. In fact, if the MP gets too carried away, it will eventually mark everything in the knowledge base, as every node in the base can be reached from any other, and we will then find paths between the wrong senses of ambiguous words as well as between the right senses.[9] For example, a connection could be found between `airplane` and `computer-terminal` simply by passing markers up the ISA chain from `airplane` through `vehicle` and the like to `mechanical-object`, and then down another ISA chain from there to `computer-terminal`. Therefore, to prevent as many "uninteresting" and misleading paths as possible, we put certain constraints on the MP and prohibit it from taking certain steps.

First, as I mentioned in section 5.2.1, Frail passes markers a maximum of *n* arcs from the origin. One would normally choose *n* to be small compared to the size of the knowledge base. Second, Frail permits the programmer to specify restrictions on passing along various types of path. For example, by default the MP will pass markers only upwards along ISA links, not downwards—that is, markers are passed to more general concepts, but never to more particular ones (prohibiting thereby the path from `mechanical-object` to `computer-terminal` mentioned above). These restrictions are specified in the form of a predicate supplied by the programmer and attached to the name of the arc. Before attempting to pass

---

[8] Howe (1983; Howe and Finin 1984) has used marker passing in a manner similar to this in an on-line help system to identify which information is relevant to a query.

[9] This statement assumes, reasonably, that the knowledge base has no disconnected subgraphs. The converse would imply that there is some piece of knowledge that is completely unrelated to any other part of the knowledge base, which would be a very peculiar situation. I also assume that all arcs can be traversed in both directions. This is the case in Frail.

a marker, the MP will evaluate the predicate, which has access to the origin, the present node, and the path between them; if the value of the predicate is `nil`, no marker is passed.

Determining exactly what restrictions should be placed on marker passing is a matter for experiment (see Hendler 1986a, 1986b). I postulate restrictions such as an ANTI-PROMISCUITY RULE: not allowing paths to propagate from nodes with more than c connections, for some chosen c. This is because nodes with many connections tend to be uninteresting ones near the top of the ISA hierarchy—`mechanical-object`, for example. We must be careful, however, not to be so restrictive that we also prevent the useful paths that we are looking for from occurring. And no matter how clever we are at blocking misleading paths, we must be prepared for the fact that they will occasionally turn up. The problem of such FALSE POSITIVES is discussed by Charniak (1981b), who posits a PATH CHECKER that would filter out many paths that are uninteresting or silly.

> This theory that I have, that is to say which is mine, is mine. My theory, that I have, follows the lines that I am about to relate. The next thing that I am about to say is my theory. Ready? My theory is along the following lines.
> —Anne Elk[10]

5.3 Polaroid Words

In section 5.1, I introduced the idea of the Polaroid Word mechanism (*PW* to its friends), which would be responsible for disambiguating each word. We saw in section 4.1 that there are many sources of information that can be used in disambiguation, and it would be up to the mechanism of the PWs to use whatever information is available to it to make a decision for each word. Often, as in the case of example (5-7) of section 5.2.2, all that is required is looking at the paths found by the marker passer. At other times, MP will return nothing overwhelmingly conclusive; or, in the case of a polysemous word, more than one meaning may be marked. It would then be necessary for PWs to use other information and negotiation between possible meanings. In this section I will describe the operation of Polaroid Words in detail.

5.3.1 What Polaroid Words look like

While it would be quite possible to operate Polaroid Words under the control of a single supervisory procedure that took the responsibility for the development of each "photograph", it seems more natural to instead put the disambiguation mechanism (and the responsibility) into each individual Polaroid Word. That is, a PW

---

[10]MONTY PYTHON. "Miss Anne Elk." *Monty Python's previous record.* Charisma, 1972.

```
[slug (noun):
    gastropod-without-shell
    bullet
    metal-stamping
    shot-of-liquor]
```

Figure 5.1. Packet of knowledge for *slug* for noun Polaroid Word.

will be a procedure, running in parallel with other PWs,[11] whose job it is to disambiguate a single instance of a word. At this point, however, we find we must stretch the Polaroid photograph metaphor, for unlike a real self-developing photograph, a PW's development cannot be completely self-contained; the PWs will have to communicate with one another and with their environment in order to get the information necessary for their disambiguation. The idea of communicating one-per-word procedures brings to mind Small's word experts, described in section 4.2.4 (Small 1980, 1983; Small and Rieger 1982). The similarity between PWs and Small's procedures is, however, only superficial; the differences will become apparent as I describe PWs in detail.

Instead of having a different PW for each word, we have but one kind of PW for each syntactic category; that is, there is a noun PW and a verb PW, and each noun uses the same disambiguation procedure as all the other nouns, each verb uses the same procedure as the other verbs, and similarly for other syntactic categories.[12] The knowledge about the meaning of each individual word is kept distinct from the disambiguation procedure itself, and indeed much of the knowledge used by PWs is obtained from the Frail knowledge base when it is necessary. When a new PW is needed, an instance of the appropriate type is cloned and is given a little packet of knowledge about the word for which it will be responsible. (Sometimes I will be sloppy and call these packets Polaroid Words as well. No confusion should result.) As far as possible, the packets will contain only lexical knowledge—that is, only knowledge about how the word is used, rather than world knowledge (already available through Frail) about the properties of the word's denotations.

The simplest packet of knowledge is that for a noun: it just contains a list of the semantic objects (frames; *see table 3.2*) that the noun could represent. Figure 5.1 shows the knowledge packet for the noun *slug*. Any information needed about properties of the senses of the noun is obtained from the Frail knowledge base.

The packet for prepositions is a little more complicated; listed with the possi-

---

[11]In the implementation described below, only one PW is active at a time, in order to simplify the implementation.

[12]At present, PWs are implemented only for nouns, verbs, prepositions, and, in rudimentary form, noun modifiers. Determiners are straightforward, and PWs for them may exist later; see section 5.3.6.

```
[with (prep):
    instrument      (and physobj (not animate))
    manner          manner-quality
    accompanier     physobj]
```

Figure 5.2. Packet of knowledge for *with* for preposition Polaroid Word.

ble semantic objects, whose semantic type is *slot (see table 3.2)*, is a SLOT RE-
STRICTION PREDICATE for each—a predicate that specifies what is required of an
instance to be allowed to fill the slot. Figure 5.2 shows the packet for the preposition *with*; it assumes that the preposition is a case flag. (PWs for prepositions of
noun-modifying PPs will be discussed in section 7.2.) A simple predicate, such as
physobj ("physical object"), requires that the slot-filler be under the specified
node in the ISA hierarchy. A complex predicate may specify a boolean combination
of features that the filler must satisfy; thus in figure 5.2, the filler of instrument
must be a physobj, but not an animate one. Predicates may also require that
a property be proved of the filler; (property sharp) is an example of such a
predicate.

The predicates for each slot are, in effect, the most restrictive predicate compatible with the restrictions on all instances of the slot in the knowledge base; thus,
in figure 5.2, the predicate for INSTRUMENT is true of all INSTRUMENTs (flagged by
with) in all verbs in the system. Clearly, the more verbs that are added, the less
restrictive these predicates will become; in fact, INSTRUMENTs do not, contrary to
figure 5.2, always have to be physical objects at all:

(5-8)   Nadia proved Loams's theorem <u>with the Marmot lemma</u>.

Thus, if we added a frame for *prove* to the knowledge base, we would have to
modify the PW for *with* as well, making the predicate for INSTRUMENT less restrictive. It does not follow, however, that the predicates will eventually become
information-free. In English, for example, an animate entity can never be an
INSTRUMENT,[13] so that particular restriction will always remain. Ideally, there
would be a process that would automatically compile the preposition information
packets from the knowledge base and would help ensure that things remain consistent when words are added or changed.

---

[13]Thus, although (i) is all right, (ii) sounds funny, and one has to say (iii) instead to convey its meaning:

(i)   Ross broke the window <u>with a potplant</u>.

(ii)   *Ross broke the window <u>with Nadia</u>.

(iii)   Ross broke the window by throwing Nadia through it.

```
[operate (verb):
    [cause-to-function
        agent          SUBJ
        patient        SUBJ, OBJ
        instrument     SUBJ, with
        method         by
        manner         with
        accompanier    with]
    [perform-surgery
        agent          SUBJ
        patient        upon, on
        instrument     with
        method         by
        manner         with
        accompanier    with] ]
```

Figure 5.3. Packet of knowledge for *operate* for verb Polaroid Word.

Verbs have the most complex knowledge packets. Figure 5.3 shows the packet for *operate*. For each meaning the case slots that it takes are listed, with the preposition or prepositions that may flag each slot. Slot restriction predicates for each slot need not be specified in the packet, because they may be immediately found in the corresponding frame. These predicates will, in general, be more restrictive than the predicates given in the PW for the corresponding preposition, but they must, of course, be compatible. For example, in the perform-surgery frame, the predicate on instrument may be (property sharp), which particularizes the predicate shown for instrument in 5.2; a predicate such as hanim ("higher animate being") would contradict that in figure 5.2 and would indicate trouble somewhere. It should be clear that if the semantics are properly characterized, contradictions will not occur, but, again, an automatic system for maintaining consistency would be helpful.

Unlike the other PW knowledge packets, the verb packets contain information that might also be readily obtained from Frail's knowledge base,[14] namely the slots that each verb frame has. This is necessary, because the knowledge packet has to include a listing of the prepositions that flag each of the verb's slots, and hence

---

[14]The preposition packets contain knowledge from the knowledge base too, namely slot restriction predicates. However, this is not easily accessible knowledge, as it requires a complete tour of the knowledge base to determine a predicate. Moreover, it may be argued that some words have slot restriction predicates that are not semantically motivated and therefore cannot be determined from the knowledge base. In this analysis, it would be argued that the restriction of inanimateness on the INSTRUMENT of *break* mentioned in footnote 13 is purely a lexical matter, that sentence (ii) of that footnote is semantically well-formed and its unacceptability is a quirk of English, and that sentence (iii) should in fact be represented as an instance with an animate INSTRUMENT.

the slots have to be listed, necessarily adding a little world knowledge to the word knowledge. The alternative, listing the flags in the Frail definition of the frame, would just be the same sin at a different site. Ideally, one would like to be able to remove this information from the individual verbs altogether and rather store generalizations about case flags as they relate to the semantic properties of verbs. That is, since verbs are classified in Frail's ISA hierarchy under such generalizations as `transitive-action` and `transfer-action` in order to support the obvious needs of inference, and since this also provides a nice generalization of slots—for example, all `transfer-actions` have `source` and `destination` slots—we could store a small table that mapped each general verb frame category to a set of flags for its slots. Alas, English is just not quite regular enough to permit this; verbs can get quite idiosyncratic about their case flags. We have already seen that the two senses of *operate* have quite different sets of case flags, although both are `transitive-actions`. Another example is the common senses of the verbs *buy* and *sell*, which are often analyzed as referring to the same frame, varying only in how the case flags are mapped to its slots; see figure 5.4 for an example. We should not complain about the idiosyncrasy of case flags, however, for it is often a great help in verb disambiguation, especially if the verb is polysemous.

5.3.2 How Polaroid Words operate

PWs operate in parallel with Absity and the parser. As each word comes in to the parser and its syntactic category is assigned, a PW process is created for it. The way the process works is described below.

There are two easy cases. The first, obviously, is that the word is unambiguous. If this is the case, the PW process merely announces the meaning and uninterestingly hibernates—PWs always announce the fact and knock off work as soon as they have narrowed their possible meanings to just one. The second easy case is that the marker passer, which has been looking for paths between senses of the new word and unrejected senses of those already seen, finds a nice connection that permits one alternative to be chosen. This was the case with example (5-7) of section 5.2.2. We will discuss in section 5.6.3 exactly what makes a marker passing path "nice"; in general, short constructed paths are nice, and immediate paths are nicer.

If neither of these cases obtains, then the PW has to find out some more about the context in which its word occurs and see which of its alternatives fits best. To do this, it looks at certain preceding PWs to see if they can provide disambiguating information; I will describe this process in a moment. Using the information gathered, the PW will eliminate as many of its alternatives as possible. If this leaves just one possibility, it will announce this fact and terminate itself; if still undecided, it will announce the remaining possibilities, and then sleep until a new word, possibly the bearer of helpful information, comes along.

```
[buy (verb):
  [purchase
        destination    SUBJ
        source         from
        sold-item      OBJ
        exchange       for
        beneficiary    for, INDOBJ] ]

[sell (verb):
  [purchase
        destination    to, INDOBJ
        source         SUBJ
        sold-item      OBJ
        exchange       for
        beneficiary    for] ]
```

Ross sold the lemming to Nadia.
```
(a ?x (purchase ?x (source=Ross)
                   (destination=Nadia)
                   (sold-item=lemming26)))
```

Nadia bought the lemming from Ross.
```
(a ?x (purchase ?x (source=Ross)
                   (destination=Nadia)
                   (sold-item=lemming26)))
```

Figure 5.4. Abbreviated packets of knowledge for *buy* and *sell*, using the same frame but different mappings of case flags to slots, and examples of their use.

Communication between PWs is heavily restricted. The only information that a PW may ask of another is what its remaining possibilities are; that is, each may see other partly or fully developed photographs. In addition, a PW is restricted in two ways as to the other PWs it is allowed to communicate with. First, since a sentence is processed from left to right, when it is initially invoked a PW will be the rightmost word in the sentence so far and may only look to PWs on its left. As new words come in, the PW will be able to see them, subject to the second constraint, namely that each PW may only look at its FRIENDS.[15] Friendships among PWs are defined as follows: verbs are friends with the prepositions and nouns they dominate; prepositions are friends with the nouns of their prepositional phrase and with other prepositions; and noun modifiers are friends with the noun they modify. In addition, if a prepositional phrase is a candidate for attachment to a

---

[15]Note that friendship constraints do not apply to the marker passer.

noun phrase, then the preposition is a friend of the head noun of the NP to which it may be attached *(see section 7.2)*. The intent of the friendship constraints is to restrict the amount of searching for information that a PW has to do; the constraints reflect the intuition that a word has only a very limited sphere of influence with regard to selectional restrictions and the like.

An "announcement" of its meaning possibilities by a PW takes the form of a list of the one or more alternatives from its knowledge packet (with their slot restriction predicates and so on if they are included in the packet) that the PW has not yet eliminated. An announcement is made by posting a notice in an area that all PWs can read; when a PW asks another for its possibilities, what it is actually doing is reading this notice. (PWs only read their friends' notices, of course.)

From the information that the notices provide, the PW eliminates any of its meanings that don't suit its friends. For example, each case slot may occur at most once in a sentence *(see section 1.1.2)*, so if one preposition PW has already decided that it is an AGENT, say, a new preposition PW could cross AGENT off its own list. A preposition PW will also eliminate from its list any cases that its dominating verb does not allow it to flag, and any whose predicates are incompatible with its noun complement. Its friends may still be only partly developed, of course, in which case the number of eliminations it can make may be limited. However, if, say, one of its cases requires a hanim filler but none of the alternatives in the partly developed noun is hanim, then it can confidently cross that case off its list. The PW may use Frail to determine whether a particular sense has the required properties. What is happening here is, of course, very like the use of selectional restriction cues for disambiguation; section 5.5 will discuss some of the differences.

Similarly, nouns and verbs can strike from their lists anything that doesn't fit their prepositional friends, and nouns and noun modifiers can make themselves compatible with each other by ensuring that the sense selected for the noun is a frame in which the slot–filler pair of the adjective sense will fit. (If a PW finds that this leaves it with no alternatives at all, then it is in trouble; this is discussed in section 5.4.)

When a PW has done all it can, it announces the result, a fully or partly developed picture, and goes to sleep. The announcement wakes up any of its friends that have not yet made their final decision, and each sees whether the new information—both the new word's announcement and any MP chain between the old word and the new—helps it make up its mind. If so, it too makes an announcement of its new possibilities list, in turn awakening its own friends (which will include the first PW again, if it is as yet undecided). This continues until none can do any more and quiescence is achieved. Then the next word in the sentence comes in, its PW is created, and the sequence is repeated.

5.3.3 An example of Polaroid Words in action

Let's consider this example, concentrating on the subordinate clause:

```
[SUBJ (prep):
     agent          animate
     patient        thing
     instrument     physobj
     source         physobj
     destination    physobj]

[OBJ (prep):
     patient        thing
     transferee     physobj]

[vending machine (noun):
     vending-machine]
```

Figure 5.5. Packets of knowledge for *SUBJ*, *OBJ*, and *vending machine*.

(5-9)   Ross found that the slug would operate the vending machine.

(5-10)   SUBJ the slug operate OBJ the vending machine.

Note the insertion of the pseudo-prepositions *SUBJ* and *OBJ*. We want to work out
that *the slug* is a metal stamping, not a gastropod, a bullet, or a shot of whiskey;
that the frame that *operate* refers to is cause-to-function, not perform-
surgery; and that *SUBJ* and *OBJ* indicate the slots instrument and patient
respectively. *Vending machine*, we will say, is unambiguous. For simplicity, we
will ignore the tense and modality of the verb. The PWs for *slug*, *with*, and *operate*
were shown in figures 5.1, 5.2, and 5.3; those for the other words are shown in
figure 5.5.

Disambiguation proceeds as follows. The first words are *SUBJ* and *slug*; their
PWs, when created, have not yet enough information to do anything interesting,
nor has marker passing from the senses of *slug* produced anything (since there are
no other words with which a connection might be found yet). Then *operate* comes
along, and tells the others that it could mean either cause-to-function or
perform-surgery. It too has no way yet of deciding upon its meaning. However, the *SUBJ* PW notices that neither meaning of *operate* uses *SUBJ* to flag the
source or destination case, so it can cross these off its list. It also sees that
while both meanings can flag their agent with *SUBJ*, both require that the agent
be hanim. None of the possibilities for *slug* has this property, so the *SUBJ* PW can
also cross agent off its list, and announce that it means either instrument or
patient.

This wakes up the *operate* PW, which notices that only one of its meanings,
cause-to-function, can take either an instrument or a patient flagged'
by *SUBJ*, so it too announces its meaning. The *slug* PW is also woken up, but it is
unable to use any of this information.

Next comes the word *OBJ*. It could be `patient` or `transferee`, but the verb *operate* doesn't permit the latter, so it announces the former. Note that if *operate* had not already been disambiguated from previous information, this would happen now, as the *operate* PW would notice that only one of its senses takes any case flagged by *OBJ*. Upon hearing that *OBJ* is going to be `patient`, the PW for *SUBJ* now crosses `patient` from its own list, since a case slot can appear but once in a sentence; this leaves it with `instrument` as its meaning. The PW for *slug* is not a friend of that for *OBJ*, so *OBJ*'s announcement does not awaken it.

The noun phrase *vending machine* now arrives, and we assume that it is recognized as a canned phrase representing a single concept (*cf.* Becker 1975, Wilensky and Arens 1980a, 1980b). It brings with it a marker-passing chain that, depending on the exact organization of the frames, might be (5-11):

(5-11)   `vending-machine` → `coin` → `metal-stamping`

since a fact on the `vending-machine` frame would be that they use `coins`, and a `coin` ISA `metal-stamping`. This is enough for the *slug* PW to favor `metal-stamping` as its meaning, and all words are now disambiguated. Now that processing is complete, all markers in the knowledge base are cleared away.

5.3.4 Recovery from doubt

Now let's consider this example, in which marker passing is not used at all:

(5-12)   The <u>crook</u> operated a pizza parlor.[16]

This proceeds as example (5-10) of the previous section did, until *operate* arrives. Since *crook* can either be something that is `hanim`, namely a `criminal`, or not, namely a `shepherd's-staff`, *SUBJ* is unable to make the move that in the previous example disambiguated both it and *operate*, though it can cross `patient` off its list. Still, when *OBJ* comes along, the *operate* PW can immediately eliminate `perform-surgery`. Let us assume that *pizza parlor* is an unambiguous canned phrase, as *vending machine* was. However, after it is processed, the PWs reach a standstill with *SUBJ* and *crook* still undisambiguated, as MP finds no connection between *crook* and *pizza parlor*.

If it happens that at the end of the sentence one or more words are not fully disambiguated, then there are three ways that they may yet be resolved. The first is to invoke knowledge of a PREFERRED or DEPRECATED MEANING for them. Preferred and deprecated meanings are indicated as an additional part of the knowledge packet for each word; a word can have zero or more of each. For example, the meaning `female-swan` of *pen* is deprecated, and should never be chosen unless

---

[16]This is exactly the same meaning of *operate* as in the previous example: `cause-to-function`. In a context like this, the action is habitual, a matter we ignore *(see section 3.8)*.

there is positive evidence for it *(see next paragraph)*; the meaning `writing-instrument` is preferred, and the meaning `enclosure` is neither preferred nor deprecated. The possibilities that remain are ranked accordingly, and the top one or ones are chosen. In the present example, therefore, the two unfinished PWs look for their preferred meanings. It is clear that in English AGENT is far more common for *SUBJ* than the other remaining possibility, INSTRUMENT, and so the *SUBJ* PW should prefer that. This, in turn, will wake up the *crook* PW, which now finds the requirement that its meaning fit *operate*'s `agent`, and therefore chooses `criminal`, completing disambiguation of the sentence.[17]

The second possibility at the end of the sentence is the use of "weak" marker passing chains. It may be the case that during processing of the sentence, MP found a path that was considered too weak to be conclusive evidence for a choice. However, now that all the evidence available has been examined and no conclusion has been reached, the weak path is taken as being better than nothing. In particular, a weak path that runs to a deprecated meaning is used as evidence in support of that meaning. In the present implementation, the trade-off between weak chains and preferred meanings is accomplished by "magic numbers" *(see section 5.6.3)*.

If neither preferred meanings nor weak chains help to resolve all the remaining ambiguities, then inference and discourse pragmatics may be invoked. It should be clear that Polaroid Words with marker passing are not a replacement for inference and pragmatics in word sense and case disambiguation; rather, they serve to reduce substantially the number of times that these must be employed. However, there will still be cases where inference must be used. For example, these sentences couldn't be disambiguated without inference about the relative aesthetics of factories and flora:

(5-13)   The view from the window would be improved by the addition of a <u>plant</u> out there.

(5-14)   The view from the window would be destroyed by the addition of a <u>plant</u> out there.

Similarly, when a president tells us (5-15):

(5-15)   I am not a <u>crook</u>.[18]

neither MP nor PW will help us discover that he or she is not denying being a shepherd's staff, though we may readily determine that shepherd's staff he or she is not.[19]

---

[17] It is possible that the results will vary depending on which PW applies its preferred meaning first. It is unlikely that there is a single "correct" order for such situations. If a sentence is really so delicately balanced, people probably interpret it as randomly as Polaroid Words do *(cf. section 1.4)*.

[18] NIXON, Richard Milhous. 11 November 1973.

[19] The present implementation does not have an inference or pragmatics system available to it.

Throughout this process, however, it should be kept in mind that some sentences are genuinely ambiguous to people, and it is therefore inappropriate to take extraordinary measures to resolve residual problems. If reasonable efforts fail, PWs can always ask the user what he or she really meant:

(5-16)   **User:** I need some information on getting rid of moles.
         System: What exactly is it that's troubling you? Is it unsightly blemishes, or those lovable but destructive insectivorous garden pests, or uterine debris, or unwanted breakwaters, or chili and chocolate sauces, or enemy secret agents that have penetrated deep into your organization?

(5-17)   **User:** Are there any planes in stock?
         System: We've got two carpenter's planes and a Boeing 747, but you'd need a requisition from Mr Andrews's office for the 747.

(PWs do not, of course, actually have such a natural language response component.)

One particular case of genuine ambiguity occurs when PWs DEADLOCK. Deadlock between two (or more) PWs is possible if one says "I can be X if you are A, and I can be Y if you are B," while the other says, conversely, "I can be A if you are X, and I can be B if you are Y." In other words, the sentence has two readings, corresponding to the choices $X+A$ and $Y+B$. This can happen if two "parallel" MP paths are found:

(5-18)   Ross was escorted from the <u>bar</u> to the <u>dock</u>. *(a courtroom scene or a harborside scene)*

(5-19)   Each <u>bill</u> requires a <u>check</u>.[20] *(each **invoice** requires a **negotiable instrument**, or each **proposed law** requires a **verification of correctness**, or various other combinations)*

Deadlock can also happen if there is more than one choice for a slot filler, and each matches a different slot for the case flag:

(5-20)   <u>SUBJ the fan</u> broke OBJ the window.

(If *SUBJ* is AGENT, *fan* is **enthusiast**; if *SUBJ* is INSTRUMENT, *fan* is **air mover**.) Deadlock cases are probably very rare—it is hard to construct good examples even out of context, let alone in a context—and PWs have no special mechanism for dealing with them.

5.3.5 *Polaroid Words for bound constituents*

When one constituent of a sentence is bound to another, the PWs for each have to be identified with one another. This occurs in relative clauses, for example, in which the *wh-* is bound to the NP to which the clause is attached. Consider (5-21):

---

[20]Readers in countries where the spelling *cheque* is used should pretend that the example was read aloud to them.

(5-21)   the club that Nadia joined

This will be parsed as (5-22):

(5-22)   [$_{NP}$the club [$_S$Nadia join *wh*-]]

where *wh*- will be bound to *the club* in the Absity representation *(see section 3.3)*. Clearly, the content of the relative clause should be used to help disambiguate the word to which the *wh*- is bound, and conversely disambiguation of other words in the relative clause can be helped by the binding of the *wh*-. A similar situation occurs in sentences in which equi-NP-deletion has applied in a subsentence *(see section 3.6)*:

(5-23)   The crook wanted to kidnap Ross.
      [$_S$[$_{NP}$The crook] [$_{VP}$[$_V$want]
          [$_{NP}$[$_S$[$_{NP}$the crook] [$_{VP}$[$_V$kidnap] [$_{NP}$Ross]]]]]][21]

Such cases are handled by identifying the PW for the *wh*- or for the head of the undeleted NP with the PW for the head of the NP to which it is bound. Each will have separate sets of friends, but any disambiguation of one will be reflected in the other.

This method assumes that it is possible to decide upon the binding of the constituent as soon as the constituent is created. In the case of the *wh*- of relative clauses, this is not true; it may not be possible to decide on the relative clause attachment (and, hence, the binding) until after the clause has been parsed and interpreted:

(5-24)   the lion in the field that frightened Nadia

(5-25)   the lion in the field that Nadia was crossing

In (5-24), the *wh*- is *the lion*; in (5-25) it is *the field*. However, Paragram (like Parsifal) incorrectly does the binding as soon as the *wh*- is detected, taking the NP presently on top of the stack *(see also sections 6.2.1 and 7.2.2)*, and PWs take unfair advantage of this. This state of affairs ought to be improved in future versions.

5.3.6 Cues unused

In section 4.1, when I listed several lexical disambiguation cues that a system should be sensitive to, I included a sensitivity to syntax and showed how the verb *keep* could be disambiguated by looking at the syntactic type of its complement (examples (4-8) to (4-10)). At present, PWs do not have this sensitivity, nor would

---

[21] In practice, it seems that the verb of the matrix sentence will usually serve to disambiguate its subject in such sentences even before the complement sentence is encountered. This is because verbs that permit this sort of construction (*want, promise, condescend, hate, refuse*, etc.—Akmajian and Heny 1975: 348) all require a sentient AGENT; there are very few homonyms that have more than one sense that fits this restriction.

the flow of information between PWs and Paragram support it even if they did. I do not anticipate major difficulties in adding this in future versions of Polaroid Words.

Because PWs are not sensitive to syntax yet, they cannot yet handle passive sentences. To be able to handle passive sentences, the PWs for verbs and for the prepositions *SUBJ* and *by* will have to be able to look at the verb's auxiliary and, if it is marked as being passive, then adjust their case flag mappings accordingly. Again, this is straightforward. Note that I am assuming a lexical analysis of passive sentences; see Bresnan 1982c. Also awaiting a sensitivity to syntax are PWs for determiners. For example, the word *the* translates as either `the` or `the-pl`, depending on whether its NP is marked as singular or plural. Determiner PWs would be particularly simple, as they do not have to deal with marker passing nor provide feedback to any other PWs. A sensitivity to syntax would also assist the resolution of nouns such as *rock*, some senses of which are [−**count**] and others of which are [+**count**]; compare:

(5-26)   Rock is the instrument of Satan. *(rock = **rock-music***)

(5-27)   Rocks are the instrument of Satan. *(rock = **stone***)

(5-28)   That rock is the instrument of Satan. *(rock = **stone***)

A second unused disambiguation cue is global context. Marker passing is used as a mechanism for local (intra-sentence) context cues, but our system has at present no representation of global context. It is my conjecture that it will not work simply to extend MP so that paths may be constructed between words of a sentence and the one before it. Rather, there should be a representation of context as a node or area in the knowledge base; this may include nodes that were senses of words of previous sentences, instances created by the semantic representations of the sentences, nodes that participated in inferences made as sentences were read, and so forth. (Such representations of context are also motivated by the need to analyze reference and connections in discourse; see Hirst 1981a, 1981b.)[22] Marker passing may then be extended to include this representation of context.

Because neither syntax nor global context are used yet, discourse focus cannot be. Strictly speaking, Polaroid Words are wrong to even TRY to disambiguate *slug* in the example of section 5.3.3, *the slug operated the vending machine*. Rather, a clever system would have first recognized that the use of the definite article *the* implies that a disambiguated referent for the NP can be found in the focus, and no other disambiguation action need be taken (unless no referent is found). Of course, this wouldn't help if the NP were *a slug*.

The last unused cue is the requirement made by some verbs that certain of their cases must be present or that certain combinations of cases are prohibited. Adding

---

[22]One possible scheme for this is Waltz and Pollack's (1985) system of microfeatures for activating elements of context.

this would allow preposition PWs to rule out possibilities in which none of them translate to a required case. In English, however, required cases are only a very weak cue, for English has few compulsory cases, and syntax serves to enforce most of them. A well-known example is the verb *break*, for which at least one of the cases AGENT, PATIENT, and INSTRUMENT must be present and be flagged by *SUBJ*. If we assume that the input is well-formed, then there will be a subject and it will be one of these three. An example of a compulsory case not enforced by syntax is the LOCATION case of the **place in position** sense of *put*:

(5-29)   Ross put the luggage on the shelf.

(5-30)   #Ross put the luggage.

An example of a prohibited combination of cases is the restriction that an action in which the PATIENT is flagged by *SUBJ* may not have an INSTRUMENT expressed unless the verb is passive *(cf. above)*:

(5-31)   The window broke.

(5-32)   #The window broke with a rock.

(5-33)   The window was broken with a rock.

5.4 What Polaroid Words can't do

It is possible, as we mentioned in section 5.3.2, that a PW could cross all its meanings off its list and suddenly find itself embarrassed. One possible reason for such an occurrence is that the word, or one nearby, is being used metaphorically, metonymically, or synecdochically:

(5-34)   His <u>pen</u> is breathing revenge.[23,24]

(5-35)   "Piper, sit thee down and write
          In a book, that all may read."
          So he vanish'd from my sight,
          And I pluck'd a hollow reed,
          And I made a rural <u>pen</u>,
          And I stained the water clear,
          And I wrote my happy songs
          Every child may joy to hear.[25]

Sometimes a word may just be used in an "extended" sense; in (5-36), we hesitate to say that *kill* is being used metaphorically, but the PW for *with* would not accept three of the four given complements as acceptable fillers of the INSTRUMENT case:

---

[23]TOLSTOI, Alexei Konstantinov. *Vaska Shibanov*. 1855–1865.

[24]Notice that the metaphor here overrides the possible literal interpretation *pen* = **swan**.

[25]BLAKE, William. "Introduction." *Songs of innocence*. 1789.

(5-36)   Yet each man kills the thing he loves,
              By each let this be heard,
              Some do it with a bitter look,
              Some with a flattering word.
              The coward does it with a kiss,
              The brave man with a sword![26]

Alternatively, it may happen that the word, or one nearby, is being used in a sense that the system does not know about (metaphor, metonymy, synecdoche, and meaning extension being special cases of this, of course). It is not possible in such cases to determine which word was actually responsible for the failure. Thus, if the **female swan** sense of *pen* is unknown, and a failure therefore occurs on (5-37):

(5-37)   The pen flew ...

there is no way of telling that the missing meaning is in *pen* rather than *fly*. Ideally, the system should try to look for possible metaphors, as in (5-38):

(5-38)   The pen flew across the page.

  Research by Gentner (1981a, 1981b) suggests that if the system is looking for a possible metaphor, it should try the verb first, because verbs are inherently more "adjustable" than nouns; Gentner found that nouns tend to refer to fixed entities, while verb meanings bend more readily to fit the context. For example, people tend to paraphrase (5-39) (Gentner 1981a: 165):

(5-39)   The lizard worshipped.

as (5-40) rather than (5-41):

(5-40)   The small grey reptile lay on a hot rock and stared unblinkingly at the sun.

(5-41)   The nasty, despicable person participated in the church service.

Thus, if a noun PW and a verb PW have irreconcilable differences, the noun should take precedence over the verb (regardless of which occurred first in the sentence— Gentner 1981a: 165).[27] If the system is still unhappy after doing its best to interpret the input metaphorically, it should ask the user for help and try again. None of this is included in present-day Polaroid Words.

---

[26]WILDE, Oscar Fingal O'Flahertie Wills. "The ballad of Reading Gaol." 1898.

[27]There are, of course, exceptions to this general strategy. In particular, some sentences cannot be interpreted metaphorically, or any way other than literally; and sometimes the verb takes precedence over the noun. Sentence (i) (due, I believe, to George Lakoff) exemplifies both cases:
(i)   My toothbrush sings five-part madrigals.
The word *madrigal* is quite unambiguous, and fits so well with the literal meaning of *sing*, that the incompatibility of selectional restrictions on `toothbrush` and the `agent` slot of `sing` is resolved in favor of the latter, and (i) gives most people an image of a toothbrush that is somehow singing. [I am grateful to Eugene Charniak for pointing this out to me.]

Note that these problems occur only in cases where slot restrictions are tested. In the case of conflicting unambiguous words, one or both being used in a new, metaphoric, metonymic, or synecdochic sense, the conflict will not be noticed until the final Absity output is sent to Frail, since there is no reason to have checked for consistency. This will also be the case when strong MP paths have caused a meaning to be chosen without checking slot restrictions, and in section 5.6.1 I show that this is a desirable state of affairs.

> We believe that the Procrustean notion of selection restrictions, supposedly stating necessary and sufficient conditions for semantically acceptable combinations of words, is fundamentally misguided.
> —Edward Kelly and Philip Stone[28]

5.5 Slot restriction predicates and selectional restrictions

It will be apparent that our use of slot-filler constraints is not dissimilar to the use of conventional selectional restrictions based on the primitives of decompositional semantics (Katz and JA Fodor 1963) *(see section 2.2.1)*. The difference is that our constraints are not just symbols in a dictionary entry, but instead are part of the knowledge base. That is, we don't mark senses of the word *slug* as [±**animate**]; rather, it is part of our world knowledge that the frame gastropod-without-shell represents something that inherits properties from the animate frame that stands above it in the ISA hierarchy, whereas metal-stamping doesn't.

There are two advantages in this. First, we avoid arbitrary and peculiar selectional restrictions. For example, *peach pit* can mean **the seed of a peach**, whereas *banana pit* cannot be **the seed of a banana**, but only **a hole in the ground to throw bananas into**. The reason for the difference is that *pit* can only mean the seed of a certain type of fruit, namely those, such as the cherry, that have a single large seed surrounded by a thick fleshy part and a thin skin. While one could posit each noun in the lexicon being marked as [± **fruit-having-a-large-seed-surrounded-by-a-thick-fleshy-part-and-a-thin-skin**], it seems more natural to require the knowledge base to decide whether the object has the necessary properties, using whatever proof techniques may be necessary. If we encounter a new fruit of the right type,

---

[28] Kelly and Stone 1975: 69. Kelly and Stone constructed a system to disambiguate words in large text corpora for content analysis. Their system employed a large lexicon in which each ambiguous word was supplemented with a hand-coded decision algorithm to discriminate its senses. The algorithms looked at surface syntax and morphology, very simple selectional restrictions on nearby words, and the exact nearby words themselves. Kelly and Stone reported that "The techniques employed in our project essentially constitute a crude analogue of the Katz and Fodor (1963) machinery for disambiguation, unsupported by syntax and employing a very simple set of markers. But we applied these techniques very energetically to real human language, and it became absolutely clear that such a strategy cannot succeed on a broad scale. It is surely ironic that the Katz and Fodor theory, for all its transformationalist invective about the productiveness of language, should erect a semantic theory which elevates the commonplace to a standard of propriety." See also section 8.3.4.

we have no hesitation in calling its seed a pit, even if we have never heard of the fruit before and therefore couldn't have its name on our seed-is-called-*pit* list.

The second, related advantage is that we now have a much cleaner organization of knowledge. We do not, for example, store in one place the fact that a knife is sharp and in another the fact that the word *knife* denotes a referent that is sharp. Rather, the frame system contains the information but once, and it can be used wherever it is needed; lexical knowledge is little more than a mapping from words into this information. This is in accord with the goal of the project of which the present work forms a part: a uniform knowledge representation suitable for both natural language understanding and problem solving *(see section 1.3)*.

5.6 Psychological reality

Although cognitive modeling is not the main goal in this work, claims of psychological reality are interesting in their own right, and, as I said in section 1.4, trying to do things the way people do them is often a good strategy in AI anyway. In this section, therefore, I look at the degree of psychological reality in Polaroid Words with marker passing, comparing them with the psycholinguistic results discussed in section 4.3. I then discuss the importance of human data in the correct use of marker passing.

5.6.1 Polaroid Words, marker passing, and psycholinguistic models

Some degree of psychological reality was built into Polaroid Words from the start, in that their design was heavily influenced by the results of Swinney (1979) and Onifer and Swinney (1981), who found that all meanings of an ambiguous word were accessed regardless of context *(see section 4.3.3)*. Similarly, PWs in all contexts start off with all their possible meanings available. This is in contrast to the prior-choice models *(sections 4.1 and 4.3.1)*, modeled by the Schank and Abelson (1977) script approach (which the weight of the evidence is now against), in which one meaning has already been selected as the right one for the context. PWs also differ from ordered-search models in which meanings are tried one at a time, in a fixed order, until one fits.

Also, in accordance with Tanenhaus, Leiman, and Seidenberg's results (1979), all PW meanings are activated even without regard for part of speech, since the MP has no access to syntactic information. Even though those meanings for what turns out to be the wrong syntactic category will be ignored, they will nevertheless have been used as the origin for marker passing, a fact which may affect later words (and probably adversely! *see section 5.6.2*).

In addition, our use of marker passing as a mechanism for finding semantic associations was intended from the start to operate so as to model the effect of semantic priming *(sections 4.3.1 and 4.3.3)*. Unlike Hayes's CSAW program *(section 4.2.3)*, which only searches its network for associations when it needs them, our

MP is continually active in the background, spreading markers around and finding and reporting associations even between unambiguous words. A node from which a marker has been passed is, of course, just like one that has been semantically primed by spreading activation, in that it has been set up to permit a rapid detection of concept association. (I will, however, qualify these remarks in the next section.) The separation of world knowledge from lexical knowledge, with marker passing occurring only in the former, suffices to prevent contextually inappropriate meanings of a word being pre-activated, in accordance with Lucas's results (1983) *(section 4.3.3)*.

However, the model is at variance with the results of Seidenberg, Tanenhaus, Leiman, and Bienkowski *(STLB)* (1982) published after the initial design of Polaroid Words (as described in Hirst and Charniak 1982) was completed. STLB found that although multiple access is the norm, selective access seems to occur for semantically primed sentences such as (5-42):

(5-42)   The farmer bought the <u>straw</u>.

(see section 4.3.3). All the same, a synthesis is possible if we make the following modification to PWs and MP. Before anything else happens, a new PW first checks whether any of its senses is already marked, that is, whether any immediate paths are available. If one is found, then that sense is chosen right away. Otherwise, things go on as before, with MP proceeding from all senses, looking for constructed paths. Since in the former case marker passing does not spread from unchosen meanings, they have not, in any real sense, been accessed. Thus, consistent with STLB's results, strong semantic priming would result in selective access but multiple access is still the norm, where strong semantic priming is (by definition) priming that results in an immediate marker passing path. With or without this change, the model predicts speed differences in the disambiguation of semantically primed sentences such as (5-42), compared with non-priming biased sentences:

(5-43)   The man walked on the <u>deck</u>.

The system will process (5-42) much faster than (5-43), because (5-42) should require only looking for MP chains, while (5-43) will look at the chains, find nothing, and then spend time dealing with slot-restriction predicates in order to choose the right meaning of *deck*. The original model predicts two speed classes, the modified model predicts three. While these predictions seem plausible, there are as yet no relevant psychological data.

Polaroid Words also have the property that they can be led astray as people are by sentences with garden-path semantics *(see section 4.3.1)*. Thus, PWs will make the same mistakes that most people do with sentences such as (5-44), in which the wrong meaning of an ambiguous word receives strong semantic priming:

(5-44)   The astronomer married the <u>star</u>.

In (5-44), MP will find the obvious chain between `astronomer` and `astro-nomical-object`; the PW for *star* will therefore choose the wrong meaning, and will not even notice that it violates the slot predicate for `marry`, because it doesn't even consider such matters if it is happy with the MP path. The error will be discovered only after the sentence is fully interpreted and Frail attempts to evaluate the erroneous frame statement that was built. Similarly, intuition suggests that people who have trouble with the sentence only detect the error at a late stage; they then invoke some kind of conscious error recovery mechanism, sometimes interpreting the sentence metaphorically *(see section 5.4)*.

However, many people do seem to be able to recover from disambiguation errors in which the garden-path pull is not as strong as that of (5-44). Daneman and Carpenter (1983: 566) gave subjects texts such as (5-45), in which subjects tended to initially choose the wrong meaning for the underlined word:

(5-45)   The lights in the concert hall were dimmed. The audience watched intently as the famous violinist appeared on the stage. He stepped onto the podium and turned majestically to face the audience. He took a <u>bow</u> that was very gracefully propped on the music stand. The enthusiastic applause resounded throughout the hall.

They found that ability to recover from erroneous disambiguation correlated with scores on a reading span test,[29] which in turn correlated with verbal SAT scores.[30] PWs thus recover from disambiguation errors like a reader with a very poor reading span.[31]

Lastly, PWs are in accord with psychological reality in that, when initially activated, they do not look at words to their right. They are thus in accord with the results of Stanovich and West (1983a: 55), who found, contrary to previous suggestions (Underwood 1981), that there is no effect in reading from semantic characteristics of words in the right parafovea, that is, words to right of the fixation point. (Stanovich and West attribute the earlier results to artifacts of Underwood's methodology.)

In general, PWs (like the rest of the Absity system) are consistent with the trend of recent psychological results strongly suggesting that human language comprehension processes are modular, with limited interaction (*cf.* Swinney 1982).

---

[29] In these tests, subjects had to read a set of sentences aloud, and then recall the last word of each. A subject's reading span is the size of the set they could handle without errors in recall.

[30] The Scholastic Aptitude Test (SAT) is a standardized test taken by applicants for college admission in the United States. It includes a test of verbal ability.

[31] And indeed, as Absity throws its input tokens away at the end of each sentence, it would score zero in the reading span test. The lowest human score that Daneman and Carpenter found was 2.

This is where my claim falls to the ground.
—Norman Voles[32]

5.6.2 Psychological non-reality

In this section, we look at ways in which the system is at variance with psychological data, or for which psychological data are not yet available but for which the predictions of PWs seem implausible (Hirst 1984).

One important way in which MP differs from psychological reality is in the decay of spreading activation. The data of Tanenhaus, Leiman, and Seidenberg (1979) and Seidenberg, Tanenhaus, Leiman, and Bienkowski (1982) show that the facilitative effect of the activation of contextually incorrect meanings lasts less than 200 milliseconds (at least in those cases where rejection can be immediate). This suggests that activation of unchosen meanings decays very quickly. On the other hand, in our system all markers remain until the end of the sentence, at which time they are all reset. This may mean that paths are found between these unchosen senses and senses of later words, a clearly misleading occurrence. While the PWs (or path filter; *see section 5.2.3*) could check for such paths and eliminate them, it would be better if they didn't occur at all. At present, Frail does not support any form of selective removal of markers, so decay of activation from unchosen meanings could not be included in the PW system; it is planned to correct this in new versions of Frail.

The length of time that an ambiguous word may remain unresolved, with several alternatives active, probably also differs in PWs from people. In the present implementation, resolution will sometimes not take place until the very end of the sentence *(see section 5.3.4)*.[33] All the psycholinguistic studies discussed in section 4.3 looked only at cases where there is sufficient information to disambiguate a word as soon as it occurs, and the data on how long people will hold off resolution, hoping that more cues will come in if there is initially insufficient information, are equivocal.

The two studies on the question of which I am aware are that of Hudson and Tanenhaus (1984) and that of Granger, Holbrook, and Eiselt (*GHE*) (1984). Hudson and Tanenhaus found that when there is no disambiguating information, both possible meanings of an ambiguous word remained active 500 msec after the word, but only one was active at the next clause boundary (even though there had been no disambiguating information). GHE's findings were quite different. They looked at two-sentence texts in which the second sentence might require re-interpretation of an ambiguous word that had occurred, with misleading bias, in the first. For example:

(5-46)   The CIA called in an inspector to check for <u>bugs</u>. Some of the secretaries had

---

[32]MONTY PYTHON. *Another Monty Python record*. Charisma/Buddah CAS 1049. 1972.

[33]In sections 7.2.7 and 7.3.2 we will see cases where a PW is forced to make early a decision that might otherwise have been left till the end of the sentence.

reported seeing roaches.

The first sentence is intended to make the reader decide that *bugs* means **hidden-microphones**, while the second requires that it actually be **insects**. After reading such sentences, subjects had to decide quickly whether a presented word was semantically related to the text. The error rate was extremely high compared to control cases when the word presented was related to the "incorrect" meaning of the ambiguous word of a sentence with misleading bias. GHE took this as evidence for CONDITIONAL RETENTION, *i.e.*, both meanings being retained for the ambiguous word, even across the sentence boundary.

The results of GHE are suspect for several reasons. First, their test for whether a word sense was active was not a proper on-line measure of activation. Second, their probe words are suspect. Thus for (5-46), their probes were *ant* (related to the text) and *spy* (unrelated to the text). Subjects who said that *spy* was related to the text were deemed to have made an "error", and this was taken as support for the hypothesis that the "incorrect" meaning of *bug* was still active. But clearly the word *spy* IS related to the text, regardless of how the subject handles the word *bug*, simply because the word *CIA* was present in the text! Indeed, it is hard to imagine how to construct a probe that is sensitive to the activity of the "incorrect" meaning of the ambiguous word but not sensitive to the global context that was deliberately introduced to create the misleading bias.

What, then, can we reliably say about when a final decision is made on an ambiguous word? Intuition (which is not exactly a reliable source) suggests that while people will delay a decision on an ambiguous word for a little while, they will, nevertheless, usually make a final decision within a few words (or constituents?) of the ambiguity.[34] That a decision may be delayed is evidenced by the fact that people do not get garden-pathed by sentences such as these:

(5-47)   Nadia's favorite <u>club</u> is the five-iron.

(5-48)   Nadia's favorite <u>club</u> is The Carlton.

(5-49)   Nadia's favorite <u>book</u> is *The House at Pooh Corner*. *(book = **literary work**)*

(5-50)   Nadia's favorite <u>book</u> is her signed first edition of *The House at Pooh Corner*. *(book = **printed volume**)*

If we made an immediate "best guess" at the meaning of the ambiguous words *club* and *book*, then at least one of each of the above pairs should be inconsistent with the way a given individual is predisposed to guess, and therefore be a garden-path sentence for that individual. (Obviously, the strategy of making an immediate best guess would make language comprehension rather difficult at times.) It seems,

---

[34]Nevertheless, there is evidence (Just and Carpenter 1980; Daneman and Carpenter 1983) for the psychological reality in reading of a "sentence wrap-up" process in which remaining loose ends, such as unresolved references, are treated. It is possible that some residual disambiguation occurs as part of this process.

therefore, that disambiguation of the examples above is incomplete until the final NP of the sentence is understood.

On the other hand, however, it is my intuition that a word such as *crook* in sentence (5-12) of section 5.3.4 is not resolved at the end of the sentence but long before, possibly by the time the verb is processed:

(5-51)   The crook operated ...

This choice seems to be based on probability: inanimate INSTRUMENT subjects are a lot less frequent than animate AGENTs, and, moreover, shepherd's staffs are rather unusual instruments for operating anything. The choice does not occur right after *crook*, relying upon the relative infrequency of shepherd's staffs as a topic of modern urban conversation, as most people have no trouble with (5-52):

(5-52)   The crook fell from the hook on which it was hanging.

This suggests that PWs should use a CUMULATING EVIDENCE approach and jettison unlikely alternatives quickly if there is no positive evidence for them. That is, one does not make an immediate best guess, but one does make a reasonable guess as soon as there is enough information to do so, even if one cannot be definite.[35] This has the advantage of helping to prevent combinatorial explosion. However, I have been loath to consider using this approach in Polaroid Words, in view of the dearth of data on the corresponding human behavior and the fuzziness of the whole notion. Any interim solution would have to fall back on "magic numbers", and we have too many of those already *(see next section)*. Nevertheless, PWs do use the relative frequency of the various meanings of an ambiguous word in some of their decisions (avoiding where possible tricks with magic numbers; *see section 5.3.4*), but since we know little of how people use frequencies,[36] we have limited their use in PWs to tidying up loose ends at the end of a sentence. Another possibility that might be considered is to retain the present timing of decision making in PWs, but add a mechanism that watches out for looming combinatorial explosion, and forces PWs to make an early guess if it senses danger.

Another prediction of Polaroid Words for which there is no psychological data is that lexical disambiguation and case selection are performed by essentially the same mechanism. It is not clear how such a prediction could even be tested. The system also predicts the psychological reality of pseudo-prepositions, a prediction that almost certainly cannot be sustained.

Lastly, a few words should be said about marker passing. While we were happy to admit it as a discrete model of spreading activation *(see previous section)*, it

---

[35] Kurtzman (1984) found that, in the case of structural ambiguity, the point of resolution varies widely, sometimes coming long before the disambiguating information, and sometimes not, in a manner very consistent with the idea of accumulating evidence. However, I know of no data addressing this issue for lexical ambiguity.

[36] We saw in section 4.3.3 that frequency does seem to be a factor even though the evidence is against the ordered search hypothesis. Little more can be said at present.

should be pointed out that there are several different competing theories of spreading activation. While these vary in their closeness to our marker passing, almost all of them differ from Frail marker passing in one important way: they assume that some links in the network are STRONGER than others, and that the strength of a link has an effect upon activation passed over it. For example, it is hypothesized that more activation spreads across strong links, or, alternatively, that the level of activation is the same across strong links but the time for the spreading is less (Collins and Loftus 1975, Lorch 1982).[37] In addition, most spreading activation theories assume that activation power decreases the further away from the origin it gets (Collins and Loftus 1975). However, in Frail (and, hence, in MP) at present, all links are of equal strength, and all markers have the same status.[38]

5.6.3 Marker passing, path strength, and magic numbers

One of the more vexed problems in using association cues for disambiguation is knowing when an association is strong enough to be considered conclusive evidence. We know from the existence of semantic garden-path sentences that associations alone should sometimes permit immediate jumping to a conclusion; we also know that this isn't true of all associations, for we do not get garden-pathed by sentences like (5-53):

(5-53)   The lawyer stopped at the bar for a drink.

We therefore need some measure of the strength of an association, so that PWs will be able to jump to conclusions (rightly or wrongly) in the same situations that people do.[39] Although frequency of the use of the concepts should be a factor in determining the strength of an association (*cf.* Anderson 1983),[40] I shall limit my remarks below to a discussion of the SEMANTIC DISTANCE between two concepts.

I mentioned in the previous section that most theories of spreading activation assume that different links have different strengths, though Frail does not attempt to model this. It is generally assumed that link strength is correlated with semantic distance—that a link between two concepts is strong exactly when they are very closely associated. Cases when this occurs may include one concept being a salient property of the other (**edibility, food**), or, possibly, a particularly good exemplar of

---

[37]Experiments by Lorch (1982) suggest that strong links receive more activation but that their activation is no faster than that of weak links.

[38]Work is proceeding on changing this in future versions of Frail. It is also planned that the amount of activation spread from a node would be inversely proportional to the number of siblings it has (Jim Hendler, personal communication).

[39]We have already identified one such situation in section 5.6.1, namely, whenever an immediate MP path is found.

[40]Eugene Charniak (personal communication) has suggested that PWs should jump to a conclusion whenever marker passing selects a preferred meaning.

the other (**robin**, **bird**);[41] a high frequency of use also strengthens a link (Collins and Loftus 1975, Anderson 1983) and hence the association between the concepts. On the other hand, de Groot (1983) has found that activation does not spread to associates of associates of a node—for example, **bull** and **cow** are linked and so are **cow** and **milk**, but activation from **bull** does not reach **milk**. Thus, PWs need a way to take an MP path and determine its strength, *i.e.*, the semantic distance between its endpoints, by looking at the links and nodes that it includes.

The present, inadequate method of measuring path strength is a function of the length of the path, the nodes it passes through, and the links it uses. I use the following heuristics:

- The shorter the path, the stronger the path.

- The more arcs that leave a node, the weaker the connections through that node (*cf.* the anti-promiscuity rule, *section 5.2.3*).

These methods, though I use them, are unsatisfactory because, like the marker passing constraints *(section 5.2.3)*, they rely heavily on MAGIC NUMBERS. For example, the second suggests that any node will not be vague if it has only n arcs, but $n+1$ arcs will invariably tip the scale. This seems unlikely. And even if there were a neat threshold like that, how do we know that n is it?—it is merely a number that we chose and that seems to work in the present implementation, but there was no principled reason for choosing it. There is, of course, well-known evidence for the psychological reality of magic numbers in certain perceptual and short-term memory processes (Miller 1956), but it is hard to believe that this carries over to marker passing in long-term memory, where activation seems to be a continuous, not discrete, variable.

It is hoped that future versions of MP will be able to include such features as path strength and the weakening of activation as it gets further from the origin, so that we won't have to worry about post hoc measurements of path strength. This would be a first step in approximating the continuous nature of spreading activation.[42]

5.7 Conclusion

I have presented a pair of cooperating mechanisms that both disambiguate word senses and determine case slots by finding connections between concepts in a network of frames and by negotiating with one another to find a set of mutually satisfactory meanings. In contrast to Hayes's CSAW system (1976, 1977a, 1977b, 1978)

---

[41] It is often reported that people are faster at making categorization judgments for typical exemplars such as **robin–bird** than atypical ones such as **chicken–bird** (Rips, Shoben and Smith 1973; Smith, Shoben and Rips 1974; Collins and Loftus 1975). This may be taken as evidence for the existence of typicality links, though Collins and Loftus (1975) show that it may be explained by the procedures by which positive and negative evidence for such decisions is gathered and evaluated.

[42] *cf.* footnote 38.

Table 5.1. *What Polaroid Words can and can't do*

SENTENCES THAT CAN BE DISAMBIGUATED

SUBJ the slug operated *OBJ* the vending machine.
SUBJ the crook operated *OBJ* the pizza parlor.
SUBJ the crook wanted to kidnap *OBJ* Ross.
SUBJ Nadia's plane taxied to the terminal.
SUBJ Ross sold *OBJ* the lemming to Nadia.
SUBJ the man walked on the deck.
SUBJ the deep philosopher threw *OBJ* the peach pit into the deep pit.

SENTENCES THAT CAN'T BE DISAMBIGUATED

The astronomer married the star.
  Marker passing is misled.
The view from the window would be improved by a plant.
  Requires inference.
I want to eliminate some moles.
  No disambiguating information.
Ross was escorted from the bar to the dock.
  Two parallel MP paths.
SUBJ the vending machine was operated by the slug.
  No passives yet.

(see section 4.2.3), PW processes work in parallel with a parser, Paragram, and a semantic interpreter, Absity, permitting them to deal with ambiguous words as if their semantic object were assigned immediately. (We shall see in chapter 7 that PWs also help in structural disambiguation.) Also unlike CSAW, the same PW control structure may be used for all syntactic categories. Polaroid Words minimize the need for separate, ill-motivated, purely linguistic knowledge; unlike Boguraev's system (1979) *(see section 4.2.2)*, PWs have access to the NLU system's world knowledge and use it wherever possible.

Polaroid Words are implemented as processes that interpret Lisp data structures containing purely lexical information that each word has in its dictionary entry. This is in contrast to approaches such as Small's (1980), where the meaning of a word is represented as a large, barely-constrained procedure, different for every word, which parses and performs semantic interpretation as well as lexical disambiguation. Rather, the parser, Absity, and the marker passer do much of the work that Small requires his "word experts" to perform. We thereby capture generalizations in disambiguation, needing only one type of PW for each syntactic category and relying almost exclusively on general world knowledge.

Polaroid Words do not yet use syntactic disambiguation cues or global context, nor can they handle metaphor and metonymy. Table 5.1 shows some examples of sentences that the system can handle and some that it can't.

In chapter 7 we will find that if we increase slightly the power of Polaroid Words, they can provide substantial help in structural disambiguation and at the same time can be helped by the structural disambiguation process.

Part III

Structural Disambiguation

6.1 Introduction

In this chapter, I discuss the problem of syntactic, or structural, disambiguation, which was first introduced in section 1.1.3. I will provide the background for the discussion in chapter 7 of the Semantic Enquiry Desk, a structural disambiguator that works with Absity and Polaroid Words.

6.2 Types of structural ambiguity

Structural disambiguation is necessary whenever a sentence has more than one possible parse. There are many classes of structurally ambiguous sentence; below I show some of the more common, but do not attempt to produce an exhaustive list. Included in the list are some local ambiguities *(see section 1.1.3)* that people can be garden-pathed by.

I will use two methods of demonstrating structural ambiguity. In some cases, I will give one sentence and show its several parses; in others, I will give two sentences such that each has a different preferred parse but each could clearly also have the structure of the other. For simplicity, when I show a parse, I will often show it only for the part of the sentence that contains the ambiguity; pseudo-prepositions *(see section 3.4)* are not usually inserted, except where necessary to make a point.

6.2.1 Attachment problems

The first class of structural ambiguity is that of ATTACHMENT AMBIGUITY: there being more than one node to which a particular syntactic constituent may legally be attached. Attachment problems are mostly problems of MODIFIER PLACEMENT. The most common example is that of a prepositional phrase that may either modify a verb (*i.e.*, be a case-slot filler) or an immediately preceding noun phrase. For example:

(6-1)   Ross wanted to phone the man with the limp.

(6-2)   Ross wanted to wash the dog with Hoary Marmot™ brand pet shampoo.

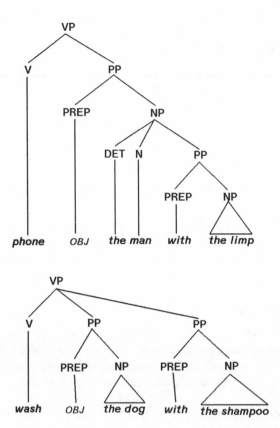

Figure 6.1. Parses of *phone the man with the limp* and *wash the dog with the shampoo.*

In sentence (6-1), the final PP is attached to the NP *the man* as a modifier: it is the man who has the limp and the preposition *with* flags an attribute of the man. In (6-2), the dog doesn't have the shampoo; rather, *with* is a case flag marking the shampoo as the INSTRUMENT of the washing action. The differing parse of each sentence reflects this; see figure 6.1. Note, however, that it is only semantic constraints that prevent each sentence from being parsed like the other.

Below I list some of the other occasions on which attachment ambiguities may occur.

1. A prepositional phrase may have more than one noun phrase available to attach it to (as well as, possibly, a verb):

(6-3)   The door near the stairs with the "Members Only" sign had tempted Nadia from the moment she first entered the club.

(The sign could be on the door or on the stairs.)

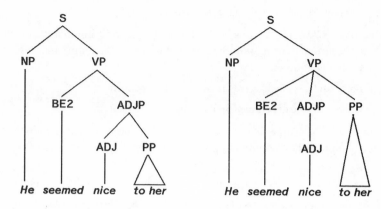

Figure 6.2. Alternative parses for *He seemed nice to her*.

2. Relative clauses have similar attachment ambiguities:

(6-4)   The door near the stairs that had the "Members Only" sign had tempted Nadia from the moment she first entered the club.

(Again, there are two possible locations for the sign.)

3. A prepositional phrase can also be attached to an adjective phrase:

(6-5)   He seemed nice to her.[1]

Depending on the parse, this could mean **he seemed to act nicely towards her** (attachment to the adjective phrase) or **he seemed to her to be nice** (attachment to the verb phrase). These parses are shown in figure 6.2.

4. When a sentence contains a subsentence, both may contain places for the attachment of a prepositional phrase or adverb:

(6-6)   Ross said that Nadia had taken the cleaning out yesterday.[2]

The word *yesterday* may qualify the saying action of the matrix sentence, or the taking action of the subsentence.

(6-7)   Nadia knew that Ross fried the chicken with garlic.

(6-8)   Nadia ate the dinner that Ross had prepared with a grace that belied her intense dislike of Venezuelan cuisine.

The preferred attachment for *with garlic* is *fried*, not *knew* or *chicken*; the preferred attachment for *with a grace . . .* is *ate*, not *prepared*.

5. An attachment ambiguity also occurs when an adverbial may modify the sentence verb or the whole sentence:

---

[1] This example is from Ford, Bresnan, and Kaplan 1982.

[2] From an example in Ford, Bresnan, and Kaplan 1982.

(6-9)   Happily, Nadia cleaned up the mess Ross had left.

The adverb *happily* could be attached to the sentence, meaning that the event was a fortunate occurrence, or it could be attached to the VP, meaning that Nadia was quite happy to clean up the mess; compare:

(6-10)   Fortunately, Nadia cleaned up the mess Ross had left.

(6-11)   Grudgingly, Nadia cleaned up the mess Ross had left.

Note, however, that some adverbs modify neither the sentence nor the VP, but rather make a pragmatic comment upon the discourse (*cf.* Whitley 1983):

(6-12)   Frankly, my dear, I don't give a damn.[3]
          (i.e., I don't give a damn, my dear, and I am being frank when I say that.)

   6. Certain participles may be attached to either the surface subject of the sentence or to the sentence node itself (Follett 1966: 121–124; see also Fowler 1965: 659–661):

(6-13)   Considering his situation likely to go from bad to worse, he decided to offer his resignation.

(6-14)   Considering the deficiencies of his education, his career has been extraordinary.

   7. On occasions, an adverbial placed between two clauses can be attached to the verb of either:

(6-15)   The lady you met <u>now and then</u> came to visit us.
          (i.e., We were visited by the lady you met now and then, or *We were visited now and then by the lady you met.)*

(6-16)   The friends you praise <u>sometimes</u> deserve it.
          (i.e., Sometimes the friends you praise deserve it, or *The friends you sometimes praise deserve it.)*[4]

Stress would disambiguate the sentences in spoken English, as may the insertion of commas in the written form. The ambiguity is restricted by permissible adverb movements; see my remarks below.

   A summary of our list of attachment ambiguities in English appears in table 6.1.

> These example sentences bear no discernible resemblance to the sentences
> that compose the text that purportedly explains them—yet the linguist's own
> sentences are also alleged (implicitly) to be drawn from the same English lan-
> guage.
> —Joseph D Becker[5]

Strangely, one occasionally finds in the literature examples of alleged attachment

---

[3] HOWARD, Sidney. *Gone with the wind* [screenplay]. 1939.

[4] Taha 1983: 260.

[5] Becker 1975: 70.

Table 6.1. *Summary of attachment ambiguities in English*

PP attachment—to noun or verb?
   Ross insisted on phoning the man with the limp.
   Ross insisted on washing the dog with pet shampoo.
PP attachment—to which noun?
   The door near the stairs with the "Members Only" sign
Relative clause attachment—to which noun?
   The door near the stairs that had the "Members Only" sign
PP attachment—to verb or adjectival phrase?
   He seemed nice to her.
PP attachment—to which verb?
   Ross said that Nadia had taken the cleaning out on Tuesday.
Adverb attachment—to verb or sentence?
   Happily, Nadia cleaned up the mess Ross had left.
Participle attachment—to surface subject or sentence?
   Considering his situation likely to go from bad to worse, he decided to
      offer his resignation.
   Considering the deficiencies of his education, his career has been extra-
      ordinary.
Adverb attachment
   The friends you praise sometimes deserve it.

---

ambiguities that are not really ambiguous at all.[6] To close this section, I list a couple:

1. In his experiments intended to determine relative sensibleness ratings for ambiguous sentences, Oden (1978) included sentences such as (6-17):

(6-17)   A good secretary can type quickly written reports.

It was alleged that this is an adverb placement ambiguity, and *quickly* could modify either *written* or *type*; that the latter is impossible, however, is shown by the unacceptability of (6-18):

(6-18)   *A good secretary can type quickly reports.

When asked to compare the correct and impossible interpretations of such sentences, subjects found them about equally acceptable, a fact that says more about the demand characteristics of the experiment than it does about the experimental hypothesis. Taha (1983:260) and Holmes (1984:240, 249) make the same mistake. The error is that in general an adverb may not be placed between a verb and its object NP; any adverb in such a position must in fact be part of the NP, if

---

[6] Any apparent instance of such a thing in this book is either a figment of the reader's imagination or the work of enemy saboteurs.

that is at all possible, and sentences in which it is not, such as (6-19), are at best marginally well formed:

(6-19)   *?Nadia closed rapidly the stopcock.

2. Ford, Bresnan, and Kaplan (1982) give examples where two clauses surround an item that may, they claim, be attached to either:

(6-20)   Though Martha claimed that she will be the first woman president yesterday she announced that she'd rather be an astronaut.

The claim is that *yesterday* could be attached to *claimed* or *announced*. I don't think such examples are ambiguous, as correct punctuation requires a comma between the subordinate and main clauses, thereby unambiguously delimiting each. In speech, intonation and a pause in the appropriate place would have the same effect.[7] Kurtzman (1984: 165–166) also had problems because of the absence of necessary commas.

6.2.2 Gap finding and filling

Gap-finding ambiguities occur when a moved constituent has to be returned to its pre-transformational starting point, and there is more than one place that it might go. For example (Ford, Bresnan, and Kaplan 1982):

(6-21)   Those are the boys that the police debated about fighting.

In this sentence, there are two possible gaps in the relative clause (which we denote by "◊") that the relative pronoun (whose referent is underlined) might fill:

(6-22)   Those are the boys that the police debated ◊ about fighting ◊.

Taking the first gap gives the meaning that **the police debated with the boys on the topic of fighting;**[8] the second gives **the police debated (among themselves) about fighting the boys**. The corresponding parses are shown in figure 6.3. The constituent that is moved into a gap is a *wh-*—either a relative pronoun, as in (6-22), or a question *wh-*, as in this example:

(6-23)   Which boys did the police debate ◊ about fighting ◊?

---

[7] Wales and Toner (1979) have shown that intonation is not always a reliable cue for disambiguation; it seems to have an effect only in certain cases of attachment ambiguity, and is often overridden by other biases; Berkovits (1982) reports further qualifications. (For a review of research on the effects of intonation upon sentence comprehension, see Cutler 1982.) In well-formed written language, however, punctuation can be an important indicator of structure.

[8] This reading assumes the North American dialect of English in which the opponent in the debate may be expressed as the direct object of the verb—*Lincoln debated Douglas*; for some British speakers, *debate* is obligatorily intransitive—*Lincoln debated with Douglas*—and the first gap would not be posited in such dialects.

The gap to which the filler belongs may be a case slot at the same level as the *wh-*, as in the examples of the previous paragraph, or it may be a case slot of a subsentence from which it has been raised, as in (6-24) (based on an example from Frazier, Clifton, and Randall 1983):

(6-24)   Mary is <u>the student</u> whom the teacher wanted ◊ to talk to the principal.

This can lead to complications when two items—the *wh-* and another constituent—have been raised from the subsentence, and each must be matched with the corresponding gap. Thus in (6-25), which is the same as (6-24) but for the addition of an extra case at the end, the gap after *wanted* takes *the teacher* instead of the *wh-*, and the *wh-* now fills the new case slot:

(6-25)   Mary is <u>the student</u> whom <u>the teacher</u> wanted ◊ to talk to the principal about ◊.

See Frazier, Clifton, and Randall 1983 for further analysis.

6.2.3 Analytical ambiguities

The attachment ambiguities that we saw above occur when it is clear what the nature of a constituent is but not where to put it. On the other hand, analytical ambiguities occur when the nature of the constituent is itself in doubt, that is, when there is more than one possible analysis of it.[9] Obviously, the two uncertainties may occur together, though often resolving one will resolve the other. For example, consider these sentences (from Ford, Bresnan, and Kaplan 1982):

(6-26)   The tourists objected to the guide that they couldn't hear.

(6-27)   The tourists signaled to the guide that they couldn't hear.

In (6-26), the preference is that the clause *that they couldn't hear* is a relative clause modifying *the guide*; in (6-27), the preference is that it is a sentential complement and modifies *signal*.

English offers many opportunities for analytical ambiguity. Here are examples of some others.

1. Particle detection—is a preposition functioning as a verb particle or as part of a prepositional phrase?

(6-28)   A good pharmacist dispenses with accuracy.
          (i.e., The way a good pharmacist dispenses is with accuracy, or What a good pharmacist dispenses with is accuracy.)

(6-29)   Ross looked up the number.
          (i.e., What Ross looked up was the number.)
          Ross looked up the elevator shaft.
          (i.e., Where Ross looked was up the elevator shaft.)

---

[9]We include here local ambiguities.

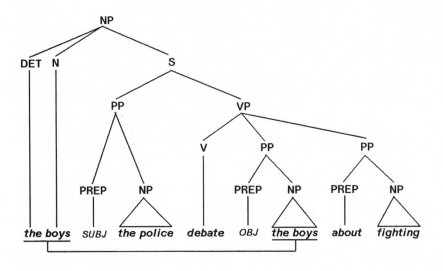

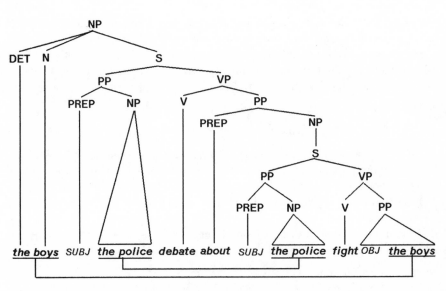

Figure 6.3. Alternative parses for *the boys that the police debated about fighting.*

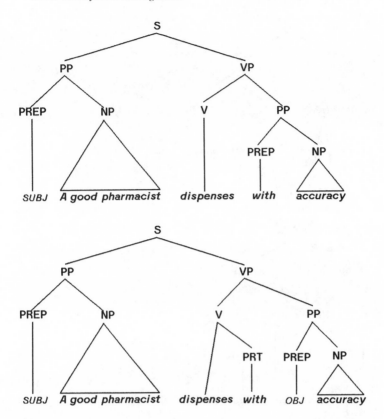

Figure 6.4. Alternative parses for *A good pharmacist dispenses with accuracy*.

See figures 6.4 and 6.5 for the parses.

2. Distinguishing a simple prepositional phrase from one that is actually an adjective phrase left after raising and *to-be*–deletion have been applied to a verb complement:

(6-30)   "You can have the music box that's in the closet or the one that's on the table," said Ross. "I want the music box on the table," said Nadia.
          (i.e., I want the music box that is on the table)

(6-31)   "I put the music box on the mantelpiece. Is that okay?" asked Ross. "No," said Nadia, "I want the music box on the table."
          (i.e., I want the music box to be on the table)

Figure 6.6 shows the alternative parses.

3. Distinguishing a present participle from an adjective:[10]

---

[10]Note that there isn't always a clear distinction between the two; see Quirk, Greenbaum, Leech, and

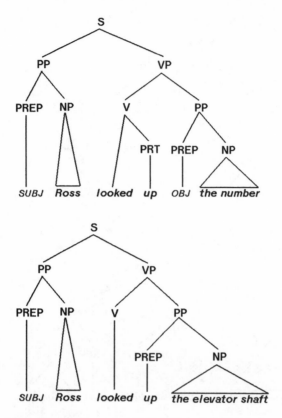

Figure 6.5. Contrasting parses of *Ross looked up the number* and *Ross looked up the elevator shaft*.

(6-32)   Ross and Nadia are singing madrigals.

(6-33)   Pens and pencils are writing implements.

The contrasting parses are shown in figure 6.7.

4. Distinguishing between a present participle and a noun. This example is from Ford, Bresnan, and Kaplan 1982:

(6-34)   We discussed running.
          (i.e., We discussed the sport of running, or We discussed the possibility of our running.)

The parses are shown in figure 6.8. In the first, *running* is a DEVERBAL NOUN (Quirk, Greenbaum, Leech, and Svartvik 1972: 133–134); that is, it has noun prop-

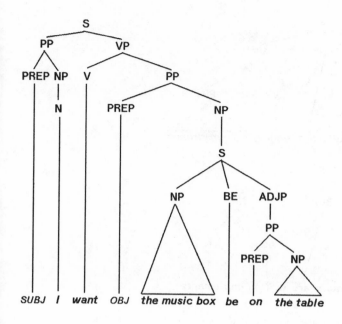

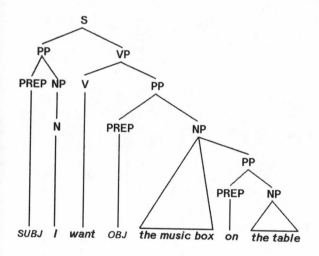

Figure 6.6. Alternative parses of *I want the music box on the table*.

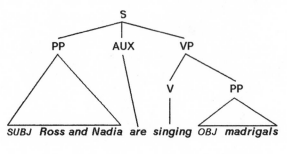

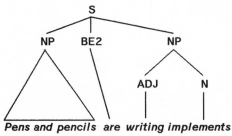

Figure 6.7. Contrasting parses of *Ross and Nadia are singing madrigals* and *Pens and pencils are writing implements.*

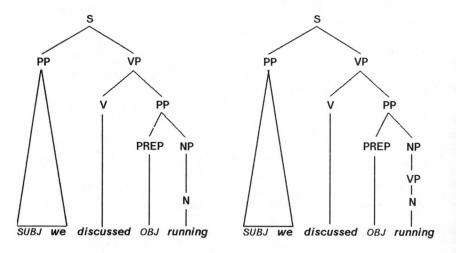

Figure 6.8. Alternative parses of *We discussed running.*

erties: it can take determiners, adjectives, and PP complements, but not *not* or NP complements (Ford, Bresnan, and Kaplan 1982):

(6-35)   We discussed the excessive running of races.

(6-36)   *We discussed not excessive running.

(6-37)   *We discussed the excessive running races.

In the second parse, it is a present participle or VERBAL NOUN, with verb properties: it can take adverbs, *not*, and direct NP objects:

(6-38)   We discussed not running races excessively.

5. Detecting the end of a noun group. Two contiguous noun phrases can appear to be a single one. Compare:

(6-39)   Ross gave the dog some water, and Nadia gave the cat food.[11]

(6-40)   Ross gave the shampoo, and Nadia gave the cat food.

The alternative parses for the second of the conjoined clauses are shown in figure 6.9. In (6-41):

(6-41)   To handle particles, we must first, obviously, add to the grammar rules that will recognize the possibility that a preposition is functioning as a particle and will ask the SED for an opinion if necessary.[12]

the string *the grammar rules that will recognize the possibility that a preposition is functioning as a particle* is actually two separate NPs, with the separation after the word *grammar*, but this is not apparent until the second occurrence of *will*, by which time recovery is very difficult. (It is also possible to read *the grammar rules that will recognize the possibility that a preposition is functioning as a particle and will ask the SED for an opinion if necessary* as a single, stylistically bad, NP.)

One particular instance of this kind of ambiguity occurs when the first of two consecutive nouns can be analyzed as an adjective. The result is often a garden path:

(6-42)   The cotton clothing is made from comes from Mississippi.[13]
          (i.e., The cotton from which clothing is made comes from Mississippi.)

6. A reduced relative clause can appear to be the VP of the matrix sentence. This leads to the "classic" garden path sentence (6-43):

(6-43)   The horse raced past the barn fell.[14]
          (i.e., The horse that was raced past the barn fell.)

---

[11]Based on an example from Marcus 1980:251.

[12]From section 7.4.1 below.

[13]I believe this example is due to Mitch Marcus.

[14]From Bever 1970:316.

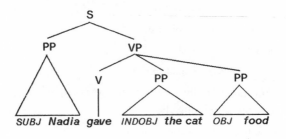

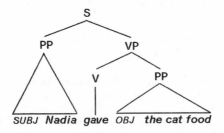

Figure 6.9. Alternative parses of *Nadia gave the cat food*.

7. Determining the structure of a complex noun group, including modifier scope.
It is well known that noun groups can have a complex internal structure. An example:

(6-44)   AIRPORT LONG TERM CAR PARK COURTESY VEHICLE PICKUP POINT[15]

This has the structure shown in (6-45), with a very complicated semantic relationship holding between the elements:

(6-45)   [[[airport [[long term] [car park]]] [courtesy vehicle]] [pickup point]]

The relationships possible between the elements of a complex noun group are
many and wonderful (Downing 1977, Levi 1978, B Warren 1978), and generally
rely heavily on pragmatics and world knowledge (Bauer 1979) *(cf. section 3.8.2)*.
Levi (1978) points out that the problem is compounded by adjectives in a noun
group that can be functioning as nouns instead of adjectives; thus *atomic bomb*,
for example, is better analyzed as if it were the also-permissible *atom bomb*, a
bomb employing the power of atoms. It is tempting to regard noun group analysis as a problem solely for the semantic interpreter, the parser's job being to do
no more than identify and delimit the group. However, we shall see below when

---

[15]Sign at Gatwick Airport; see *Verbatim*, **8**(3), Winter 1982, p. 12.

we look at disambiguation in Marcus's Parsifal parser (1980) that the parser can, with the aid of a semantic process, discover some of the structure.

> He thought he saw a Banker's Clerk
>   Descending from the bus;
> He looked again, and found it was
>   A Hippopotamus.
> —Lewis Carroll[16]

8. Participles and adjectivals can be particularly troublesome when they occur at the end of a clause. It is not even clear exactly when they engender an ambiguity, and there seem to be wide idiolectic differences. Consider the following examples, where small caps indicate stress, from Quirk, Greenbaum, Leech, and Svartvik (hereafter *QGLS*) (1972: 762):

(6-46)   The manager apPROACHED me, SMILing.

(6-47)   The manager approached me SMILing.

In both sentences, it is the manager, not the speaker, who is smiling. These seem best treated as a supplementive clause (QGLS 1972: 760–764), and parsed as being derived from (6-48), a conjunction of two main clauses:

(6-48)   The manager$_i$ approached me, and he$_i$ was smiling.

The same analysis seems correct for clause-final adjectivals, which QGLS regard as verbless supplementive clauses:

(6-49)   The manager approached us <u>full of apologies</u>.

(6-50)   He drove the damaged car home <u>undismayed</u>.

Two types of ambiguity can arise from this. The first occurs when the subject and the object of the matrix sentence both could be the subject of the supplementive; informants found (6-51) and (6-52) (QGLS 1972: 724, 763) ambiguous as to who was leaving the room and who was going home:

(6-51)   We met him leaving the room.

(6-52)   I saw him going home.

Compare also:

(6-53)   He drove the car home <u>undismayed</u>.
            (i.e., The driver was undismayed.)

(6-54)   He brought the car back <u>undamaged</u>.
            (i.e., The car was undamaged.)

---

[16]*Sylvie and Bruno.* 1889. Chapter 7.

The second type of ambiguity arises when the participle, instead of being a supplementive, could be attached to the object NP either as a reduced restrictive relative clause or as a verb complement:

(6-55)   The manager approached the boy smoking a cigar.
          (i.e., The manager, smoking a cigar, approached the boy, or *The boy smoking a cigar was approached by the manager.)*

(6-56)   The manager caught the boy smoking a cigar.
          (i.e., The manager caught the boy in the act of smoking a cigar, or *The manager caught the boy who was smoking a cigar (but the boy smoking a pipe escaped).)*

Note the difference between (6-55) and (6-56): in (6-55), *smoking a cigar* can be supplementive—the manager was smoking—but not a verb complement; in (6-56), the verb complement reading is available (since *catch*, unlike *approach*, can take a complement), but the supplementive reading is not. (QGLS (1972:763) claim a three-way ambiguity for (6-56), including the supplementive, but this is not possible in my idiolect; even a comma after *boy* doesn't seem to help. Informants I asked about these sentences mostly just became confused.)

This leads us into the murk surrounding clause-final participles. The problem can be seen in the sentences with alleged participle attachment problems that were used in Oden's experiments on ambiguous sentences (1978) *(see section 6.2.1)*:

(6-57)   A boy saw a pilot driving to the airport.

Supposedly, the boy or the pilot could have been driving to the airport. However, the former interpretation requires a comma after *pilot*, and even then is a highly deprecated usage; hence we find the well-known example (6-58) funny and semantically nonsensical:

(6-58)   #I saw the Grand Canyon flying to New York.

But, as we have seen, clause-final participles CAN be supplementive, with the subject of the sentence as their elided subject, even without a guiding comma. It is unclear to me why this reading should be blocked in (6-57) and (6-58).[17]

9. Apparent cleft sentences may also admit a non-cleft subject–verb–object analysis. Thus, (6-59):

---

[17]It is my intuition that clause-final participles of this form can qualify only the surface subject, in sentences such as (6-51) and (6-52), when the subject is the speaker and the participle describes the speaker's movement at the time. Moreover, this seems to be a convention of informal speech rather than a "real" rule of the language—a convention that lets one abbreviate a sentence like (i):

(i)   I saw him while I was driving home.

Obviously this is a tenuous and dangerous argument. For one thing, what is the difference between a convention of informality and a "real" rule? I'm not sure, but I think the former is exemplified by the fact that people will say (ii) to mean (iii), despite the apparent anomaly, a fact that I don't think I want to include in a competence grammar:

(ii)   Nadia just left, because I saw her leaving.

(iii)   Nadia just left; I know this because I saw her leaving.

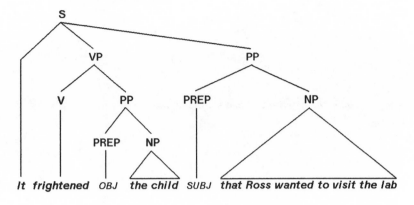

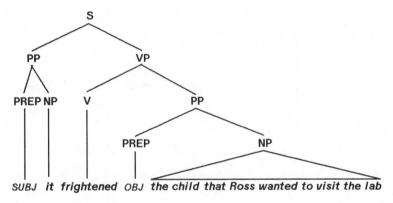

Figure 6.10. Alternative parses of *It frightened the child that Ross wanted to visit the lab.*

(6-59)   It frightened the child that Ross wanted to visit the lab.[18]

has the two parses shown in figure 6.10. The corresponding meanings are **that Ross wanted to visit the lab frightened the child** (the cleft analysis), and **the child, whom Ross wanted to visit the lab, was frightened by X**, where **X** is some entity in the discourse focus (the subject–verb–object analysis).[19]

10. In a few cases, a past participle can look like a gapped VP, rendering a question indistinguishable, but for punctuation or intonation, from a command:

(6-60)   Have the crystals dissolved?

---

[18] From Crain and Steedman 1985.

[19] There is also another cleft reading, in which the complement is instead parsed as a relative clause followed by an infinitive. The resulting sense is **to visit the lab frightened the child that Ross wanted**. There seems to be a strong bias against this reading. [I am grateful to Jim Hendler for pointing this out to me.]

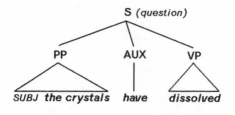

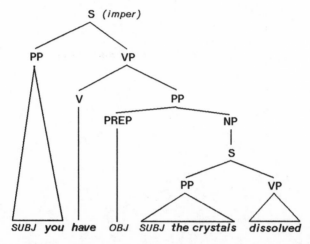

Figure 6.11. Parses of *Have the crystals dissolved?* and *Have the crystals dissolved.*

(6-61)   Have the crystals dissolved.

The two parses are shown in figure 6.11.

11. There are at least four different structures that can underlie sentences of the form *NP be ADJ to V*, reflecting various ways that the predicate may have been formed. The following examples are well known:

(6-62)   Ross is eager to please.
          (i.e., Ross be [eager [Ross please ∅]]; Ross is eager that he please someone.)

(6-63)   Ross is ideal to please.
          (i.e., Ross be [ideal [∅ please Ross]]; Ross is ideal for someone to please him.)

(6-64)   Ross is easy to please.
          (i.e., [∅ please Ross] be easy; pleasing Ross is easy.)

(6-65)   Ross is certain to please.
          (i.e., [Ross please ∅] be certain; that Ross will please someone is certain.)

The correct parse is not always determined uniquely by the adjective and verb, as the ambiguity of (6-66) shows; it may be parsed like (6-62) or like (6-63):

Table 6.2. *Summary of analytic ambiguities in English*

Relative clause or complement?
   The tourists objected to the guide that they couldn't hear.
   The tourists signaled to the guide that they couldn't hear.
Particle detection
   A good pharmacist dispenses with accuracy.
Prepositional phrase or adjectival phrase?
   I want the music box on the table.
Present participle or adjective?
   Ross and Nadia are singing madrigals.
   Pens and pencils are writing implements.
Present participle or noun?
   We discussed running.
Where does an NP end?
   Nadia gave the cat food.
Reduced relative clause or VP?
   The horse raced past the barn fell.
Determining noun group structure
   airport long term car park courtesy vehicle pickup point
What is the subject of the supplementive?
   He drove the car home undismayed.
   He brought the car back undamaged.
Supplementive, restrictive relative, or verb complement?
   The manager approached the boy smoking a cigar.
   The manager caught the boy smoking a cigar.
Cleft or not?
   It frightened the child that Ross wanted to visit the lab.
Question or command?
   Have the crystals dissolved?
   Have the crystals dissolved.
How is the predicate formed?
   Ross is eager to please.
   Ross is ideal to please.
   Ross is easy to please.
   Ross is certain to please.

(6-66)   The chicken is ready to eat.
          (i.e., The chicken is ready to eat something, or The chicken is ready to be eaten.)

This completes our long, yet not exhaustive, list of structural ambiguities in English. A summary of the list appears in table 6.2.

6.2.4 *The interaction between categorial and structural ambiguity*

If a word is categorially ambiguous, a sentence containing it can be structurally ambiguous, and the possibilities will correspond to those for the word. For example:

(6-67)   The Japanese push bottles up the Chinese.[20]

(6-68)   Charles Wallace sat there tucking away turkey and dressing as though it were the most delicious thing he had ever tasted.[21]

In (6-67), the words *push* and *bottle* could be verb and noun respectively, or noun and verb; the writer intended the latter (the context of the sentence is a report on a World War II battle), though there is a strong preference for the former. In (6-68), *dressing* is a noun, but could have been a verb:

(6-69)   Charles Wallace sat there tucking away turkey and dressing himself at the same time.

Clearly, not all categorial ambiguities result in structural ambiguities, since the syntactic context will often admit only one of the alternatives; and, as we saw in the previous section, some create only local ambiguity, with a possible garden path.

6.2.5 *Structural ambiguity as a closure problem*

Another way to look at many structural ambiguities is to view them as CLOSURE PROBLEMS (Ford, Bresnan, and Kaplan 1982). In parsing, a constituent of the parse tree is said to be OPEN if it has not been declared complete, and so other constituents may still be attached to it. When a constituent is complete, it is CLOSED, and that subtree may no longer be changed. In English (and most other natural languages; *but see exercise 5.3 in section 9.5*) it is almost always true that if several constituents are open, then the attachment of another constituent to one of them causes the closure of all open constituents at a lower level of the tree.

For example, suppose (6-70) has been parsed up to the point marked by the vertical bar, with the partial parse shown in (6-71):

(6-70)   Nadia told the man with the limp | about Ross's indiscretion.

(6-71) $[_S [_{NP} \text{Nadia}] [_{VP} [_V \text{told}] [_{NP} [_{DET} \text{the}] [_N \text{man}] [_{PP} [_{PREP} \text{with}]$
          $[_{NP} [_{DET} \text{the}] [_N \text{limp}] |$ about Ross's indiscretion.

At this point, the open constituents are the S, VP, NP, PP, and second NP that are as yet missing their right brackets; the closed constituents are the NP *Nadia*, the V, and both DETs. Now let us suppose that the parse proceeds, and a PP is built from the words *about Ross's indiscretion*. This PP has to be attached somewhere, and the candidates are exactly those constituents that are still open. Clearly, the "correct" choice is the VP, and performing this attachment has the side-effect of

---

[20]Quoted by Wilks (1982b) as a well-known example.

[21]L'ENGLE, Madeleine. *A wrinkle in time*. New York: Farrar, Straus and Giroux, Inc. 1962.

closing all those constituents that are dominated by this VP, namely the two NPs and the PP. The VP itself, and the S that dominates it, are not closed. To show that the NPs and PP are closed, we need only show the inadmissibility of sentences that attempt a subsequent attachment to them:

(6-72) *Nadia told the man with the limp about Ross's indiscretion due to gout.
        (*i.e., the limp that was due to gout*)

(6-73) *Nadia told the man with the limp about Ross's indiscretion that she met at the laundromat.
        (*i.e., the man with the limp that she met at the laundromat*)

There are a couple of minor counterexamples to the above generalizations. The first is that under certain circumstances a noun phrase that contains an NP-like quantifier phrase can be split in two (Akmajian and Lehrer 1976); thus all the following are generally considered acceptable:

(6-74) A number of stories about Watergate soon appeared.

(6-75) A number of stories soon appeared about Watergate.

(6-76) A sizable herd of large African elephants was discovered last year.

(6-77) A sizable herd was discovered last year of large African elephants.

In parsing, such splits require the initial noun phrase to be reopened when its second part is discovered. The second, more tenuous, counterexample is the possibility in some idiolects of breaking a modifier off a subject NP and placing it further down the sentence:

(6-78) Are you good men and true?[22]

(6-79) ?Many students failed that were expected not to.

Such sentences are, strictly, ill-formed. They seem to be least bad in cases such as the ones just given, where none of the open constituents permit the attachment of the new one, so a closed one has to be reopened. Compare:

(6-80) *Are you good men with no serious criminal record and true?

(6-81) *Many students failed the comprehensive exams that were expected not to.

Awkward counterexamples aside, it can be seen that attachment disambiguation is equivalent to deciding which open constituents should be closed. That is, instead of saying that we close all constituents below the chosen point of attachment, we can say that we attach at the lowest level that we have chosen not to close. This view also accounts for many analytical ambiguities, insofar as determining the attachment point will often eliminate all but one analysis—this is the case with

---

[22]SHAKESPEARE, William. *Much ado about nothing.* 1598. III, iii, 1.

the examples (6-26) and (6-27) above[23] even before the ambiguous constituent has been analyzed. One of the disambiguation methods we will look at in the next section, that of Ford, Bresnan, and Kaplan (1982), works by trying to decide which constituents should be closed. Clearly, gap-finding ambiguities cannot in general be resolved by closure decisions, nor could analytical ambiguities such as present participles that look like adjectives, or vice versa. Nevertheless, it happens that the closure decision mechanism of Ford, Bresnan, and Kaplan that we will look at in section 6.3.3 is also helpful in gap finding.

6.3 Current theories of structural disambiguation

In this section we look at present approaches to the resolution of structural ambiguities by a parser.[24]

6.3.1 Structural disambiguation in ATN parsers

It is possible for a parser to perform structural disambiguation without the ambiguity ever being explicitly apparent to it. This is the case, for example, when an ATN parser *(see section 1.3.2)* has to make a choice between two alternative paths but has no way of knowing the validity of either; it chooses one at random, and if that path succeeds it will never come back to try the other. If the unchosen path would also have led to a valid parse, then the sentence was ambiguous, and the random choice amounted to blind disambiguation. The unseen path, however, might have produced a preferable parse. It has therefore been suggested (Wanner 1980) that the ATN's random choice be replaced by trying the arcs in a particular fixed order, thus modeling the syntactic bias of English that leads to a preference for one particular parse *(see section 1.1.3)*; that is, the arc that would lead to the preferred parse would always be tried first, and only if this fails would others be tried.

In addition, one could eliminate semantically anomalous parses by the addition of a semantic checker at the end of the parse. The checker's finding the parse to be semantically ill-formed could be treated exactly like a syntactic failure: the parser would back up and try another path. This method was used in the LUNAR system (Woods, Kaplan and Nash-Webber 1972); the checker relied mostly on selectional restrictions.

---

[23] (6-26) The tourists objected to the guide that they couldn't hear.

(6-27) The tourists signaled to the guide that they couldn't hear.

[24] Since we will not be making any claims of psychological reality for the disambiguation mechanism that we discuss in chapter 7, we will not discuss here much psycholinguistic research on structural disambiguation. It is worth noting, however, that, as in research in lexical ambiguity *(see section 4.3)*, there are single-reading, multiple-reading, and ordered search hypotheses, and our computational mechanism will be closest to the multiple-reading hypothesis. For a detailed review of the literature, the interested reader may consult Kess and Hoppe 1981.

Unfortunately, these disambiguation strategies are both inadequate. Ford, Bresnan, and Kaplan (1982) show that arc-choice ordering is not adequate because it does not take into account the effects of lexical bias seen, for example, in the differing analyses of sentences (6-26) and (6-27) in section 6.2.3. Marcus (1980: 224) points out that the semantic checker is not good enough because it cannot make COMPARATIVE judgments; it will accept the first result that is minimally acceptable, never knowing whether something better might appear were it to reject the parse under consideration. Moreover, even if the checker can say exactly why it doesn't like a particular parse, the ATN parser is unable to use this information, and may present the checker with other parses that turn out to have exactly the same problem.

Boguraev's (1979) ATN-based disambiguation system *(see also section 4.2.3)* countered these objections by having both ACTIVE and PASSIVE structural disambiguation strategies, which were invoked as part of the semantic interpretation procedures at the completion of each noun phrase and each clause (on the ATN's POP arcs). Passive tests were similar to those of the LUNAR system: checks that a completed structure is (or isn't) SEMANTICALLY COHERENT with respect to case frames, selectional restrictions, and so on. Active disambiguation procedures took a partial sentence structure and some additional items and attempted to identify the permissible structures that could be built. Some of the blind non-determinism of ATN parsers was thus avoided. The system always tried to eliminate possibilities as soon as possible, in order to minimize backing up and to avoid making the same mistake twice. The system could distinguish relative clauses from verb complements and make decisions about PP attachments.

6.3.2 Structural disambiguation in Marcus parsers

Unlike an ATN parser, a Marcus parser *(see section 1.3.2)* cannot back up, and must therefore detect structural ambiguity whenever it arises and decide immediately and irrevocably which alternative is the better. As Marcus (1980) points out, this has the advantage that the judgment can be comparative—unlike an ATN parser, a Marcus parser can take the better alternative instead of being happy with the first minimally acceptable one it finds.

In Marcus's Parsifal parser, there are three different ways in which semantics is used to guide the parse. The first is absolute selectional restrictions, used for deciding upon prepositional phrase attachments. A case-frame interpreter runs in parallel with the parser, and the parser rules may ask whether a particular PP fits any of the empty slots left in a particular case frame, or whether it fits as a modifier on a sentence or noun phrase. As in the case of an ATN parser, the order in which possible attachments are tried can account for syntactic bias in the disambiguation, though, as we saw above, this is not fully adequate.[25]

---

[25]The order of attempted attachments is VP, S, NP; Marcus is quite aware (1980: 305) that this is not correct in general.

Table 6.3. *Example of Marcus's noun-noun algorithm operating on* water meter cover adjustment screw

The Buffer	$[N_2\ N_3] > [N_1\ N_2]$?
1) water | meter | cover |	no
2) [water meter] | cover | adjustment	no
3) [[water meter] cover] | adjustment |screw	yes
4) [[water meter] cover] | [adjustment screw]	(Rule for 2 nouns applies)
5) [[[water meter] cover][adjustment screw]]	(Finished)

(From Marcus, Mitchell P. *A theory of syntactic recognition for natural language.* The MIT Press, 1980, p.253. Copyright © 1980 by The Massachusetts Institute of Technology.)

The second use of semantics is in gap finding. In this case, comparative semantic judgments are made. They are used in a gap-finding algorithm developed by Marcus (1980: 233–234) that is sensitive to both syntactic and semantic bias and uses rules of the form of (6-82) (Marcus 1980: 288):

(6-82)   If semantics prefers X filling slot A {much better |
          somewhat better | no better} than Y filling slot A,
          then ..., else ....

The semantic preference takes into account the sentence verb and the nature of the gap-filler. Marcus gives this example (1980: 235), with two possible gaps:

(6-83)   Which dragon did the knight give ◊ the boy ◊?

The semantic process considers the possibilities, one for each gap:

(6-84)   X give **higher animate entity** to **animate entity**.
          X give **animate entity** to **higher animate entity**.

and finds the second preferable to the first; the second possible gap is therefore chosen. Parsifal did not contain a complete semantic process for this kind of judgment, but faked it with selectional restrictions (Marcus 1980: 320–322).

The third use of semantics in Parsifal is in finding the structure in noun-noun compounds, that is, in complex noun groups with no adjectives. Again this relies on comparative semantic judgments. Marcus's algorithm uses a buffer three items long. If only the first two items in the buffer are nouns, they are simply combined. If all three items are, then the semantic process is asked to report its preference for combining N_1 with N_2 or N_2 with N_3 (where N_1; N_2, and N_3 are the three buffer items). The preferred grouping is chosen, and the two items are combined into a single one. Table 6.3 (from Marcus 1980: 253) shows the algorithm operating on the noun group *water meter cover adjustment screw*.

Marcus does not really justify this algorithm, and indeed Finin (1980) points out that there are many exceptions to it; for example, the following, where brackets indicate the desired structure, require more than three buffer elements:

(6-85)　[solid state] [RCA [color television]]]

(6-86)　[plastic [toy [fire truck]]]

Also, it is hard to see how a semantic process could make the required decisions at such a local level. Why, for example, is *adjustment screw* better than *water meter cover adjustment* in table 6.3? The latter is what one uses the former for, so both are equally semantically unimpeachable. Even if the buffer were longer, what would prevent the premature grouping of *plastic toy*, a very nice group, in (6-86)? Note also that the algorithm only brackets the structure, and does not actually find the relationships between the elements; this is left to the semantic interpreter. But since the semantic component will have been forced to hypothesize these relations anyway in order to provide the required semantic preference, there seems to be little use in the parser bothering about any of this.

6.3.3 Ford, Bresnan, and Kaplan's theory of closure

Ford, Bresnan, and Kaplan (hereafter *FBK*) (1982) propose that, at least in neutral contexts, preferences for when constituents should be closed are given by case preferences or expectations on the verb; that is, each verb in the lexicon has marked on it the cases for which fillers are normally provided (based, presumably, on frequency).[26] For example, *discuss* would be marked with (6-87):

(6-87)　[AGENT discuss PATIENT]

while *keep* would be marked with (6-88):

(6-88)　[AGENT keep PATIENT STATE]

This would explain why the preferred analysis of (6-89) is with *on the beach* attached to *the dogs* as part of the PATIENT, while that of (6-90) has it attached to *kept* as the STATE case:[27]

(6-89)　The women discussed the dogs on the beach.

(6-90)　The women kept the dogs on the beach.

---

[26] I have modified FBK's terminology and notation to make it similar to that used in this book. I hope that I haven't thereby introduced any misrepresentation of their claims.

[27] The data on attachment preferences come from experiments that FBK performed, in which subjects were asked for their first impression of the meaning of structurally ambiguous sentences.

That is, the preferred analysis of each sentence is the one that gives it exactly the cases expected.

FBK thus propose a closure theory based on LEXICAL PREFERENCE. An important principle of the theory is that of the FINAL EXPECTED ARGUMENT: in the parsing of the structure that is to become the last of the expected cases, closure is delayed as long as possible, so that as much of the rest of the sentence as possible is swallowed up into that case; if the structure being parsed is not the last one expected, then closure is early. (After the final expected argument is closed, attachment to the VP continues to have low priority.) Thus, in (6-89), *the dogs* is the final expected case, so closure of the NP is delayed, and the PP that follows gets sucked into it. In (6-90), *the dogs* is not the last expected case, so it is closed immediately. Note that this theory accounts not only for attachment ambiguity, but also some analytic ambiguity. Consider again these examples:

(6-91)   The tourists objected to the guide that they couldn't hear.

(6-92)   The tourists signaled to the guide that they couldn't hear.

The preferred form for the verb *object* is (6-93):

(6-93)   [AGENT object to PATIENT]

while for *signal* it is (6-94):

(6-94)   [AGENT signal PATIENT MESSAGE]

Therefore, in (6-91) *the guide* is the final argument, and so *that they couldn't hear* gets attached to it as a relative clause. In (6-92), *the guide* is not final and is closed early, forcing *that they couldn't hear* to be analyzed as a sentential complement.[28] If the preferred structure is simply not possible:

(6-95)   The tourists signaled to the guide that they didn't like.

the parser backs up, and takes the other path. SYNTACTIC PREFERENCE—trying alternative parsing rules in a particular order—is invoked only when lexical preference does not give a choice between alternative parses. Thus there is a preference for deverbal nouns over verbal nouns, and (6-34)[29] is analyzed accordingly.

FBK point out that lexical preference can also be used in gap finding.[30] Consider again these examples of theirs, where "◊" marks the preferred location of the gap:

(6-96)   Those are <u>the boys</u> that the police warned ◊ about fighting.

---

[28]This also explains why (i) is not analyzed as a raised form of (ii), which would require early closure of the final argument:

(i)   The woman wanted the dress on that rack.

(ii)   The woman wanted the dress to be on that rack.

[29](6-34) We discussed running.

[30]The role of lexical expectations in gap finding was first suggested by JD Fodor (1978).

(6-97)   Those are the boys that the police debated about fighting ◊.

If *warn* is marked as preferring (6-98) to (6-99):

(6-98)   [AGENT warn PATIENT about OBJECT]

(6-99)   [AGENT warn about OBJECT]

while *debate* has the reverse preference, with (6-100) preferred to (6-101):

(6-100)   [AGENT debate about OBJECT]

(6-101)   [AGENT debate PATIENT about OBJECT]

then the preferred gap can be located.

This theory of closure assumes that the verb of the sentence has been identified. It cannot, therefore, be applied in cases where categorial or lexical ambiguity makes it a problem just to determine where the verb is *(see section 6.2.4)* or what its case structure is.

Ford, Bresnan, and Kaplan have implemented their theory in a parser by Kaplan. In addition, Shieber (1983) has shown that lexical and syntactic preferences can be incorporated in a simple LALR(1) context-free parser for English that, given an ambiguous grammar, gives the preferred structural disambiguations.

It should be noted that FBK's theory is presented as a theory of competence for out-of-context sentences. It does not attempt to explain how lexical preferences interact with context and discourse pragmatics, or under what circumstances one may override the other. The theory assumes that a verb will have a set of preferred cases, and does not take into account the possibility that some verbs—perhaps many or most—will have no strong preference. For example, FBK's own data *(see footnote 27)* show that the preferred reading for (6-91) won by a vote of only 11 to 9—hardly an overwhelming victory.[31] Moreover, there seem to be counterexamples to their theory. For example, the preference in (6-89) can be changed simply by making the object NP indefinite:

(6-102)   The women discussed dogs on the beach.

It may be argued that this is one of the cases where discourse pragmatics overrides the lexical preference, but unless some indication can be given of when this happens, the lexical preference theory comes dangerously close to being unfalsifiable: "Lexical preferences determine the attachment, except in cases where they don't".

---

[31] FBK offer no statistical analysis of their data. However, for each sentence 14 out of their 20 subjects would have to be in agreement to have $p<.05$ for the hypothesis that there is any preference at all for one structure over another (Walpole 1974:218–219; Nadia Talent, personal computation). Twelve of the 51 test sentences upon which they support their theory, including (6-91) and (6-97), did not meet this criterion. Also necessary is an analysis to see whether there is a significant difference in the results for pairs of verbs for which different preferences are alleged.

6.3.4 Structural disambiguation as presupposition minimization

A very different theory of structural disambiguation from that of Ford, Bresnan, and Kaplan has been proposed by Crain and Steedman (1985; Steedman 1982). FBK's theory, as we saw, assumes a null context and does not incorporate any considerations of discourse. Crain and Steedman, on the other hand, claim that discourse context and, in particular, PRESUPPOSITION, are paramount in structural disambiguation.

The presuppositions of a sentence are the facts that a sentence assumes to be true and the entities that it assumes to exist (see the papers in Oh and Dinneen 1979, in particular Karttunen and Peters 1979). For example:

(6-103)   There were two reasons I didn't want to marry Mark.[32]

This sentence presupposes that the reader knows who the writer is, who Mark is, and that either they are married or the possibility of their marrying has been mooted. If a sentence presupposes information that the reader does not have, she has to detect and invoke these UNSATISFIED presuppositions. People have no trouble doing this,[33] though there is evidence that it increases comprehension time (Haviland and Clark 1974), and it is a common literary device that the opening sentences of a story (such as (6-103)) contain many unsatisfied presuppositions, thereby drawing the reader straight into the story.

Now, there is a simple trick, first used by Winograd (1970, 1972), for determining many PP attachments: try each possibility and see if it describes something that is known to exist. For example, (6-104):

(6-104)   Put the block in the box on the table.

could be asking that **the block** be placed in **the box on the table**, or that **the block in the box** be placed on **the table**. The first reading can be rejected if *the block* does not in context uniquely identify a particular block, or if there is no box on the table, or if *the box on the table* does not uniquely identify a particular box. Similar considerations may be applied to the second reading. (If neither reading is rejected, or if both are, the sentence is ambiguous, and Winograd's program would seek clarification from the user.) Similarly, we can disambiguate an earlier example if we happen to know the layout of the club involved:

(6-105)   The door near the stairs with the "Members Only" sign had tempted Nadia from the moment she first entered the club.

Crain and Steedman have called this technique "THE PRINCIPLE OF REFERENTIAL SUCCESS: If there is a reading which succeeds in referring to an entity already

---

[32]EPHRON, Nora. "Once burned." *Vanity Fair*, **46**(1), March 1983, 80–81. Opening sentence.

[33]Weischedel (1979) has shown how the presuppositions of a sentence may be computed as the sentence is parsed.

established in the hearer's mental model of the domain of the discourse, then it is favored over one that does not".

The Principle of Referential Success deals with a very limited range of structural ambiguities. But Crain and Steedman hypothesize that it can be generalized, noting that success in finding a referent is just one kind of PRESUPPOSITION SATISFACTION. The generalization, then, is that the reading that satisfies the most presuppositions (or, more precisely, leaves the fewest unsatisfied)[34] is the one to be favored: "THE PRINCIPLE OF PARSIMONY: If there is a reading which carries fewer unsatisfied but consistent presuppositions or entailments than any other, then, other criteria of plausibility being equal, that reading will be adopted as the most plausible by the hearer, and the presuppositions in question will be incorporated in his or her model".

This principle can explain garden-path sentences such as (6-106):

(6-106)   The horse raced past the barn fell.

The correct parse presupposes the existence of a particular horse and that this horse is known to have raced past a barn, presuppositions unsatisfied in the null context. The incorrect parse, the one that garden-paths, only presupposes the first of these; the other is taken as the new information that the sentence is conveying. The Principle of Parsimony claims that the garden-path parse is chosen just because it makes fewer unsatisfied presuppositions.

If this is indeed the case, then it should be possible to attenuate the garden-path effect by reducing the unsatisfied presuppositions without changing the sentence structure. This prediction was confirmed in experiments by Crain and Steedman, who found that (6-107) was judged ungrammatical in rapid presentation significantly more often than (6-108) (55% and 29% respectively), even though both have the same structure as (6-106):

(6-107)   The teachers taught by the Berlitz method passed the test.

(6-108)   Teachers taught by the Berlitz method pass the test.

Because it is generic, (6-108) does not presuppose the existence of any particular set of teachers the way (6-107) does. Similarly, there were fewer garden paths on sentences such as (6-109):

(6-109)   The students taught by the Berlitz method passed the test.

where, presumably, *students* is more plausibly the object of *taught* than *teachers* was in (6-107). In another experiment, Crain and Steedman were able to induce garden-pathing in a sentence structure that is not normally a garden path. For example, (6-110) can be made into a garden path:

(6-110)   It frightened the child that John wanted him to visit the lab.

---

[34]But *cf.* section 7.2.1.

by providing a cóntext with a plausible referent for *it* and no unique referent for *the child*:

(6-111)   Several children heard the explosion. It frightened the child that John wanted him to visit the lab.

Similarly, Milne (1982b) has shown that semantic plausibility affects categorial disambiguation of word pairs that could be either ADJ + N or N + V. For example, people tend to parse *the granite rocks* as a noun phrase, DET + ADJ + NP, and can get garden-pathed by sentences in which it requires the analysis DET + N + V:

(6-112)   The granite rocks during the earthquake.

The converse preference is shown, for example, by *the chestnut blocks*, people having no trouble with (6-113), but tripping on (6-114):

(6-113)   The chestnut blocks the sink.

(6-114)   The chestnut blocks are red.

(Some pairs, such as *building blocks*, showed no bias.)[35]

The Principle of Parsimony is a particular case of Crain and Steedman's PRIN- CIPLE OF A PRIORI PLAUSIBILITY: "If a reading is more plausible in terms of either general knowledge about the world, or of specific knowledge about the universe of discourse, then, other things being equal, it will be favored over one that is not". This principle is implicit in the results of Milne mentioned above. It is, of course, an extremely vague principle, generalizing techniques such as checking selectional restrictions that have already been used in both ATN and Marcus parsers *(see sections 6.3.1 and 6.3.2)*. Nevertheless, we will be able to make some computational use of it in chapter 7.

If we accept that presupposition and plausibility have strong effects in structural disambiguation, the question then arises whether structural or lexical preferences in fact play a role at all. Since the null context is in no way neutral with respect to presuppositions, studies such as that of Ford, Bresnan, and Kaplan (1982) *(see section 6.3.3)* that used it to look for such context-independent preferences may have just found artifacts of this non-neutrality. To test this, Crain and Steedman took sentences with local ambiguities of relative clause versus complement. They con- structed contexts for the sentences so that both of their readings had, in the context, the same number of unsatisfied presuppositions; thus the Principle of Parsimony could not be used to choose a reading, and any preference for one reading over the other must come from structural disambiguation strategies. However, they found

---

[35]These results could be interpreted as showing a form of lexical preference similar to the verb pref- erences of Ford, Bresnan, and Kaplan (1982) *(see previous section)*. Milne's data do not rule out the possibility that the N + V or ADJ + N reading is chosen solely on the basis of a categorial preference of the first word, even if this reading is less plausible or contains more unsatisfied presuppositions. (The choice could not be a function solely of the second word, as *granite rocks* showed an ADJ + N preference, but *jeep rocks* showed N + V.)

subjects preferred neither structure over the other, and concluded that, at least for this type of ambiguity, structural preferences are not used.

This result should be regarded as only suggestive, however; it is very difficult to construct materials so that presuppositions and plausibility are matched in different readings,[36] and Crain and Steedman used only five sets of stimuli.[37] Moreover, we saw in section 1.1.3 that some sentences seem to have a structural bias toward their less plausible reading. In addition, some of the data of Ford, Bresnan, and Kaplan (1982) do seem to require an explanation in terms of lexical preference rather than presupposition or plausibility. For example, the preferred structure for (6-115), favored by 90% of their subjects:

(6-115)   The women discussed the dogs on the beach.

was (6-116):

(6-116)   [AGENT discuss PATIENT]

instead of (6-117):

(6-117)   [AGENT discuss PATIENT LOCATION]

It is hard to explain this difference as one of presupposition or plausibility. The choice is between the equally plausible and equally unsatisfied presuppositions that either the dogs or the women are on the beach, yet subjects showed a very strong bias. Similarly, sentence (6-118) is amusing exactly because the lexical expectation of participants rather than a place leads to an implausible reading:

(6-118)   One witness told the commissioners that she had seen sexual intercourse taking place between two parked cars in front of her house.[38]

In addition, there is some evidence that structural or lexical preferences do affect the order in which the possible readings of a sentence are considered.[39] Rayner, Carlson, and Frazier *(RCF)* (1983) studied the eye movements of people as they read garden-path sentences of varying plausibility, similar to those such as (6-107) and (6-109) that Crain and Steedman used. They found that plausibility did not affect the tendency to initially choose the wrong structure for such sentences, and concluded that pragmatics does not affect the initial, preferred choice for the structure, though it can veto the structure afterwards. In a second experiment on eye

[36]It is also difficult to evaluate the materials one has constructed. Crain and Steedman mention that they did not notice a third possible reading for some of their stimuli until it was pointed out to them—nor did I *(see footnote 19)*.

[37]See also Ferreira 1985 for a discussion of problems with Crain and Steedman's experiments.

[38]*The Press* (Atlantic City, New Jersey), 14 June 1979. Quoted in COOPER, Gloria (compiler). *Squad helps dog bite victim, and other flubs from the nation's press.* Garden City, New York: Dolphin Books, 1980.

[39]Crain and Steedman do not claim that pragmatics determines the order, but rather that there is no particular preferred order (Stephen Crain, personal communication).

movements, they found that reading times were shorter for sentences in which the more plausible reading was the one that permitted use of the MINIMAL ATTACH-MENT disambiguation strategy, which they believe to be the basis for many structural disambiguation preferences.[40] Unfortunately, RCF's results must, like Crain and Steedman's contrary result, be taken as suggestive only, because of serious flaws in their experimental materials.[41] Much more work will be needed before the question of exactly what, if any, structural preferences there are can be satisfactorily resolved.

6.4 Conclusion

There are many different kinds of structural ambiguity, and there is at present no agreement on any general principles that can be used for disambiguation. It seems clear, however, that knowledge from several different sources is used. In the next chapter we will present a system that works with Paragram, Absity, and Polaroid

---

[40] The minimal attachment strategy is to resolve an attachment ambiguity in the manner that creates the fewest non-terminal nodes in the parse tree, whenever semantics allows it; thus, for example, PPs are wherever possible attached to the dominating VP instead of an NP below it. Example (6-115) above is a counterexample to the generality of the principle (Ford, Bresnan, and Kaplan 1982).

[41] RCF used rather subtle differences in plausibility in their sentences. For example, *the performer* is said to be more plausibly the indirect object than the subject of *sent the flowers*; but I find it hard to believe that there could be a significant difference. Similarly, they rate (i) plausible but (ii) implausible:

(i)   The tourist [that was] wired the money managed not to misplace it this time.

(ii)   The bank [that was] wired the money managed not to misplace it this time.

Presumably RCF's experience with wiring money is from banks to people. However, as it happens, my only experience with wiring money was when a friend wired money TO a bank, and the bank misplaced it! Similar difficulties arise for many of their other test sentences. If plausibility varies in this way from one individual to another, then RCF's results would be explained by their failure to control this variation.

Moreover, two-thirds of their test sentences were ill-formed in common dialects that prohibit reduced relative clauses whose *wh-* has undergone dative movement, to the apparent confusion of 20% of their subjects. (Such dialects find (i) and (ii) above ill-formed, and not merely garden-path–prone, when the *that was* is deleted; *cf.* Langendoen, Kalish-Landon, and Dore 1973.) One of their sentences even included dative movement with the verb *deliver*, which is not allowed in many (most?) dialects.

See also Kurtzman 1984: 209–214 for discussion of problems with RCF's experiments.

Similarly, Holmes (1984) also claims to have shown that context has no effect on processing strategies and structure preferences. Her subjects were asked to say rapidly whether a structurally ambiguous sentence was or wasn't consistent with a preceding three-sentence "short story" that was biased toward either the preferred or non-preferred reading of the target sentence. She found that, in general, subjects' responses indicated that they computed the preferred reading of the target even when the short story was consistent with the non-preferred reading. However, it is unclear that subjects were motivated to actually process the target sentence IN THE CONTEXT OF the short story (of which it was not itself a part); rather, they may have adopted the strategy of processing it in the null context, thereby producing the preferred reading, and then checking it for consistency with the story. Indeed, since consistency was not assured, a neutral, "open-minded" strategy like this seems a very reasonable one for a subject to adopt.

Words to resolve several kinds of structural ambiguity. It includes among the methods that it uses some that we have seen in preceding sections.

A year working in Artificial Intelligence is enough to make one believe in God.
—Alan Perlis[1]

7.1 Introduction

In this chapter, I will show how structural disambiguation may be added to the Paragram–Absity–Polaroid Words system. I will do this in two stages. First, I will consider the present version of the system and the structural ambiguities that it handles, a small subset of those that I listed in section 6.2. (Not all of the sentence types that I listed can even be parsed by the present Paragram grammar.) The disambiguation methods will include a synthesis of some of the ones that we saw in section 6.3, as well as my own. Then, second, I will consider methods for extending the system's present limited range of abilities.

Although Paragram is basically a Marcus parser *(see section 1.3.2)*, it has a somewhat different approach to semantics from that taken by Parsifal (Marcus 1980), which we saw in section 6.3.2. The two are similar in that they both assume the existence of a semantic process that they can ask for guidance when they need it. However, unlike Parsifal, Paragram is a trifle paranoid: it will never attach anything to anything, whether an ambiguity is possible or not, without first asking for permission from semantics. The semantic process that Paragram uses is called the SEMANTIC ENQUIRY DESK (SED); it is the operation of this process that we discuss in the remainder of this chapter.

At present, Paragram knows about two types of structural ambiguity for which it requires assistance from the SED: prepositional phrase attachment and gap finding in relative clauses. In the following sections, I will show how the SED handles each of these. We will see that the SED, in turn, gets considerable help from Polaroid Words.

---

[1] PERLIS, Alan J. "Epigrams on programming." *SIGPLAN notices*, **17**(9), September 1982, 7–13.

7.2 Prepositional phrase attachment

In this section, I consider those occasions on which the parser will require guidance from the SED to deal with a prepositional phrase.

7.2.1 Where prepositional phrases may be attached

Not all prepositional phrases really require the parser to send off for a semantic attachment decision, though Paragram asks anyway. English syntax prohibits VP attachment of PPs that occur between the subject and verb of a sentence or between the indirect and direct object:

(7-1)   *Nadia for his birthday gave her secretary a gyroscope.

(7-2)   *Nadia gave her secretary for his birthday a gyroscope.

PPs in these positions are always NP-attached:

(7-3)   The gyroscope for Nadia's secretary gave him great pleasure.

(7-4)   Nadia gave the secretary on the second floor a gyroscope.

and the SED reminds Paragram of this basic fact when necessary. English also prohibits restrictive PPs from being attached to NPs that consist of a proper name or a pronoun, or, in general, to NPs with a unique definite referent:

(7-5)   The girl with brown hair didn't know what she wanted to prove.

(7-6)   *Nadia with brown hair didn't know what she wanted to prove.

(7-7)   Ross was rather amused by the girl with brown hair.

(7-8)   *Ross was rather amused by her with brown hair.

This is not true, however, of non-restrictive PPs, whether appositive or not *(see section 3.8)*:

(7-9)   When I am sad and weary,
           When I think all hope has gone,
           When I walk along High Holborn
           I think of <u>you with nothing on</u>.[2]

(7-10)   Ross thinks of <u>Nadia with nothing on</u>.

(7-11)   Nadia thinks of <u>her house with a new coat of paint</u>.

(7-12)   Nadia thinks that <u>her house, in Toronto's trendy Withrow Park area</u>, is an architectural masterpiece of the early 1900s.

---

[2]MITCHELL, Adrian. "Celia Celia." [1] *Out loud*. London: Cape Goliard Press, March 1968. [2] *For beauty Douglas*. London: Allison and Busby, 1982. 128.

The SED rules that I will develop below will, however, always attach the PP to the VP if the NP has a unique definite referent and VP attachment is at all possible. In (7-9) and (7-10), this would incorrectly attach *with nothing on* to the VP as the MANNER case (an attachment that would be plausible in (7-10) but is probably not the preferred one). Except when commas are provided, determining the correct attachment in such cases is very difficult (as are the semantics of the attachment— see section 3.8), and I will have no more to say about it.

7.2.2 *Determinants of prepositional phrase attachment*

In a few lucky cases, the preposition itself will suffice to determine the PP attachment by having no meanings at all for one attachment or the other. Obviously, the pseudo-prepositions *SUBJ*, *OBJ*, and *INDOBJ* cannot be attached to NPs, for that would contradict the syntactic position they represent. This is also the case for some ordinary prepositions. For example, *into*, *onto*,[3] and *despite* never[4] have NP-attachment meanings.[5] Other prepositions are precluded from VP-attachment by certain verbs; *with* cannot flag any case of *know*, for example:

(7-13)   *With his microscope, Ross knew that the diamond was counterfeit.[6]

(7-14)   *With care, Ross knew that the diamond was counterfeit.

(7-15)   *With Nadia, Ross knew that the diamond was counterfeit.

Similarly, not many verbs have a case flagged by *of*.[7] If the SED is given a case like one of these, it can easily return the correct answer to the parser, even if the PP complement remains undisambiguated.

But let us suppose that it is not a simple case. How is the SED to decide what to tell the parser? The SED will be given the PWs, which may or may not be fully disambiguated, for the following: the elements of the PP itself, the verb of the VP

---

[3] *cf.* Fowler 1965:420.

[4] Hirst 1981a[1]:86, fn.

[5] What, never? Well, hardly ever. Nominalized verbs CAN take these prepositions, but strictly speaking the attachment comes before the nominalization:
(i)   The stealing of the gem despite the security measures mystified the police.

(ii)   ?The attendance despite the rain was surprisingly high.

Compare:
(iii)   The attendance was surprisingly high despite the rain.

[6] But:
(i)   With his telepathic powers, Spock knew the thoughts of all the people on the space ship.

(Barbara Brunson, personal communication).

[7] Among the exceptions: *smell of, die of, talk of, approve of, know of*. All these verbs are intransitive, and *of* usually occurs right after the verb, so there is no ambiguity.

to which it might be attached, and the head noun of the NP or NPs for which it is a candidate.[8] I will refer to this verb and these nouns as the potential attachment heads. In the following discussion, I will first assume that the PWs (other than, of course, the preposition) are disambiguated, later relaxing this assumption.

If the SED is going to decide whether a given prepositional phrase is best attached to the VP of the sentence or to an NP, it must first know how that PP will function in each of its possible locations. Now, in the description of preposition Polaroid Words in section 5.3.1, I said that their meaning was either a case flag of one kind or another (in prepositional phrases attached to a verb phrase) or some appropriate slot of the noun (in PPs attached to a noun phrase).[9] A preposition PW will work on both the set of VP-attachment meanings and the set of NP-attachment meanings until it knows where the PP is to be attached and can eliminate the inappropriate set.

Now, we saw in section 6.3 two types of strategy for deciding whether a PP should be attached to the verb head or the noun head. The first was Ford, Bresnan, and Kaplan's Final Expected Argument Principle (1982) *(section 6.3.3)*, which says that (if semantics or pragmatics doesn't overrule it) the parser should attach PPs to the VP until no more cases are expected, after which point the current NP gets them. (The principle does not give a way of choosing between NP heads if there is more than one.) The second kind of strategy was pragmatic: Crain and Steedman's Principles of Referential Success, of Parsimony, and of A Priori Plausibility (1985) *(section 6.3.4)*, which say that the attachment should be done so as to minimize the number of unsatisfied references and presuppositions while maximizing plausibility. While we were not wholly satisfied with either kind of strategy, we shall have the SED use a synthesis of the two to decide on PP attachments.

There are several things we must have before we can implement these strategies:

- An annotation on each verb sense as to which of its cases are "expected".

- A method for deciding on the relative plausibility of a PP attachment.

- A method for determining the presuppositions that would be engendered by a particular PP attachment, and for testing whether they are satisfied or not.

- A method for resolving the issue when the strategies give contradictory recommendations.

---

[8] At the point when the parser calls the SED for help, the parser will have just finished parsing the PP, which will be the first element of the buffer. The open NP to which it might be attached will be the current constituent on the parser's stack; the open VP will be above it on the stack. By the strict rules of Marcus parsing, the open VP should not be available for examination at this point (Marcus 1980: 41); however, Marcus breaks the rule himself (1980: 305), claiming (1980: 311) that case-frame semantics are not within the scope of the rules of strict determinism. Paragram is also unhappy about looking at the open VP, and an escape into Lisp code is required to do it.

[9] Recall from table 3.2 that in either case the semantic type of the translation of a preposition is *slot*.

7.2.3 Verb annotations

The first requirement, annotating verbs for what they expect, is straightforward once we have data on verb preferences. These data could come from textual analysis or from formal experiments on people's preferences, such as the one Ford, Bresnan, and Kaplan (1982) ran. (Connine, Ferreira, Jones, Clifton, and Frazier (1984) have presented a large set of suitable data.) However, for a small, experimental system such as ours, the intuitions of the author and his friendly informants suffice. We will classify cases as either COMPULSORY, PREFERRED, or UNPREFERRED *(cf. section 5.3.6)*.

7.2.4 Plausibility

Now let's consider the use of plausibility to evaluate the possible attachments. Often, SLOT RESTRICTION PREDICATES *(see section 5.3.1)* will allow the preposition Polaroid Word to immediately eliminate many or all of its NP- or VP-attachment possibilities, even before the SED becomes involved. For example:

(7-16)   Ross loves the girl with brown eyes.

The preposition *with* can be attached to a VP with *love* only as the MANNER case, but requires the filler to be a `manner-quality`, which `eye` isn't *(cf. Ross loves the girl with a passion)*; when this is eliminated, only NP-attachment possibilities remain.

Slot restriction predicates are a simple form of plausibility testing. In the most general case, deciding whether something is plausible is extremely difficult, and I make no claims to having solved the problem. In the best of all possible worlds *(see section 2.2.2)*, Frail would be able to answer most questions on plausibility. Slot restriction predicates would be DEFINED to guarantee plausibility. The predicate on INSTRUMENT, for example, would not require merely that it take a physical object, but that it take a physical object that could plausibly be used for the action in question. But, of course, we don't know how to specify that. What, for example, should the slot restriction for the INSTRUMENT of *cut* be *(cf. section 5.4)*? Some of the items in (7-17) are plausible, some are implausible, and some are difficult even for a human to decide upon the plausibility of:

(7-17)   Ross cut the salami with a knife / a screwdriver / a pencil / a laser beam / an elephant / a sword / a chain saw / a computer / a dandelion / Fermat's last theorem / a pas de bourrée.

However, there are two easy methods of testing plausibility that we can use that, though non-definitive, will suffice in many cases. The first of these, which we just saw, is the slot restriction predicates that we do have in present-day Frail. Note that the work of handling these is already done for us by Polaroid Words—the SED will not even see possibilities that violate them *(see above)*. While satisfying the predicates does not guarantee plausibility, failing the predicates indicates almost certain implausibility. The second method is what we shall call the EXEMPLAR PRINCIPLE: an object or action should be considered plausible if the knowledge base contains an instance of such an object or action, or an instance of something similar.[10] The SED can easily construct from the semantic objects supplied to it the Frail call to do this.[11;12]For example, if the SED wants to test the plausibility of *a cake with candles* or *operate with a slug*, it looks in the knowledge base to see if it has run across such a thing before:

(7-18)   (a ?x (cake ?x (attr=(some ?y (candle ?y))))))

(7-19)   (a ?x (operate ?x (instrument=(a ?y (slug ?y))))))

If it finds an instance, it takes the attachment to be plausible. If no such item is found, the matter is unresolved.[13] Thus the results of plausibility testing by the SED will be either EXEMPLAR EXISTS or CAN'T TELL.[14]

---

[10]Notice that the Exemplar Principle is simply a weak form of the Principle of Referential Success.

[11]It is the SED rather than the preposition PW that does this because the PW is able to see only the heads of the NPs it deals with, not the whole NP. If this were to change, as it might in future versions, then PWs may take over this task from the SED.

[12]Frame determiners do not yet have a general frame matcher of the kind described by Finin (1980) or DG Bobrow and Winograd (1977), so calls such as (7-18) and (7-19) are taken more literally than they ought to be.

[13]Various recovery strategies suggest themselves. For example, the SED might try asking Frail for items similar to the one being tested by replacing one of the frames in the search with a sibling or ancestor in the ISA hierarchy. Thus, if *operate with a slug* draws a blank, it could try *operate with a coin* or *operate with a metal-stamping*. The problem with this, of course, is that it is hard to know where to stop if plausibility remains unproved. Also, there is the danger of turning an implausible search item into a plausible one, or vice versa.

Ideally, the SED should also be able to see if the entailments of an attachment lead to an implausibility or contradiction. For example, the AGENT of an action is usually located at the same place that the action occurs; thus attachment of the PP to the VP would lead to a contradiction in (i):

(i)   The women discussed the dogs on the beach.

if it were known that the women were not at the beach.

What we really need is a theory of implausibility that could prove a Frailframe statement implausible. One component of such a theory would be the construction of "mental images" of things whose plausibility is to be tested (*cf.* Waltz 1978). I believe, however, that the exemplar principle is what people use most of the time; their enormous knowledge bases permit a conclusion of implausibility to be drawn when a modest amount of searching fails to find an exemplar for plausibility.

[14]With a large knowledge base it may be possible to assign ratings based on the number of exemplars found; an item that has a hundred exemplars would be considered more plausible than one with only one exemplar, other things being equal. It would be necessary to take into consideration how many instances can be found of the frame with slot values DIFFERENT from those sought. If only one cake could be found with (attr=flowers), but a hundred without, a cake with flowers on it could be considered plausible but unusual. On the other hand, if there were just one cake known, but with (attr=flowers), then flowers on cakes would be considered perfectly normal.

Once an instance has been determined to be either common or unusual, it could be marked as such for future reference. A marking of *unusual* would have to be revised if too many more instances like it turn up. Intuition suggests that people operate in this way.

7.2.5 *Testing for presupposition satisfaction*

The next requirement is a method for deciding whether a particular PP attachment would result in an unsatisfied presupposition. I will show that the Principle of Referential Success *(section 6.3.4)* suffices. We observe the following.[15] First, a definite NP presupposes that the thing it describes exists and that it is available in the focus or knowledge base for felicitous (unique) reference;[16] an indefinite NP presupposes only the plausibility of what it describes. Thus, *a blue chipmunk* presupposes only that the concept of a **blue chipmunk** is plausible; *the blue chipmunk* further presupposes that there is exactly one blue chipmunk available for ready reference. Second, the attachment of a PP to an NP results in new presuppositions for the new NP thus created, but cancels any uniqueness aspect of the referential presuppositions of both its constituent NPs. Thus, *the ocelot with the blue chipmunk* presupposes that there is just one such ocelot available for reference (and that such a thing is plausible); the plausibility and existence of an **ocelot** and a **blue chipmunk** continue to be presupposed, but their uniqueness is no longer required. Third, the attachment of a PP to a VP creates no new presuppositions,

---

[15]The proof of the generality of these observations is by absence of counterexample. If the reader has a counterexample, she or he should notify me promptly.

[16]When I say "exists" here, I am conflating two things: actual existence in the world, represented by an instance in the knowledge base, and conceptual existence, which is not quite so straightforward. For example, one can say:

(i)   The conference on linguistic meteorology will not be held this year.

apparently denying the existence of the entity whose existence is seemingly *(cf. chapter 4, footnote 16)* presupposed by the sentence's own subject NP! But there is no paradox; what the NP really presupposes is the existence of the conference AS A CONCEPT. If (i) is uttered to someone who had heard of the plans of the conference, it would be a perfectly valid reference to the concept, in their knowledge base, of the conference, in exactly the same manner as I describe above for entities with represented real-world existence. If (i) is uttered to someone who has not heard of the conference, the presupposition is still there, albeit unsatisfied. The problem of representing non-existence of a particular instance of a generic frame, or of any instance of it, is left to the knowledge base designer. [I am grateful to Yorick Wilks, Xiuming Huang, and Dan Fass for drawing my attention to this problem; see Wilks, Huang, and Fass 1985.]

When I say "available" here, I am also conflating two things: being already explicitly represented in the knowledge base, and being implicitly represented, that is able to be generated from available information. An example of the latter: the NP

(ii)   The address of my brother who lives in Melbourne

(cf. Winograd 1972: 156, Ritchie 1980: 103) might not refer to an existing node in the knowledge base, but if my brother is known and it is known that people have addresses, then the existence of the presupposed address may be inferred and is thus available in the knowledge base. This suffices to satisfy the presupposition.

It should be emphasized that nothing I am saying here denies that definite NPs can introduce new information, as Ritchie (1980: 103) has pointed out. My point is only that, even in such cases, there is a presupposition (unfulfilled) of prior knowledge. Such usage is not in any way pathological.

but rather always indicates new (unpresupposed) information.[17]

These observations allow us to "factor out" most of the presupposition testing: the candidate attachments will always score equally for unsatisfied presuppositions, except that VP attachment wins if the NP candidate is definite but NP attachment would result in reference to an unknown entity. On the other hand, if NP attachment would result in a felicitous definite reference, the number of unsatisfied presuppositions will remain the same for both attachments, but by the Principle of Referential Success we will prefer the NP attachment.[18] Testing for this is particularly easy for the SED because of the property of Absity that the semantic objects associated with the syntactic constituents are all well-formed Frail objects (or, to be precise, Polaroid Word "pictures" of them). The SED can therefore just put them into a call to Frail to see whether the mooted NP-attachment entity exists in the knowledge base or not. (The entity may be there explicitly, or its existence may be inferred; that is up to Frail.) If the entity is found, the presupposition is SATISFIED, and the PP should be attached to the NP; otherwise, if the presupposition is UNSATISFIED or if NO PRESUPPOSITION WAS MADE, the VP gets the PP.

As an example, let's suppose the SED needs to decide on the attachment of the PP in (7-20):

(7-20)   Ross saw the man with the telescope.

It will have the semantic objects for *the man* and *with the telescope*, the latter having two possibilities:

(7-21)   (the ?x (man ?x))

---

[17]This is not quite true; sentences asserting a change of state presuppose that the new state did not previously hold. For instance, (i):

(i)   Ross flew to New York.

presupposes that Ross isn't already in New York. Such presuppositions can be the complement of the presuppositions engendered by NP attachment of the PP:

(ii)   Throw the ring in the tub.

The PP of (ii) can be NP-attached, implying that the ring is in the tub, or VP-attached, implying, conversely, that the ring is not (yet) in the tub. [I am grateful to Eugene Charniak for these examples and for discussion of these points.] I will ignore these complications; but note that the PP-attachment procedure to be discussed below will nevertheless handle most of these cases correctly.

[18]A corollary of this is that a PP is never attached to an indefinite NP if VP attachment is at all possible, except if the Final Expected Argument Principle applies. This seems too strong, and the rule will probably need toning down. The corollary is not completely out of line, however, as definiteness certainly influences attachment. For example, the preference for NP attachment in (i) is changed to a VP preference in (ii) just by making the NP indefinite (even though the Final Argument Principle still applies!):

(i)   The women discussed the dogs on the beach.

(ii)   The women discussed dogs on the beach.

```
(7-22)    (instrument=(the ?y (telescope ?y))
          (attr=(the ?y (telescope ?y))))
```

It therefore constructs the Frail statement (7-23) for the NP attachment:

```
(7-23)    (the ?x (man ?x (attr=(the ?y (telescope ?y))))))
```

If this returns some instance, `man349` say, then the SED knows that presupposition considerations favor NP attachment; if it returns `nil`, then it knows they favor VP attachment.

7.2.6 Making the attachment decision

The SED's last requirement is a method for deciding on the PP attachment, given the results of verb expectation and presupposition and plausibility testing. If all agree on how the attachment should be made, then everything is fine. However, as Ford, Bresnan, and Kaplan (1982) make clear, verb expectations are only biases, not absolutes, and can be overridden by conflicting context and pragmatic considerations. Therefore, the SED needs to know when overriding should occur. Table 7.1 shows a decision algorithm for this. The algorithm assumes (unrealistically) that there are one VP and one NP available and that implausibility judgments can be made; we will get rid of these assumptions in a moment. The algorithm gives priority to ruling out implausible readings, and favors NP attachments that give referential success (referential success is tried first, since it is the stronger condition); if these tests don't resolve matters, it tries to use verb expectations.[19] If these don't help either, it goes for VP attachment (*i.e.*, Minimal Attachment; *see sections 1.1.3 and 6.3.4*), since that is where structural biases seem to lie, but it is more confident in its result if an unsatisfied presupposition contraindicates NP attachment.

Now, table 7.1 makes two assumptions that it shouldn't. The first is that we can recognize plausibility with some confidence at the SED level, whereas we saw earlier that the best we can really do is say "yes" or "maybe". We shall therefore rearrange the priorities to take account of this. The second assumption is that there is only one NP candidate for attachment. We will amend this by adding a preference in NP attachment for the most recent NP, that is, a preference for Low Right Attachment *(see section 1.1.3)* when there is more than one NP available.[20] The

---

[19] We saw in section 1.1.3 that some sentences, such as (i):

(i)   The landlord painted all the walls with cracks.

show verb expectations prevailing over plausibility. Ideally, the SED would react to this sentence the way most people do; however, the procedure we present tends to err on the side of common sense.

[20] When checking for referential success in the attachment of a PP to an NP that is, in turn, part of a PP attached to an NP, we check the entire matrix NP; however, for plausibility exemplars, we only check the immediate attachment. For example, suppose we wish to attach the underlined PP in (i), where *in*

Table 7.1. *Decision algorithm for restrictive PP attachment (one VP and one NP)*

[Referential success]
if NP attachment gives referential success
    then attach to NP

[Plausibility]
else if VP attachment is implausible
    then attach to NP
else if NP attachment is implausible
    then attach to VP

[Verb expectations]
else if verb expects a case that the preposition
    could be flagging
    then attach to VP
else if the last expected case is open
    then attach to NP

[Avoid failure of reference]
else if NP attachment makes unsuccessful
    reference
    then attach to VP
else sentence is ambiguous, but prefer VP
    attachment anyway.

---

amended algorithm is shown in table 7.2. It is simpler than it looks. Its priorities are referential success, known plausibility, verb expectations, and avoidance of unsatisfied presuppositions, and there is an "inner loop" with these same priorities for handling the final expected argument.

Sentences for which the algorithm gives the correct answer are shown in table 7.3. I also show a few sentences on which the algorithm fails. That the algorithm is a little ragged around the edges, especially in its more desperate clauses towards the end, is not bothersome; it seems to me that the fault is not in the algorithm but rather in the system's inability to use world knowledge for disambiguation as well as people do. I can't believe that people have some sophisticated mental algorithm that tells them how to attach PPs in those awkward cases where several different possibilities all rate approximately the same *(cf. section 1.4)*; rather, they use a simple algorithm and lots of knowledge, and in the rare awkward (and, probably, artificial) case, either ask for clarification, choose an attachment almost at random

---

the park has already been attached to *the man*:

(i)   the man in the park <u>with the chain saw</u>

The two entities we check for referential success will be *the man with the chain saw* and *the man in [the park with the chain saw]*. For plausibility, we will check *a man with a chain saw* and *a park with a chain saw*.

Table 7.2. *Decision algorithm for restrictive PP attachment (one VP and more than one NP; imperfect plausibility judgments)*

[Referential success]
if some NP attachment gives referential success
    then attach to most recent such NP

[Plausibility]
else if there is exactly one attachment known to be plausible
    then make that attachment

[Verb expectations]
else if verb expects a case that the preposition could be flagging
    then attach to VP
else if the last expected case is open or past
    then if there is an NP attachment known to be plausible that
        doesn't give referential failure
      then make the rightmost such attachment
    else if VP attachment is known to be plausible
      then attach to the VP
    else if there is an NP attachment that doesn't give referential failure
      then make the rightmost such attachment
    else attach to the rightmost NP

[Avoid failure of reference]
else if there is an NP attachment known to be plausible that
    doesn't give referential failure
  then make the rightmost such attachment
else if there is an NP attachment that doesn't give referential failure
  then make the rightmost such attachment
else sentence is ambiguous, but prefer VP attachment anyway.

(perhaps using a stochastic technique; *cf.* Heidorn 1982, Fujisaki 1984), or use conscious higher-level inference (perhaps the kind used when trying to figure out garden paths) to work out what is meant.

The algorithm does not treat the case where there are two verbs available for the PP to be attached to. It seems that the verb closer to the PP is preferred, other things being equal. To see this, consider the following sentences,[21] in which it must be decided whether the final PP is attached to the main verb, *put*, or to the verb of the relative clause, *read*:

(7-24)   Ross put the book Nadia had been reading <u>in the study</u>.

(7-25)   Ross put the book Nadia had been reading <u>behind the couch</u>.

Most people experience a mild garden-path effect with (7-24), initially attaching *in the study* to *read*, and then backing up after they find that this leaves *put* without

---

[21] The examples are from Marilyn Ford (personal communication).

Table 7.3. *PPs that are and aren't correctly attached*

PPS THAT ARE CORRECTLY ATTACHED

The women discussed the dogs <u>on the beach</u>.
 NP-attached.
The women discussed the tigers <u>on the beach</u>.
 NP-attached if there are tigers on the beach, but VP-attached if tigers on the beach
 is not found plausible and discussed on the beach *is.*
The women discussed tigers <u>on the beach</u>.
 VP-attached if tigers on the beach *is not found plausible.*
Ross bought the book <u>for Nadia</u>.
 NP-attached if there is a book for Nadia available for reference, and VP-attached
 otherwise.
Ross included the book <u>for Nadia</u>.
 NP-attached.
Nadia saw the man in the park <u>with the telescope</u>.
 Attached to in the park *if there is a park with a telescope with a man in it, or if*
 there is a park with a telescope even if there is a man with a telescope; attached to
 the man *if there is a man with a telescope but no park with a telescope; attached*
 to the VP otherwise.

PPS THAT ARE NOT CORRECTLY ATTACHED

The women discussed dogs <u>on the beach</u>.
 NP-attached because dogs on the beach *is plausible and doesn't fail referentially,*
 though VP attachment seems to be preferred by informants.
The women discussed the dogs <u>at breakfast</u>.
 NP-attached like the dogs on the beach, *because the subtle implausibility of* the
 dogs at breakfast *as a topic of conversation is not detected.*
The landlord painted all the walls <u>with cracks</u>.
 NP-attached (contra informants) if walls with cracks are deemed plausible; oth-
 erwise, VP-attached (contra common sense) by lexical expectations.

---

its obligatory LOCATION case. No such effect is felt with (7-25). The verb *read* can take a PLACE modifier, and, in (7-24), grabs the PP accordingly—an error that results in the garden path. In (7-25), the PP is judged an implausible PLACE for reading, and so is left for attachment to *put*. The implication is that local attachment is preferred, but is subject to plausibility considerations. The SED does not yet handle PP attachment problems with two competing verbs.

7.2.7 *Muffling combinatorial explosions*

The preceding discussion assumed that while the meaning of the preposition of the PP whose attachment is to be decided may be unresolved, the potential attachment heads and the prepositional complement were all either lexically unambiguous or already disambiguated. Now let's consider what happens if they are not, that is, if the Polaroid Words that must be used by the SED to decide on an attachment are not yet fully developed. We will see that the SED's decision will often as a side effect allow the PWs to become disambiguated as well.

In principle, the number of combinations of meanings of the undisambiguated words could be large. For example, if the two potential attachment heads, the preposition, and the prepositional complement all have three uneliminated senses, then 81 (*i.e.*, 3^4) combinations of meanings could be constructed. In practice, however, many combinations will not be semantically possible, as one choice will constrain another—the choice for the verb will restrict the choices for the nouns, for example. Moreover, such multiple ambiguities are probably extremely rare. (I was unable to construct one that didn't sound artificial for use as an example in this paragraph.) It is my intuition that verbs are almost always disambiguated by the prepositional phrase (possibly *OBJ*+ NP) that immediately follows them, before any PP attachment questions can arise, thereby reducing substantially the number of combinations. Moreover, the SED could use the strategy that if the verb remains ambiguous when PP attachment is being considered and combinatorial explosion seems imminent, the Polaroid Word for the verb is REQUIRED by the SED to resolve itself forthwith, even if it has to guess *(cf. section 5.3.4)*.[22] (This is in accord with Just and Carpenter's (1980: 340) model of reading, in which combinatorial explosion is avoided by judiciously early choice of word senses.)

Given, then, a manageably small number of lexical ambiguity combinations, structural disambiguation by the SED may proceed as before. Now, however, each attachment must be tried for each combination. The type of attachment that scores best for some combination is then chosen, thereby also choosing that combination as the resolution of the lexical ambiguity. For example, if combination *A* suggests NP attachment on the basis of referential success, thus beating combination *B*'s suggestion of VP attachment on the basis of plausibility, then both NP attachment and the word senses in combination *A* are declared winners. Ties are, of course, possible, and may well indicate genuine ambiguity; the SED has at present no mechanism for handling them. One possible resolution method would be (as discussed above) to force the PWs involved to make a guess one by one about their meanings until a clear solution is apparent; this obviously risks being overzealous if the ambiguity is genuine. Of course, if all or a majority of the tied combinations agree on what the PP attachment should be, there is no problem for the SED even if the PWs are left none the wiser.

---

[22]This strategy is not implemented in the SED at present.

> To shrink with horror from ending [a clause] with a preposition is no more
> than a foolish superstition.
> —H. W. Fowler[23]

7.3 Gap finding in relative clauses

7.3.1 Why gap finding is difficult

As I mentioned in section 6.2.2, there is an interaction between ambiguities of relative clause attachment and of gap finding: the former requires deciding what the relative pronoun refers to, and the latter requires deciding where to put it. Unfortunately, just finding the gaps in relative clauses is a source of severe difficulty for Marcus parsers such as Paragram and Parsifal. To see the problem, consider (7-26) and (7-27):[24]

(7-26)　The mansion that the Hearsts moved $\Diamond$ to California was monstrous.

(7-27)　The mansion that the Hearsts moved to California for $\Diamond$ was monstrous.

Both Paragram and Parsifal try to place the *wh-* as soon as they find a potential gap that their semantic consultants will let them use. Thus (7-27) will be treated like (7-26), with the *wh-* placed after the word *moved*, despite the fact that the correct gap occurs later in the sentence. Even if the parsers tried to look out for such cases (which they don't), their deliberately limited lookahead would often prevent them seeing the later gap, since it can be arbitrarily far from the "false" gap (though there does seem to be a performance limitation):

(7-28)　the mansion that the Hearsts moved to California last summer for $\Diamond$

(7-29)　the mansion that the Hearsts moved to California last summer against the advice of their attorneys for $\Diamond$

Because of this problem, we will not be able to use Ford, Bresnan, and Kaplan's (1982) proposals for applying lexical preference to gap finding *(section 6.3.3)*; the parser requires a decision to be made on whether or not to use an apparent gap before it is known whether an expected case will turn up later.[25] The system, therefore, will have a systematic bias towards erroneously early placement of *wh*-s, and this seems unavoidable in a (present-day) deterministic system.[26]

Paragram and Parsifal are also a little overeager in deciding which constituent the *wh-* should be bound to; both take the most recent NP on the parser's stack. For example, in (7-30):

---

[23]Fowler 1965: 626.

[24]These examples are from Frazier, Clifton, and Randall (1983), who use them to make a different point.

[25]Experiments by Clifton, Frazier, and Connine (1984), Stowe (1984) and Tanenhaus, Stowe, and Carlson (1985) suggest that lexical expectations are used; see exercise 5.10 in section 9.5.

[26]Sometimes it will erroneously AVOID early placement; see next section.

(7-30)   the lions in the field that ...

the NP that the *wh-* will be bound to is *the field* (PP attachment of *in the field* to *the lions* will not have occurred yet). This choice is made as soon as the *wh-* occurs *(cf. section 7.4.2)*.

In what follows, I will limit the discussion to fairly simple cases. I will consider only the case of one filler and one gap, and look for gaps only in the top level of the relative clause. (Neither Paragram nor Parsifal can handle subsentential gaps or multiple gaps.) Examples of cases that we won't look at:

(7-31)   the boy whom the girl wanted $\Diamond$ to die[27] *[gap in subsentence of relative clause]*

(7-32)   the boy$_i$ whom the girl$_j$ wanted $\Diamond_j$ to die for $\Diamond_i$ *[two gaps and fillers]*

(Notice that the gap after *wanted* takes *the boy* in (7-31), but *the girl* in (7-32); this creates a problem similar to that in examples (7-26) and (7-27).)

7.3.2 How to find gaps

Some of the principles that we used for prepositional phrase attachment will also serve for finding the gap in a restrictive relative clause. The gap location is constrained by plausibility and a preference for avoiding unsatisfied presuppositions, just as PP attachments are, and the tests can be done in the same way, with the Exemplar Principle and the Principle of Referential Success. We will also rely on preposition Polaroid Words to screen out wildly implausible hypotheses with the aid of slot restriction predicates, as they did in PP attachments.

Initially, we will assume that the binding of the *wh-* is lexically unambiguous. If the gap is in the subject position, it is immediately apparent, and English requires that it be taken without question:

(7-33)   the cat that $\Diamond$ sat on the mat

(7-34)   *the cat that sat $\Diamond$ on the mat

After the verb, gap finding gets more complicated. Either there is a noun phrase following the verb or there isn't. If there isn't, then there are two possibilities:

- the *wh-* is the object of the verb: *the company that Ross moved $\Diamond$ to California*;

- there is no object of the verb, and the gap is somewhere later in the sentence: *the company that Ross moved to California for $\Diamond$*.

(We have already seen that the second possibility will not be considered unless the first is semantically inadmissible.) If a noun phrase does follow the verb, then that may be the object of the verb, and the first possibility above is eliminated; but if the verb is one that can take an indirect object, then there are four possibilities (*cf.* Marcus 1980: 226–228 for the first three; *see also section 6.3.2*):

---

[27]From Frazier, Clifton, and Randall 1983, with syntax corrected.

- the NP is the indirect object, and the *wh-* is to be used as the direct object: *the book that Ross gave ◊ the girl*;

- the NP is the direct object, and the *wh-* is to be used as the indirect object: *the girl that Ross gave ◊ the book*;[28]

- the NP is the direct object, there is no syntactic indirect object, and the gap is somewhere later in the sentence: *the girl that Ross gave the book to ◊*;

- the NP is the indirect object, a direct object will follow, and the gap is somewhere later in the sentence: *the book that Ross gave the girl the money for ◊.*[29]

The decision in each case is, of course, made by the Semantic Enquiry Desk by asking Polaroid Words to check the acceptability of slot-fillers and by testing for referential success and exemplars.

Suppose that we have (7-35), that the parser has just finished analyzing *the girl*, and that the words are all unambiguous:

(7-35) the book that Ross sold the girl

The competing parses are these:

(7-36) Ross sold INDOBJ the girl OBJ the book

(7-37) Ross sold INDOBJ the book OBJ the girl

(7-38) Ross sold OBJ the girl

(7-39) Ross sold INDOBJ the girl

Notice that the second two are weak versions of the first two. The SED sets up HYPOTHETICAL PWs for *INDOBJ* and *OBJ* corresponding to the first two parses (that is, two different *INDOBJ* PWs and two *OBJ* PWs), and looks to see whether there are any total failures. In this case, there will be a failure in parse (7-37), because the slot restriction predicates of `sell` require that *INDOBJ* flag a `destination` that is `hanim` (a "higher animate being");[30] `(the ?x (book ?x))` fails this test, leaving *INDOBJ* with no possible meaning. On the other hand, parse (7-36) succeeds; parses (7-38) and (7-39) are therefore not considered (despite, as already mentioned, the possibility of error).

Now let's consider an example in which slot restriction predicates don't give the answer and other tests must be used:

---

[28] This construction varies widely across idiolects in acceptability. Some people, including most speakers of non–North American English, disallow this construction, and allow only the form given as the third possibility. Marcus (1980: 226–228) provides an analysis of the idiolectic variation; see also Langendoen, Kalish-Landon, and Dore 1973. A computer NLU program should be able to handle a wide variety of idiolects.

[29] Neither Paragram nor, I think, Parsifal, can parse this.

[30] Ambiguities can result with things like companies that are both `hanim` and salable; for example, *the company that Ross sold IBM* could be parsed like (7-36) or like (7-37).

(7-40)   the book that Ross gave the girl

Let's assume that the dest ination of give, unlike sell, need not be hanim (*e.g.*, it could be a dog), so the counterparts of both (7-36) and (7-37) will succeed. The SED then constructs the Frail objects that correspond to these parses and tries for referential success.

```
(7-41)    (the ?x (book ?x
                  (a ?y (give ?y
                              (agent=Ross)
                              (patient=?x)
                              (destination=(the ?z (girl ?z)))))))


(7-42)    (the ?x (book ?x
                  (a ?y (give ?y
                              (agent=Ross)
                              (destination=?x)
                              (patient=(the ?z (girl ?z)))))))
```

If one of these succeeds referentially, the corresponding possibility is chosen. If neither does, then the SED constructs calls to look for exemplars of the concepts. (If both succeed, the discourse is an extremely weird one.) The calls that search for exemplars are made by ABSTRACTING the previous calls. Continuing the example:

```
(7-43)    (a ?x (book ?x
                (a ?y (give ?y
                            (agent=(a ?w (person ?w)))[31]
                            (patient=?x)
                            (destination=(a ?z (girl ?z))))))))
(7-44)    (a ?x (book ?x
                (a ?y (give ?y
                            (agent=(a ?w (person ?w)))
                            (destination=?x)
                            (patient=(a ?z (girl ?z))))))))
```

In the exemplar search, the thes have been replaced by as. (This is not entirely satisfactory; see below.) If these also both fail, the third and fourth possible parses are tried, with the *wh-* not being used in the present position. If they both had found exemplars, the one that found the greatest number would be preferred (*cf. footnote 14*); this would happen, for instance, in cases like Marcus's *dragon–knight–boy* example.[32]

The last case to consider is when early use of the *wh-* has been rejected. In this case, the *wh-* is necessarily used at the site of the next preposition that is missing

---

[31] This is the "indefinite" form of Ross, since Ross is an instance of a person.

[32] *the dragon that the knight gave the boy [cf. (6-83)].*

its complement and that can possibly accept it.[33] If no such gap eventuates, then
the *wh-* should have been used earlier; recovery, however, is not possible, and the
parser has been garden-pathed.[34]

Now let's relax the assumption that the words involved are lexically unambiguous and suppose that some are, instead, undeveloped Polaroid Words. In this case,
each of the words' remaining meanings will have to be included in the semantic
tests, as with lexical ambiguity in PP attachment *(see section 7.2.7)*. If only one
sense of a word gives good results, the gap is used, and, as a side effect, the PW
is disambiguated appropriately. If more than one sense is good, the gap is chosen,
but the PW continues to look for disambiguation cues *(cf. section 5.3.5)*. Again,
as with PP attachment, some of the PWs should, if necessary, be forced to make an
early decision, but this is not yet implemented. Similar principles could be used
in deciding between alternative bindings for the *wh-* when a method of obtaining
the possibilities is provided *(see above and section 7.4.2)*.

We now return to the problem of exactly what should be sought when looking for
exemplars to prove plausibility. When the SED is testing for referential success,
no problem arises—it just looks for the exact semantic object specified. However, if this does not succeed, the SED has to look for "something similar". For
prepositional phrase attachment *(see section 7.2.4)*, this is not so difficult, since the
semantic object is simply a frame with a specified slot value; the question of "similarity" doesn't really arise.[35] Relative clauses describe more complex and specific
situations than PPs, and it would be silly to require an exemplar to match exactly;
rather, a suitable abstraction needs to be created. For example, the plausibility of
the book that Ross gave the girl should not rest on knowing of some book that
some person gave some girl; people accept as plausible *the sewing machine that
Ross gave the librarian*, but not *the escalator that Ross gave the baby*, though they

---

[33] It is necessary to distinguish such prepositions from particles, but at the moment we don't—we
always take loose prepositions as indicative of a gap if a gap is sought; see section 7.4.1.

[34] These garden paths do not seem to have psychological reality. For example, (i) would give the system
a garden path:

(i)   Ross likes the horse that Nadia knitted ◊ on Monday.

but people don't seem to have any trouble analyzing (i) and deciding that the horse was a knitted toy.
Compare:

(ii)   Ross likes the horse that Nadia knitted near ◊ on Monday.

(iii)   #Ross fed the horse that Nadia knitted ◊ on Monday.

Note that (iii) can be parsed by people, even though it is nonsensical.

[35] But see footnote 13. Notice also that in the VP–PP plausibility tests, the SED does not test for
implausibility in the entire case structure. For example, in testing the attachment of *with the telescope*
to *saw* in (i):

(i)   The squirrel saw a man with a telescope.

the SED looks only for an exemplar of **see with a telescope**, not **squirrel see with a telescope**, and
makes the obvious mistake.

are unlikely to have an example of either in their knowledge bases. They do, however, have exemplars of giving something suitable as a gift to something suitable
as a gift recipient—a concept very hard for us to characterize in Frail—and use
knowledge and inference in attempting to make a match in the knowledge base.
Ideally, the SED should have a principled method of abstracting from a semantic
object to an exemplar search pattern, and also the necessary inference mechanisms
for the search; this is a matter for further research.

> The two kinds of relative clause, to one of which "that" and to the other of
> which "which" is appropriate, are the defining and the non-defining; and if
> writers would agree to regard "that" as the defining relative pronoun and "which"
> as the non-defining, there would be much gain both in lucidity and in ease.
> —H. W. Fowler[36]

I have spoken above solely of restrictive relative clauses. The problems of gap
finding are similar in non-restrictive relative clauses:

(7-45)   The mansion, which the Hearsts had moved ◊ to California, was monstrous.

(7-46)   The mansion, which the Hearsts had moved to California for ◊, was monstrous.

The Principle of Referential Success, however, does not apply in testing for gaps
in such clauses, because (by definition) the clause contains new information about
the *wh-*. The SED is therefore limited to weaker methods, such as the Exemplar
Principle, to test for plausibility in non-restrictive relatives.

7.4 Methods for other structural ambiguities

To deal with all the different types of structural ambiguity listed in section 6.2 is
a large task, and the Semantic Enquiry Desk presently handles only two of them,
albeit two particularly important ones. In this section I give some preliminary
thoughts on how some of the other ambiguities might be handled.

7.4.1 Particle detection

There are three classes of verb in English that take particles: PREPOSITIONAL VERBS,
PHRASAL VERBS, and PHRASAL-PREPOSITIONAL VERBS. Each class has a different
syntactic behavior, varying in the movements the particle may make with respect to
the verb and its object; see Quirk, Greenbaum, Leech, and Svartvik 1972: 811–819
or Cowie and Mackin 1975 for a detailed discussion of the classes, their syntax,
and their distinguishing characteristics. A verb usually has a distinct sense when

---

[36]Fowler 1965: 625–626.

```
[look (verb):
   [look-deliberately
        agent        SUBJ
        patient      at
        direction    up, down, out, ...
           ... ]

   [search-for-info
        PHRASAL      up
        agent        SUBJ
        patient      OBJ
           ... ]

   [be-wary-of
        PHRASAL      out
        agent        SUBJ
        patient      for
           ... ]]

[up (prt)]

[out (prt)]
```

Figure 7.1. Partial Polaroid Words for *look* with particles, and *up* and *out* as particles.

used with a particle—compare *look* and *look up [a phone number]*, for example—so particle detection is closely related to lexical disambiguation.

To handle particles, we must first, obviously, add to the grammar rules that will recognize the possibility that a word is functioning as a particle and will ask the SED for an opinion if necessary. Listed in the Polaroid Word for each verb will be the words that can act as particles with that verb; thus the PWs for *look*, *up*, and *out* may appear in part as shown in figure 7.1. (Notice that particles are taken as being semantically empty; this does not threaten Absity's compositionality if they are suitably typed.)

Let's suppose that the parser is working on (7-47) or (7-48):

(7-47)   Ross looked up the number.

(7-48)   Ross looked the number up.

The parser notes that *up* in these positions could be a particle. It therefore asks the SED whether *look up the number* is better regarded as verb–particle–object-NP, or as verb–PP. The SED decides that no sense of *number* makes a good direction and reports accordingly. As a side-effect, the PW for *look* is resolved. (No PW process is created for *up*.)

Ideally, the SED should be able to take context and plausibility into account in such decisions. It is, however, restricted by the parser's limited lookahead, and would probably analyze (7-50) erroneously as being like (7-49):

(7-49)   Ross looked up the elevator shaft.

(7-50)   Ross looked up the elevator shaft in the inventory of the building's conduits.

7.4.2 Relative clause attachment

To determine the attachment of a relative clause, the possible ambiguity of the *wh-* must be added to the SED's gap-finding methods. First, of course, it must be determined what the possibilities for the *wh-* are. We saw in section 7.3.1 that Marcus parsers always immediately assume it to be the most recent NP on their stack, but there is no reason why the decision couldn't be delayed and all possibilities considered in conjunction with the content of the relative clause. This would, however, require the SED to figure out exactly what *wh*-s could be constructed from constituents on the stack, in effect doing some of the parser's work for it, which might be considered inelegant.

The best way to handle ambiguity in the *wh-* seems to be to make it a Polaroid Word once its syntactic possibilities are discovered. It can then be disambiguated with no need of extra mechanisms or rules, except that at the end of the clause the SED will have to look at its result in order to tell the parser where to attach the relative clause.[37]

7.4.3 Adverb attachment

Adverb and adverb phrase attachment is conditioned by both lexical preferences and the position of the adverb in the sentence. Some adverbs insist on being attached always to the sentence or always to the VP, and these may be handled easily by the SED if they are so marked in the lexicon:

(7-51)   Fortunately, the bad guys couldn't get across the river.
          (≠ *The bad guys were fortunate that they couldn't get across the river.*)

(7-52)   One day, when Princess Mitzi was out in the garden, hopefully kissing frogs …[38]
          (*i.e., Princess Mitzi was kissing frogs in a hopeful manner; ≠ It is hoped that Princess Mitzi was kissing frogs*[39] *or #The fact that Princess Mitzi was kissing frogs was full of hope.*)

---

[37] It might be objected that even this is unnecessary, as once the *wh-* is disambiguated, the attachment of the relative clause is of no further interest. This is not true in all cases, since the attachment of the clause may result in the closure of intermediate constituents, and thus affect later attachment possibilities.

[38] MONTY PYTHON. *Monty Python's previous record.* Charisma, 1972.

[39] My tolerance for a wide range of idiolects *(cf. footnote 28)* does not extend to the discourse-comment use of *hopefully.* "Such use is not merely wrong; it is silly" (Strunk and White 1979:48).

Webster (1983) attempts to defend the admissibility of the use of *hopefully* as a discourse comment by the following amazing argument: *interestingly* can be used as a sentence modifier; therefore, so can *hopefully.* This is both a non sequitur and an ignoratio elenchi. Whitley's arguments (1983), though at least informed, are also unconvincing.

Adverbials that admit both attachments are sensitive to their position in the sentence. Generally, clause-initial position implies sentence attachment, and clause-final implies VP attachment; compare:

(7-53)   In accordance with the law, Ross ate his breakfast.
          (i.e., The law obliged Ross to eat his breakfast, and he did so.)

(7-54)   Ross ate his breakfast in accordance with the law.
          (i.e., The particular way that Ross ate his breakfast was legal.)

However, adverbials are easily moved about. The following examples mean the same as (7-53); note that (7-56) differs from (7-54) only in its comma:

(7-55)   Ross, in accordance with the law, ate his breakfast.

(7-56)   Ross ate his breakfast, in accordance with the law.

This suggests the following rule for the SED: an adverbial modifies the sentence if set off from the clause by commas (and if lexically permitted to do so).[40] This assumes that adverbials such as *in accordance with the law* may be reliably distinguished from ordinary prepositional phrases, for otherwise the rule will be erroneously applied to preposed PPs such as (7-57):

(7-57)   On Monday, Ross ate his breakfast.

I hypothesize that such adverbials are a small (but not closed) class concerning obligation and happenstance, and are flagged by constructions such as *in accordance with*, *as instructed by*, *as predicted by*, and the like.

Unfortunately, there are a few adverbs for which the rule does not work and for which the SED will need to use something more subtle. Sentence (7-58) admits both attachments:

(7-58)   Happily, Nadia frolicked in the meadow.

Such sentences cannot be reliably disambiguated without inference on the context.

---

[40]Discourse comment adverbials (*i.e.*, those not attached at all) behave rather as sentence modifiers do:

(i)   Frankly, I don't like him. *(discourse comment)*

(ii)   I don't like him, frankly. *(discourse comment)*

(iii)   He gave his opinion frankly. *(VP-attached)*

(iv)   He frankly gave his opinion. *(VP-attached)*

Note, however, the use of *literally* in (v):

(v)   Ross and Nadia literally fell over with laughter. *(discourse comment)*
         (i.e., Ross and Nadia fell over with laughter, and I mean that literally)

(vi)   I mean that literally. *(VP-attached)*

7.5 Conclusion

The Semantic Enquiry Desk gains its power from the design of Absity and Polaroid Words. It is able to make semantic judgments with Frail because the constituents with which it works have already been assigned well-formed semantic objects by Absity. Even if the correct choice of object for an ambiguous word is not yet known, the alternatives will be well-formed and easily accessible from the Polaroid Word.

Part IV

Conclusion

8   Conclusion

8.1 Towards a conclusion

The goal of this chapter is to put the work described in previous chapters into perspective. First, I summarize the virtues of the work, and its potential. Then I compare it with similar work carried out concurrently by others. Finally, I list some of the questions that it leaves unanswered that ought to be answered.

8.2 The work in review

8.2.1 What has been achieved

I have presented a semantic interpreter and two disambiguation systems: one for lexical ambiguity and one for structural ambiguity. The systems have been designed to work closely with one another and with an existing parser and knowledge-representation system.

The semantic interpreter, Absity, is "Montague-inspired", in that it adapts to AI several aspects of Montague's (1973) way of thinking about semantics: it is compositional; it has a strong notion of "semantic object"; it operates in tandem with a parser; its partial results are always well-formed semantic objects; and it imposes a strong typing upon its semantic objects. The semantic objects are objects of the knowledge representation, and the types are the types that the representation permits (which, we saw, correspond to the syntactic categories of English).

The structural disambiguator is the Semantic Enquiry Desk. It tells the parser what to do whenever the parser needs semantic help to decide between two or more alternative structures. The SED makes its decisions by looking at the semantic objects in the partial results of the semantic interpreter, and, if necessary, by calling the knowledge base for information on plausibility and referential success.

Polaroid Words are the individual, one-per-word processes for lexical disambiguation. Each process figures out the meaning of the word for which it is responsible through negotiation with its "friends" (certain nearby Polaroid Words), using the knowledge base to find simple properties of semantic objects when necessary. Even when "undeveloped", Polaroid Words can be regarded by Absity as semantic objects that it can manipulate, and both the SED and other Polaroid Words can obtain well-formed partial information from a PW that has not been able to terminate.

8.2.2 Implicit claims

Implicit in my remarks about semantic objects is the claim that objects in a knowledge representation, although they are just bits in a computer, are somehow qualitatively different from "mere symbols", and I am critical (especially in section 2.3.1 and 8.3.1 below) of systems in which, I allege, the symbols of natural language are merely translated into other symbols instead of being interpreted into semantic objects (in the strict Montague 1973 sense of these terms). This claim needs some defense.

To build the defense, we must consider what a semantic object is, or could consist of. It seems to be generally agreed these days that semantic objects are not merely mental images or "capsules of thought" (Sapir 1921: 13; see Kempson 1977: 16 for discussion; but also see Rapaport 1985 on Meinongian semantics in AI); rather they are thought to be things like formal mathematical entities (Montague 1973) or situations and entities in the world (Barwise and Perry 1983). However, when people comprehend language, they do not "do semantics" with real objects, but rather with PERCEPTS of these objects. When we consider an agent understanding language, we must posit some internal representation of those semantic objects, a representation in which meanings of new sentences can be constructed, facts stored and retrieved, and inferences made—in other words, a knowledge representation in the AI sense.

It is not necessary to discuss here the many outstanding issues concerning the nature of mental representations. Rather, the point is that when we speak of an agent performing semantic computations, we are committing ourselves to an identification of the agent's percepts, or cognitive semantic objects, with the "real" semantic objects (whatever their nature may be) that are external to that agent. Thus I am arguing for a psychologically oriented semantics, in the style of Jackendoff (1983, 1984), and claiming, additionally, that once the identification of internal and external objects is made, the distinction between the two may, for most purposes, be ignored.

We can thus claim that Frail objects are fully fledged, first-class semantic objects; they may be made of silicon bits, but we can nevertheless identify them with things out there. Conversely, "mere symbols" (by definition) don't have the properties to permit this; they are just words. They can be stored and retrieved, even used in formal inference, but no direct correspondence to real semantic objects inheres in them. The difference between semantic objects and mere symbols is the same as the difference between a knowledge base and a database.

Also implicit in this work is the idea that an NLU system should be composed of interacting processes in which everything looks as well-formed as possible to everything else. Thus Absity always keeps the semantic objects that it is building well-formed, even when they are not final, so that the SED and the Frail representation can use them. Similarly, a PW represents a semantic object, and even if it can't decide which particular object it is, it will have a set of well-formed possibilities visible for other processes to make use of, while at the same time being manipulable as a single object by processes that don't care about its eventual meaning.

A third implicit idea is that, while not compromising the previous principle, things should generally happen in their own sweet time but as soon as possible. Thus, a Polaroid Word is not obliged to decide upon its final answer either immediately upon its creation or at any particular time thereafter (except in certain special circumstances; see sections 5.3.4 and 7.2.7). Nevertheless, a PW is expected not to dawdle, but to announce its answer as soon as it possibly can (*cf.* Mellish 1982b, 1985: 27; Just and Carpenter 1980).

A fourth aspect of the approach is that the design of each of the interacting processes must accede to the demands of the design of the other processes, and the design and development of each must therefore be coordinated. Thus, the parser demands of the structural disambiguator that it be able to make semantic decisions halfway through the parse. The disambiguator therefore requires of the semantic interpreter that it be incremental and have well-formed partial results that can be used for inference in and retrieval from the knowledge base. The semantic interpreter thus requires that the knowledge representation be compositional and support the concept of typed semantic objects. It also requires of the parser (thereby completing a circle of demands) that it support tandem processing; this, in turn, requires that lexical disambiguation appear to be immediate. Lexical disambiguation requires that the parser be able to insert pseudo-prepositions where necessary and do categorial disambiguation.

In the present research, the parser, Paragram, and the knowledge representation system, Frail, were the given starting points. Nevertheless, they too were forced to change: the grammar for Paragram had to accommodate pseudo-prepositions and Frail had to be given frame determiners. In addition, many of the requirements for the next version of Frail were discovered.

Nevertheless, many of the main ideas in the system and its components are independent of the other components of the system, and should be adaptable to other systems. Absity, for example, should be able to work with other parsers and with other knowledge representations, provided only that they support its requirements of compositionality and support of semantic objects; most frame-based representations—in particular, Sowa's (1984) conceptual graphs—should meet these requirements.

Where available data permitted it, the design of the system was also influenced by considerations of psychological reality. All else equal, we preferred the approach for which reasonable (but modest) claims of cognitive modeling could be made. Also, we have resisted the influences of "artificial difficulty" upon our design; we have not added any complexities just in order to be able to handle strange ambiguities that would also give people trouble or would be improbable in natural discourse.

8.2.3 Applications of the work

My hope for this research is that it be applicable in the development of general text understanding systems in wide domains of discourse. (To some extent, it is also applicable to the development of narrow-domain system interfaces, but problems such as lexical ambiguity are generally less of a worry in such cases.) There are three applications, all a long way off yet, that interest me in particular:

1. The digestion of large corpora of text. Enormous volumes of information in natural language are now available in machine-readable form. It would be useful to have a system that could really understand and integrate the information, in order to answer questions about it. Present systems simply use key words, or clever tricks based on key words, to find and present potentially relevant slabs of text. This is quite inadequate, for example, in legal information systems, where the search for a precedent case will often require matching at some very abstract level of the argument, and key words are of little or no help.[1]

2. Improving machine translation. High-quality translation without human assistance will never be possible. However, there is still much that could be done to improve the machine's part in the system. Moreover, high-speed, low-quality, unassisted machine translation may yet become practical, and acceptable in many situations.

3. Keeping expert systems up-to-date. How nice it would be if the medical expert systems of the future could keep their knowledge bases up-to-date by reading the medical journals each week. This poses additional problems beyond just digesting text: the relevant parts must be picked out from the rest, and then integrated with the existing knowledge base. Moreover, this knowledge base might not be Frail-like, or, indeed, be in any form suitable as a target for semantic interpretation. (For example, the production rules of present-day diagnosis systems are not a suitable target.) Further interpretation may therefore be necessary.

8.3 Related work of others

In this section, I discuss other recent work whose goals or methods are similar to those of the present project. For most of these, it is not possible to do much more than mention similarities and differences; I cannot as a rule compare merits, as both the present work and those mentioned below are as yet insufficiently mature to permit judgments any less vague than "seems promising" or "seems problematic".

---

[1] For this example I am grateful to Judy Dick, who is presently working at the University of Toronto on the development of suitable representations for arguments.

8.3.1 Semantic interpretation and disambiguation

The present approach to semantic interpretation is distinguished from that exemplified by van Bakel (1984). Van Bakel describes a system, AMAZON/CASUS, in which Dutch sentences are converted into a case-structure representation. However, there is no interpretation per se; words remain words, and no knowledge representation or concept of semantic object is introduced, nor is there any attempt at ambiguity resolution. In our terms, this is a translation into other symbols rather than an interpretation into semantic objects *(see section 8.2.2).*[2]

One project on semantic interpretation whose motives are similar to ours is that of Jones and DS Warren (1982), who attempt a conciliation between Montague's (1973) semantics and a conceptual dependency representation (Schank 1975). Their approach is to modify Montague's translation from English to intensional logic so that the resulting expressions have a canonical interpretation in conceptual dependency. They do not address such issues as extending Montague's syntax nor whether their approach can be extended to deal with more modern Schankian representations (*e.g.*, Schank 1982a, 1982b). Nevertheless, their work, which they describe as a hesitant first step, is similar in spirit to ours and it will be interesting to see how it develops.

Another project that shares some of the spirit of the present work is that of Hendler and Phillips (1981; Phillips and Hendler 1982), who have implemented a control structure for NLU based on message passing. Their goal is to run syntax and semantics as parallel (but not tandem) processes and provide semantic feedback to the parser. The parser (Phillips 1983) follows in parallel all paths that it can find until either a unique one succeeds syntactically or a semantic decision is needed. Constituents are passed to a "moderator", which chooses from the parser's alternatives when necessary, translates the accepted syntactic constructs to their semantic representation in a Phillips network (Phillips 1975), and passes them on for further semantic processing. The system operates in the domain of patent descriptions, and is strongly expectation-driven. The approach is essentially ad hoc, in that the interpretation of syntactic constituents into various kinds of semantic object is not governed by any form of typing—though without tandem processing, the motivation for a strong typing is lessened.

After Polaroid Words were first reported in Hirst and Charniak 1982, Pazzani and Engelman (1983) described an apparently[3] similar system used in a military question-answering program called KNOBS. Like Polaroid Words, KNOBS had words as procedures that tried to find their sense in context, working in conjunction with a parser, a semantic interpreter,[4] and a frame-like representation of knowledge

---

[2] See Hirst (1985) for further discussion of this work.

[3] Unfortunately, the paper is rather hazy about many basic details.

[4] Pazzani and Engelman first seem to suggest that the system takes Small's (1980) word-expert approach to parsing, but the rest of the paper and its oral presentation at the Conference on Applied Natural

(that, in the case of KNOBS, also contained elements of conceptual dependency). Marker passing is not used, however, and when selectional restrictions fail it, the system falls back on looking at the currently active script *(cf. section 4.1)*.

The motivation behind the use of this approach to disambiguation is unclear, since KNOBS seems intended to operate solely in domains so constrained that they have scarcely room for any lexical ambiguity other than pronouns (which the system treats in a manner similar to other lexical ambiguities).[5] The only examples shown of disambiguation in the system are of the abbreviation *A/C*, which can mean either **aircraft** or **air conditioner**; the examples shown are these:

(8-1)   What A/C can fly from Hahn?

(8-2)   Send 4 A/C to BE70701.

(8-3)   What is an A/C?

In sentence (8-1), *A/C* is resolved as **aircraft** by the selectional restrictions of *fly*. In sentence (8-2), selectional restrictions can't be used, so *A/C* is resolved as **aircraft** by noting that sending **aircraft** to coordinates is part of the "offensive counter air" script that defines the system's domain, while sending **air conditioner**s isn't. And in sentence (8-3), where the complete lack of disambiguating cues calls for desperate measures, *A/C* is resolved as **aircraft** by noting that **air conditioner**s do not participate in the system's script at all and that the system has nothing sensible to say about them. One might be forgiven for thinking that the ambiguity of *A/C* was introduced solely so the system would have something to disambiguate, and that the strategy applied in desperation to (8-3) might better have been the one used first on all of the examples.[6]

Since the publication of the present work as Hirst 1983b, Lytinen (1984) has reported a system, MOPTRANS, with several similar features. Lytinen's system, like the present work, is concerned with determining how syntax and semantics can

---

Language Processing seem to indicate a control structure like that of Polaroid Words and Absity rather than Small's Word Expert Parser.

[5] Polaroid Words, on the other hand, are intended for use in general text understanding systems.

[6] Notice further that if the system DID have something to say about **air conditioner**s, then trying to disambiguate (8-3) would be wrong. Presumably the user does NOT want a reply like (i):

(i)   An A/C is a winged vehicle that can fly to places, carry passengers and cargo, drop bombs, and intercept other aircraft.

but rather one like (ii) or (iii):

(ii)   The abbreviation "A/C" means "aircraft" or "air conditioner", depending upon the context.

(iii)   When I used it just now, I meant "aircraft"; in other contexts, it can mean "air conditioner".

I'm afraid I worry about artificial intelligence and artificial stupidity in military control systems. I have visions of systems like KNOBS ordering air conditioners to be sent to strategic locations to intercept the bad guys. Let's hope that the systems provide suitably unambiguous feedback to their users (*e.g.*, *air conditioners sent* rather than *A/C sent*).

work well together to create an unambiguous language-independent representation (which he uses as an interlingua for simple machine translation). Although he describes it in rather different terms, working in the Yale conceptual dependency paradigm (Schank 1975), the principles of MOPTRANS are quite similar to Absity's *(see section 1.1.1)*. However, Lytinen does not attempt a compositional semantics, and it is not always clear why the resulting representation is "correct". For instance, he gives this (not very well formed) example (1984: 112–113):

(8-4)   Les ambulances de la Croix Rouge ont transporté d'urgence deux jeunes filles, dont les mains avaient été blessées par suite d'une bombe, à l'hôpital Manolo Morales.
(My translation: Red Cross ambulances rushed two girls, whose hands had been injured by a bomb, to Manolo Morales Hospital.)

The representation of this input (shown in figure 8.1) carefully includes the facts about the ambulance, but not the name of the hospital or the hands as the injured body part. Strangely, hands are nevertheless mentioned in the system's English translation, (8-5), though not its (not very well formed) German translation, (8-6):

(8-5)   2 young women who were injured by a bomb in the hands [sic; *see exercise 6.2 in section 9.6*] were rushed by an ambulance owned by the Red Cross to the hospital.

(8-6)   2 junge Frauen wurden nach das Spital mit einem Krankenwagenen von dem Rotkreutz, gehastet. Sie wurden mit einem Bombe verwundet.

The approach to lexical ambiguity in MOPTRANS includes rules similar to those employed by Polaroid Words, and uses simple world knowledge, especially ISA relationships. However, there is nothing in the system like marker passing for disambiguation by association. Lytinen, rather, was more concerned with deciding upon the exact meaning of a vague word in context. Thus,

(8-7)   Gunmen seized control of the American embassy.

is recognized as an instance of the frame `take-over-building`, whereas

(8-8)   Gunmen seized control of a Boeing 727.

is an instance of `hijack`. By contrast, Absity and PWs (if *seize control* could be recognized as a canned phrase; *cf. section 5.3.3*) would simply invoke the frame `seize-control`, and leave it to other processes (such as Bruin; *see section 1.3*) to make any further inferences or script instantiations that may be warranted. Thus, Absity takes an approach to vagueness similar to that of situation semantics (Barwise and Perry 1983; *cf.* Winograd 1984).

The MOPTRANS approach to structural ambiguity is to look for the attachment that is best semantically, and see if syntax will permit it. The system is not sensitive to lexical preferences.

```
Exp0 =
  Concept   Explode-Bomb
  Inst      Obj6 =
                Concept Bomb
                Inst-of Exp0
  Object    Hum21 =
                Concept Person
                Gender  Female
                B-Part  Obj5 =
                                Concept Bodypart
                Age     Young
                Number  2
  Result    Inj2 =
                Concept Injured
                R1 Hum21
                Result-Of Exp0
Ptr99 =
  Concept   Ptrans-by-Ambulance
  Object    Hum21
  To        Loc7 =
                Concept Hospital
  Inst      Obj4 =
                Concept   Ambulance
                Owned-By  Org5 =
                                Concept Medical-Org
                                Owns    Obj4
                                #Name   Red Cross
                Inst-Of   Ptr99
  Precond   Inj2
```

Figure 8.1. Lytinen's (1984) conceptual dependency representation of sentence (8-4).

The well-known BORIS system by Dyer (1983) also uses non-compositional semantics; the emphasis of this research is on "deep" understanding of texts and the knowledge structures required for this task. To resolve lexical ambiguity, BORIS looks at the surrounding context, using both top-down expectations created by preceding text and bottom-up processes for particular ambiguous words that look at subsequent text (Dyer 1983: 180–182). These are both implemented as demons, and the latter kind resemble Polaroid Words in some ways. The two methods cooperate in the system, with the bottom-up demons deferring to top-down expectations; this deference is in contrast to the results of Marslen-Wilson and Tyler (1980; Tyler and Marslen-Wilson 1982), which suggested the priority of bottom-up processes *(see section 2.4)*. For example, the word *gin* is resolved by BORIS as an **alcoholic drink** and a **card game**, respectively, by the expectations of ingest (from *drinks*) and competitive-activity (from *plays*) in the following sentences:

(8-9)   John drinks gin.

(8-10)   John plays gin.

Bottom-up processes would also be created for *gin*, but would terminate after noticing that top-down expectations already have the matter in hand. The bottom-up demons would, however, get to do the work in sentences like the following, where no expectations are yet created and the demons must look at the interpretation of what follows:

(8-11)   The gin spilled.

(8-12)   The gin players ...

It is not clear what would happen with a sentence like:

(8-13)   John played with his gin.

Important recent work that extends the syntactic complexity of Montague's work is that on generalized phrase structure grammars (GPSGs) (Gazdar 1982). Such grammars combine a complex transformation-free syntax with Montague's semantics, the rules again operating in tandem. Gawron *et al* (1982) have implemented a database interface based on a GPSG. In their system, the intensional logic of the semantic component is replaced by a simplified extensional logic, which in turn is translated into a query for database access. Schubert and Pelletier (1982) have also sought to simplify the semantic output of a GPSG to a more "conventional" logical form, and Rosenschein and Shieber (1982) describe a similar translation process into extensional logical forms, using a context-free grammar intended to be similar to a GPSG;[7] Popowich (1984) has done similar work in logic grammars.

The GPSG approaches differ from mine in that their output is a logical form rather than an immediate representation of a semantic object; that is, the output is not tied to any representation of knowledge, and the process is therefore, as with van Bakel's work above, only translation rather than interpretation. In Gawron *et al*'s system, the database provides an interpretation of the logical form, but only in a weak sense, as the form must first pass through another (apparently somewhat ad hoc) translation and disambiguation process. Nor do these approaches provide any semantic feedback to the parser. (Gawron *et al* produce all possible parse trees for the input sentence and their translations and then throw away any that don't make sense to the database; Church and Patil (1982) have shown that this is not a good idea.) These differences, however, are independent of the choice of GPSG; it should be easy, at least in principle, to modify these approaches to

---

[7] Rosenschein and Shieber's semantic translation follows parsing rather than running in parallel with it, but it is strongly syntax-directed and is, it seems, isomorphic to an in-tandem translation that provides no feedback to the parser.

give Frail output, or, conversely, to replace Paragram in my system with a GPSG parser.[8]

The work of Mellish (1985) on the semantic interpretation of noun phrases addresses issues largely orthogonal to those treated in this book. However, Mellish's approach, the interpretation being refined incrementally as more information becomes available, is very like that of Polaroid Words, which, I think, meet his stated requirements for semantic analysis (1985:27).

The PSI-KLONE system of RJ Bobrow and Webber (1980a, 1980b; Sondheimer, Weischedel, and RJ Bobrow 1984) also has a close coupling of syntax and semantics. Rather than operating in tandem, though, the two are "cascaded", with an ATN parser handing constituents to a semantic interpreter, which is allowed to return them (causing the ATN to back up) if the parser's choice is found to be semantically untenable. Otherwise, a process of INCREMENTAL DESCRIPTION RE-FINEMENT *(cf. previous paragraph)* is used to interpret the constituent; this relies on the fact that the syntactic constituents are represented in the same formalism, KL-ONE (Brachman 1978), as the system's knowledge base. The semantic interpreter uses PROJECTION RULES to form an interpretation in a language called JAR-GON, which is then translated into KL-ONE. Bobrow and Webber are particularly concerned with using this framework to determine the combinatoric relationship between quantifiers in a sentence.

Bobrow and Webber address several of the issues that I do, in particular the relationship between syntax and semantics. The information feedback to the parser is similar to the Semantic Enquiry Desk, though because the parser is deterministic in my system, semantic feedback cannot be conflated with syntactic success or failure. Both approaches rely on the fact that the objects manipulated are objects of a knowledge representation that permits appropriate judgments to be made, though in rather a different manner in each case.

Other than Absity, the main piece of work in AI that has been inspired by Montague semantics is Nishida's (1983, 1985) prototype English-to-Japanese translation system. English sentences are translated into a formal language called EFR ("English-oriented Formal Representation"), which is a typed, higher-order logic with a lambda operator; this plays the same role as Montague's intensional logic, and may be, in turn, either interpreted by a semantic network or translated into Japanese. For translation, the English words in the representation are replaced with their Japanese counterparts (which may be structures of arbitrary complexity), and the resulting logical expression is evaluated to give a case-structure representation for the output sentence. Heuristic rewriting rules for topicalizing, eliminating re-

---

[8] The choice of Paragram was largely pragmatic—it was available—and represents no particular commitment to transformational grammars. An Absity-inspired semantic interpreter for an ATN parser is presented in Charniak and McDermott 1985. Except for the type of grammar that it uses, the DIA-LOGIC system of Grosz *et al* (1982) is similar to that of Rosenschein and Shieber with regard to the properties discussed here.

dundancies, and the like then create the tree for the final Japanese output. For interpretation into a network structure, the English words in the EFR are replaced by pieces of network structure before the expression is evaluated.

Like Absity, Nishida's system runs syntax and semantics in tandem and is compositional. The syntax is extended from that of Montague's fragment. Parses are constrained by simple selectional restrictions, but the system relies on a human operator to decide between alternative parses when necessary.

Of the work mentioned above, only that of Dyer, Lytinen, and Pazzani and Engelman addresses issues of lexical ambiguity as ours does, though Bobrow and Webber's incremental description refinement could possibly be extended to cover it. Also, Gawron *et al* have a process to disambiguate case roles in the logical form after it is complete; this operates in a manner not dissimilar to the case-slot part of Polaroid Words.

8.3.2 Knowledge representation for language understanding

Sowa has recently described a representation of knowledge that is based on conceptual graphs (Sowa 1984). This system combines many of the advantages of frames *(see section 1.2)* with those of decompositional representations such as conceptual dependency (Schank 1973, 1975; *cf.section 2.2.1*). Sowa shows (1985) how his conceptual graphs support an approach to semantics and word and case slot disambiguation that is quite similar in spirit to that of Absity.

8.3.3 Spreading activation in natural language systems

If a spreading activation mechanism is to be included in an NLU system, perhaps it can do more than just lexical disambiguation. Pollack and Waltz (1982; Waltz and Pollack 1985) have described a system in which spreading activation simultaneously chooses the meaning of ambiguous words and a structure from among the alternatives presented to it by a chart parser. The system operates by building a network in which both activation and inhibition may spread, starting from nodes representing the input words. As the system proceeds, nodes representing the constituents of the correct parse rise in their activation level, while incorrect nodes become more inhibited, and eventually the system becomes consistent. (The initial activation levels of the nodes vary, in order to account for syntactic, lexical, and case preferences.) The result is a network that represents the parse of the input. Unlike people and Polaroid Words, the system is not fooled by garden-path sentences such as *The astronomer married the star*. Pollack and Waltz apparently regard this as a feature, because the system initially entertains the incorrect interpretation and then rejects it, doing a sort of "double take".

In a similar vein, Small, Cottrell, and Shastri (1982; Cottrell 1985a) developed a system that uses spreading activation and inhibition for both semantic interpretation and lexical disambiguation. The system is based on the connectionist processing and representation models of Feldman and Ballard (1982). As in Small's

Word Expert Parser *(see section 4.2.4)*, syntactic knowledge is not distinct, but rather is integrated with the system's other knowledge sources. Again, the goal is to spread activation and inhibition until a stable network is formed; this network is the interpretation, rather than just the parse, of the sentence. McClelland and Kawamoto (1986) have created a similar system that uses a distributed rather than localist representation.[9]

Charniak (1985) has taken the idea of spreading activation even further by suggesting that almost all aspects of language comprehension can be performed by a marker passer, along with a checker that discards anomalous marker-passing chains *(see section 5.2.3)*. Included are determining case from selectional restrictions, attaching PPs, disambiguating words (of course), analyzing the structure of nominal compounds, and determining the referents of NPs. The basic ideas are that much of conventional parsing may be eliminated, that marker passing can deal with such remaining structural analysis as is necessary, and that vague, imprecise representations will often suffice in the analysis.

There has also been some preliminary work on parsing by spreading activation in a network. The idea is that given a sentence, the network would settle into an equilibrium state representing the parse tree, which could then be used by a system such as Pollack and Waltz's *(above)*. Selman (1985; Selman and Hirst 1985, 1987) and Fanty (1986) have developed algorithms for constructing such a network from a context-free grammar. For related work, see Cottrell 1985b.

These systems are still in an early stage of development, and it remains to be seen whether parsing by spreading activation will be able to deal with the complexities of English syntax that more traditional parsers such as ATNs and Marcus parsers can (but see Jones 1983, Jones and Driscoll 1985), or the various semantic complexities that Absity can (or can't) interpret. Claims of psychological reality for this approach must be treated with caution, however; Auble and Franks (1983) have presented results suggesting that spreading activation plays only a limited role in sentence comprehension in people.

8.3.4 Lexical disambiguation in text databases

The use of on-line dictionaries for lexical disambiguation is being studied by Amsler (1982a) and Lesk (1986). Amsler's goal is analyzing the meaning of large on-line text corpora, with a view to information science applications. Amsler's previous research (*e.g.*, Amsler 1980, 1981) has shown that the structure of the texts of dictionary definitions makes the computational establishment of ISA and PART-OF relations among word senses quite easy. These can then be used to create suitable knowledge structures. For example (Amsler 1982a), a computational

---

[9]The other systems described above, like Polaroid Words, use LOCALIST representations in which each concept is represented by a single node in their formalism. In contrast, DISTRIBUTED representations use a pattern of activation in a set of nodes.

analysis of descriptors used in word senses that describe various vehicles leads to a description of what the vehicle frame is like, that is, what slots it should have and what the slots' typical and default values should be. The structure of definition texts may also be used in lexical disambiguation by following the ISA and PART-OF links. The text of the on-line *Merriam-Webster pocket dictionary* was itself disambiguated (by hand), so that it can be used in automatic disambiguation (Amsler 1980, 1981). In Lesk's version (1986), textual similarities between the definitions are sought directly.

This disambiguation technique is not unlike the marker passing used by Polaroid Words, except that the domain includes both words (possibly ambiguous, if the dictionary is not disambiguated) and concepts (*i.e.*, definitions). Clearly, dictionary processing has the potential for being extremely useful in NLU (*cf.* Amsler 1982b). In particular, the automatic generation of frame structures would greatly assist the development of large-scale knowledge bases. (Dictionary processing could not produce knowledge bases containing all that is necessary for, say, problem solving, but it could eliminate a lot of tedious work by producing a foundation for such bases.)

9 Speculations, Partially Baked Ideas, and Exercises for the Reader

---

When there is light at the end of the tunnel, order more tunnel.
—Anonymous[1]

But in our enthusiasm, we could not resist a radical overhaul of the system, in which all of its major weaknesses have been exposed, analyzed, and replaced with new weaknesses.
—Bruce Leverett[2]

The research I have described in this book necessarily leaves unanswered many questions, big and small. Many sections, especially 3.8, 5.3.6, 5.4, and 7.4 have discussed things left undone by Absity, Polaroid Words, and the Semantic Enquiry Desk. In this chapter, I list a number of other open questions, partially baked ideas, and wild speculations, sometimes with my thoughts on how they might be answered or developed. Some could be dissertation topics; others may be good subjects for a term paper or course project. Several are psycholinguistic experiments. At the start of each question (if appropriate) I give in brackets the section or sections of this book in which the matter is discussed.

9.1 The representation of knowledge

Exercise 1.1 [1.1.2, 1.3.1, 5.2, 5.6.3] Could a non-discrete representation of knowledge be developed for AI? Such a representation would be able to handle close similarities and differences, such as the **head of a pin** compared with the **head of a hammer**. Consider the possibility of pseudo-continuous representations that are to discrete representations as floating-point numbers are to integers. Candidates

---

[1] Found in the 'fortune' database distributed with 4.1c BSD UNIX. *UNIX* is a trademark of AT&T Bell Laboratories.

[2] LEVERETT, Bruce W. *Register Allocation in Optimizing Compilers*. Doctoral dissertation [available as technical report CMU–CS–81–103], Department of Computer Science, Carnegie–Mellon University, February 1981. 134.

to consider include some kind of network of neuron-like nodes (*cf.* Feldman and Ballard 1982; Feldman 1985), a value-passing machine such as Fahlman, Hinton and Sejnowski's (1983) Thistle system, and a simulated-annealing or Boltzmann network (Kirkpatrick, Gelatt and Vecchi 1983; Fahlman, Hinton and Sejnowski 1983; Smolensky 1983) *(see also exercise 4.8).* A concept would be represented by a very large number of nodes and connections instead of just a few as in Frail, and no one node would be essential to the representation of any concept. Two concepts would be similar to the extent that they incorporated the same nodes.

How could Absity and its friends operate with such a representation? For example, in lexical disambiguation, how could a relationship between two concepts, such as **astronomer** and **star**, be found? Can marker passing operate between groups of nodes? What about relationships implied by two concepts incorporating the same node?—such relationships are not necessarily relevant to lexical disambiguation.

Exercise 1.2 [5.2.3] Despite all efforts to the contrary, some of the paths found by a marker passer will be uninteresting or misleading. Give an example of such a path that could not have been prevented without also losing desirable paths. Charniak (1982, 1985) has proposed that the output of a marker passer should be filtered though a path checker that would attempt to remove undesirable paths. Characterize as formally as possible what characteristics make a path undesirable. Can undesirable paths be categorized into easy-to-recognize classes?

Exercise 1.3 [7.3.2] The SED's gap-finding methods ideally require that Frail be able to take a frame statement and search for "something similar". This requires a better and more formal idea than we presently have of what similarity of instances is. Can you develop such a formalization? To begin, consider that if the frame statement to be matched does not describe an extant instance (which will usually be the case, or there wouldn't be a need to search for a similarity), it can be given a "phantom instantiation" and thereupon treated as extant. Then marker passing from the phantom could be a simple way to find candidates for similarity, though each candidate would have to be tested, as even careful marker passing (presumably with constraints different from those used to find simple relationships by Polaroid Words) would probably find a large number of spurious candidates. Would marker passing be adequate for finding candidates? Or would it be common for instances to be distant from others to which they are similar? Techniques such as Winston's (1978) transfer frames may also be applicable to this problem.

Exercise 1.4 [4.3, 4.3.1] **Literary criticism made simple:** Many styles of poetry operate simply by forcing the user to make a mental connection that he or she did not previously have, viewing the world in a slightly different way. When the poet succeeds in making a felicitous long-distance connection in the user's head, the latter experiences a 'delight' response. This is best seen in minimalist poems such as those of Richard Brautigan. Consider, for example, these poems:

(9-1)   **The pill versus the Springhill mine disaster**

When you take your pill
it's like a mine disaster.
I think of all the people
    lost inside of you.[3]

(9-2)   **The net wt. of winter is 6.75 ozs.**

The net wt. of winter is 6.75 ozs.
and winter has a regular flavor
with Fluoristan to stop tooth decay.

A month ago I bought a huge tube
of Crest toothpaste and when I put it
in the bathroom, I looked at it
    and said, "Winter."[4]

(9-3)   **Romeo and Juliet**

If you will die for me,
I will die for you

and our graves will
be like two lovers washing
their clothes together
in a laundromat.

If you will bring the soap,
I will bring the bleach.[5]

(9-4)   **Kafka's hat**

With the rain falling
surgically against the roof,
I ate a dish of ice cream
that looked like Kafka's hat.

It was a dish of ice cream
tasting like an operating table
with the patient staring
up at the ceiling.[6]

---

[3] BRAUTIGAN, Richard. "The pill versus the Springhill mine disaster." *The pill versus the Springhill mine disaster*, New York: Dell, 1968. 100. Copyright © 1968 by Richard Brautigan. Reprinted by permission of Delacorte Press / Seymour Lawrence and Helen Brann Agency, Inc.

[4] BRAUTIGAN, Richard. "The net wt. of winter is 6.75 ozs." *Rommel drives on deep into Egypt*, New York: Delta, 1970. 12. Copyright © 1970 by Richard Brautigan. Reprinted by permission of Delacorte Press / Seymour Lawrence and Helen Brann Agency, Inc. *Crest* is a trademark of Proctor and Gamble.

[5] BRAUTIGAN, Richard. "Romeo and Juliet." *Rommel drives on deep into Egypt*, New York: Delta, 1970. 7. Copyright © 1970 by Richard Brautigan. Reprinted by permission of Delacorte Press / Seymour Lawrence and Helen Brann Agency, Inc.

[6] BRAUTIGAN, Richard. "Kafka's hat." *The pill versus the Springhill mine disaster*, New York: Dell, 1968. 89. Copyright © 1968 by Richard Brautigan. Reprinted by permission of Delacorte Press / Seymour Lawrence and Helen Brann Agency, Inc.

The reader probably did not previously have a mental connection between tooth-paste and winter; the poem's purpose is to make one. Whether or not such poems 'work' for a particular reader must depend on whether that person's knowledge base has a structure that permits the association to be made, and it is probably the case that for any one poem, a hit rate of at best about 25% can be expected—the other 75% of readers won't get it. (I hope that at least one of the above examples worked for you.)

Exercise: Write a Brautigan appreciater—a program very willing to make con-nections. Extend it to handle Eliot or Yeats or Leonard Cohen. For extra credit: Write a program that generates Brautigan-like poems. (Do not attempt to extend it to handle Eliot or Yeats or Leonard Cohen.)

Wax and gold—Literary criticism made difficult: Donald Levine (1965, 1985: 21–28) describes the importance of deliberate linguistic ambiguity in a large number of non-Western cultures. He writes that, for example,[7]

> in one African variant of Islamic culture, that of the Somali nation, a love for am-biguity appears particularly notable in the political sphere. David Laitin reports that the Somali boast that "the Somali language is sinuous", because it permits words to take on novel shapes that accommodate a richness of metaphors and poetic allusions. Political arguments and diplomatic messages take the form of alliterative poems, mastery of which is a key to prestige and power. These poems typically begin with long, vague, circumlocutory preludes, introducing the theme at hand, which is then couched in allegory. Of these poems, Laitin writes:
>
> > A poetic message can be deliberately misinterpreted by the receiver, with-out his appearing to be stupid. Therefore, the person for whom the mes-sage was intended is never put in a position where he has to answer yes or no, or where he has to make a quick decision. He is able to go into further allegory, circling around the issue in other ways, to prevent direct confrontation. (Laitin 1977: 39)

Levine is particularly struck by the Amhara culture of Ethiopia.

> In what is perhaps the most characteristic expression of the Amhara genius, a genre of oral literature known as "wax and gold", the studied use of ambiguity plays a central part. Wax and gold (*sam-ennā warq*) is the formula with which the Amhara symbolize their favorite form of verse. The form consists of two semantic layers. The apparent, superficial meaning of the words is called "wax" (*sam*); their hidden, deeper significance is the "gold" (*warq*).
>
> The following Amharic couplet exemplifies the *sam-ennā warq* figure:
>
> > Since Adam your lip did eat of that Tree
> > The Savior my heart has been hung up for thee.

---

[7] The following excerpts from Levine 1985: 23–27 and Laitin 1977: 39 are copyright © 1977, 1985 by The University of Chicago, by whose kind permission they are reprinted here.

In this secular couplet the "wax" of Adam's sin and Christ's crucifixion in his behalf has been used as a mold in which to pour a love message. A literal translation of the "wax" of the couplet is:

Because Adam ate of the apple from the Tree of Knowledge
The Savior of the World has been crucified for thee.

To appreciate the "gold" of the couplet, one must know that the verb meaning "was crucified", *tasaqqala*, may also mean "is infatuated with". A literal translation of the "gold" content would be:

Because of your (tempting) lips
My heart is infatuated with thee.

In other figures, the duplicity of the message is rendered less explicit. In figures known as *hiber* and *merimer*, the "wax" and "gold" are combined in the same word or phrase instead of being put side by side. These figures thus correspond to the English pun. For example:

Your father and your mother have vowed to keep from meat
But you, their very daughter, innards do you eat.

"To eat someone's entrails" is an Amharic idiom which means "to capture his heart". The hidden meaning of the couplet is thus: "You made me love you".

Exercise: Write a wax-and-gold appreciater—a program that can find both the surface and hidden meanings of a text. The program should also appreciate puns in English.

Exercise 1.5 [8.2.3] Must a knowledge representation for medical diagnosis necessarily be different from the compositional frame-like representations we require as a target for semantic interpretation? If so, how can people learn or amend their rule bases from reading? Is a synthesis of the two kinds of representation possible? (Recall that Frail itself was developed as a synthetic representation for both language understanding and problem solving.)

Exercise 1.6 [5.5] I have argued that selectional restrictions are better accounted for as slot restriction predicates in the knowledge base than as symbols on words in the lexicon.[8] This may be a slight oversimplification, however; that is, there may be words that are essentially synonymous, pointing to the same frame in the lexicon, and yet have different selectional restrictions. For example, *eat* and the intransitive sense of *feed* are probably both best represented by the `eat` frame, yet *feed*, unlike *eat*, requires its AGENT to be an animal:

(9-5)   Cows feed on hay.

(9-6)   #Ross feeds on pancakes.

---

[8] Lytinen (1984: 33) also argues for this.

Sentence (9-6) seems slightly metaphorical, implying that Ross is voracious or animal-like in his approach to pancakes.[9]

Our approach can be saved by making distinct frames for *eat* and *feed*; but is this reasonable? The fact that some other languages make the same distinction (*e.g.*, *essen* and *fressen* in German) suggests that it may be—indeed, it may be necessary in an interlingua for machine translation. What other possible counterexamples are there? Could a system with separate lexical selectional restrictions and slot restriction predicates be feasible? How should one handle the restrictions on words like *board*, where one can only use *board* for a vehicle that one can stand in or on—a boat, airplane, hovercraft, or bus, for example, but not a canoe or a car?

Exercise 1.7 [1.3.1, 3] We have shown Frail to be a reasonable target for semantic interpretation. However, for many applications, such as machine translation, this is insufficient; it must also be a suitable starting point for language generation. What are the necessary properties? Does Frail have them?

9.2 Semantic formalisms

Exercise 2.1 [2.2.1, 3.8] Although we have been very critical of decompositional semantics, frame-based semantics is vulnerable to many of the same criticisms. The frame to define a chair, for example, is little more than a structured version of the decompositional representation in (2-8); the symbols have now become slots, frames, and ISA relations. Still remaining are such problems as how an inherently vague concept such as **chair** can be adequately defined and what a suitable set of primitives is. The problem of choosing primitives is especially important in systems like Frail that, unlike, say, KRL *(see section 1.2)*, maintain a strict ISA hierarchy without overlap of subclasses. Investigate possible solutions to these problems. How can inherent vagueness be handled in a frame system? Methods to discuss include defining a concept as a procedure that tests whether an object meets the necessary criteria or as a prototype with tolerances for variation from it (*cf.* Winograd 1976: 13–14), and using the mechanisms of fuzzy logic (Zadeh 1983). Remember that we wish to retain the full inference power of frames and our ability to use them as compositional semantic objects. Compare network frame systems and strictly hierarchical frame systems for expressive power, deductive abilities, and implementation efficiency.

Exercise 2.2 [2.1] A new approach to meaning, SITUATION SEMANTICS, has recently been made popular by Barwise and Perry (1983; Barwise 1981; Israel 1983;

---

[9]Transitive uses of *feed* do not follow this pattern; the feedee may be human or animal:

(i)   Nadia fed the geese corn.

(ii)   Ross fed Nadia pancakes.

Even so, sentence (ii) seems to suggest that the situation lacked a certain gentility, for otherwise *served* would have been a more natural verb to use.

Cooper 1985). Situation semantics is a REALIST theory, in that it takes meaning to be something actually in the world, and linguistic meaning to be simply a special case of a more general phenomenon. Absity is based on the Montague (1973) way of thinking about semantics; could situation semantics similarly form the basis for a compositional computational semantic formalism (*cf.* Winograd 1984)? What would the resulting semantic interpreter be like? What would its advantages and disadvantages be compared to those of Absity? (For some work on these questions, see Fenstad, Halvorsen, Langholm, and van Bentham 1985, and Lespérance 1986.)

Exercise 2.3 [2.2.2, 3.3] Chierchia (1982, 1983) has pointed out certain problems with maintaining consistency in Montague's (1973) typing system. For example, the NP *Ross* and the infinitive verb *to run* have different types—*individual* and *property of individual*, respectively—which in turn obliges *is nice* to be of different types in (9-7) and (9-8), a clearly undesirable and counterintuitive effect:

(9-7)   Ross is nice.

(9-8)   To run is nice.

Chierchia's solution is a less prolific, three-level system of types in which properties such as *to run* may be used interchangeably with individuals such as *Ross*. The typing of Absity, also much simpler than Montague's, is able to handle the particular example above, because an NP is a frame statement, and a verb is a frame (which may be turned into a frame statement by combining it with the determiner *NULLDET* to make an NP—though to deal with (9-8) properly, its intensionality must also be handled). But Absity may have consistency problems nevertheless. Can you find such a case? Could consistency be dependent upon the particular knowledge representation? If so, could Chierchia's solution be adapted for use in Absity? What are the ramifications for Frail?

Exercise 2.4 [2.2.2, 3.3; continues previous exercise] Just as Montague semantics makes counterintuitive type distinctions *(see previous exercise)*, it also fails to make distinctions that we intuitively feel it ought (Chierchia 1982, 1983). For example, in (9-9) and (9-10), *slowly* and *try to* both turn out to be functions from properties to properties:

(9-9)   Ross eats the ice cream slowly.

(9-10)   Ross tries to eat the ice cream.

Since Absity maps different syntactic types to the same semantic type (*e.g.*, adverbs and auxiliaries are both slot–filler pairs), it is vulnerable to the same criticism. Show that Absity's type mappings are intuitively well motivated. A fortiori, show that their motivation is not unlike that for Chierchia's approach to types *(see previous exercise)*.

Exercise 2.5 [3.2] Is there a principled way in which it may be decided which rules of a grammar should have semantic rules associated with them?

Exercise 2.6 [3.8, 7.2.1, 7.2.6] Frail has no way of representing counterfactual states, as in (9-11):

(9-11)   Nadia thinks of <u>her house with a new coat of paint</u>.

The underlined phrase describes an instance that is the same as an extant instance except for a slot value or two but has only conceptual existence, though it doesn't seem to be merely an intension. Implement a suitable representation for such things, and show how your representation can be used to determine attachment of non-restrictive prepositional phrases to uniquely defined noun phrases, as in (9-11).

9.3 Semantic interpretation and discourse pragmatics

The Absity system derives the literal meaning of its input, and is almost completely devoid of knowledge of discourse pragmatics. The following exercises address these deficiencies.

Exercise 3.1 Polaroid Words provide a suitable place to handle finding the referents of pronouns. The PWs for words such as *she*, *it*, and *they* could externally appear to be like an ordinary noun Polaroid Word. Internally, they could use whatever methods were appropriate (Hirst 1981a, 1981b) to determine the set of candidate referents, and then be disambiguated like any noun PW (*cf.* Pazzani and Engelman 1983; *see section 8.3.1*). Non-pronominal definite references require a different approach: appropriate extension of the abilities of frame determiners in Frail. This gives the appearance of having two separate reference resolution mechanisms, but this need not be the case; internally, the PW for a pronoun may use frame determiners. For example, the PW for *she* could behave just like the Frail call (the ?x (female ?x)). Implement these additions to Polaroid Words and Frail. You will need to be able to determine which of the concepts previously mentioned in the discourse are candidate referents and which in particular have been highlighted by the speaker or writer as the discourse topic. See if the various methods described in Hirst 1981a, 1981b can be adapted for use with Frail.

Exercise 3.2 [5.3.3] Neither Absity nor the Polaroid Word system has any method for dealing with the various categories of "canned phrase" in English, except that in section 5.3.3 we conceptually incorporated by fiat the "phrasal recognizer" of Wilensky and Arens (1980a, 1980b). Such an incorporation will not necessarily be straightforward. The more rigid expressions, especially ungrammatical ones such as *by and large*, could well be handled with a little lookahead at lexicon lookup time and replaced by a single token in the input stream; this would fit well with the present system. On the other hand, some canned phrases, such as *kick the bucket* (= **die**), may also be taken literally or be subject to syntactic and morphological processes; these cannot be handled at the initial lexicon-lookup level, but can only be recognized after some parsing and interpretation. This could lead to control and interaction problems with both Absity and Polaroid Words. For example, the system will faithfully interpret (9-12) literally:

(9-12)   Ross kicked the ...

and, upon finding the next word to be *bucket*, will first have to ask whether Ross is really kicking a real bucket or not; if he isn't, it will then have to get rid of its partially built literal interpretation. Could Absity handle this? Consider also Weischedel's (1983) method of using Horn clauses to map from one semantic representation of a sentence to another (in this case from its literal to its intended meaning).

A slightly different approach, however, is suggested by psycholinguistic evidence that people do not process idioms or canned phrases in such a two-stage process, trying first the literal meaning and then the idiomatic one. Rather, Ortony, Schallert, Reynolds, and Antos (1978) found that idioms were processed as fast as control phrases and that processing was slowest when the context indicated the literal meaning of the canned phrase. It seems likely that canned phrases are stored as a single unit in the mental lexicon and accessed very early; thus, *cross that bridge* would be enough to cause access to the phrase *cross that bridge when one comes to it*. Similarly, McDonnell (1982) found that an appropriate context can prime the meaning of idioms, just as ordinary words can be primed. However, Rakowsky (1985) has found that idioms themselves do not prime their idiomatic senses, and, further, seem to inhibit ("negatively prime") their literal senses. Rakowsky suggests a model in which processing of an idiomatic sense starts as soon as the sense can be accessed. Processing of the literal sense, however, remains incomplete, but a trace of it remains so that it may be completed if it turns out to be needed.

It should be possible to do something similar in Absity. A process would look out for canned phrases, and when it found one it would take over from Absity for the duration of the idiom (but saving Absity's state, just in case) and insert a structure with the appropriate meaning in the interpretation. The structure would be Polaroid Word–like to the extent that it would detect whether or not it fitted properly; if it found, sooner or later, that it didn't, it would restore Absity. This of course makes semantic interpretation no longer deterministic, which might be regarded as too drastic.

Exercise 3.3 [5.4] How may metaphor be detected and resolved by Polaroid Words?

Exercise 3.4 [continues previous exercise] Not all constructs that violate slot restriction predicates are metaphoric. Consider:

(9-13)   Ross believes that <u>rocks</u> can fly.

(9-14)   Nadia doubts that <u>rocks</u> can fly.

Neither meaning of *rocks*, **stones** and **rocking movements**, fits with *fly*, but of course the sentences are perfectly acceptable and **stones** is the sense chosen by informants. This could be simply because it is the more frequent sense, or it could be that, as a **physical object**, it is still the better choice for **flying**. Experiment: Determine which.

The problem for Polaroid Words here is deciding when to relax slot restrictions and allow a literal interpretation. In the examples above, we might say that the context, a belief report, gives "permission" for this, just as children's story or fantasy may permit talking animals and the like. Matters are not this simple, however, or else we couldn't use metaphors in belief reports:

(9-15)   Nadia believes that computers are the rocks in the bowling green of life.

More importantly, there is simply a lot of nonsense in the real world:

(9-16)   **Go on, have your fun. It's always the children that suffer later:** Los Angeles secretary Jannene Swift married a 50-pound pet rock in a formal ceremony in Lafayette Park.[10]

The context is strong enough to force the reading that Ms Swift went through the motions of marriage, even if the preconditions were not fulfilled and there is no marriage, legally or semantically. Again, it may help that *rock* can be a **physical object**;[11] it is hard to assign a literal interpretation, no matter how anomalous, to (9-17):

(9-17)   Ross was married to his career.

Exercise: Investigate the conditions under which anomalous sentences are and aren't interpreted figuratively.

Exercise 3.5 Subtleties of meaning are conveyed in a speaker's or writer's exact choice of words (Lanham 1974); to translate (9-18) and (9-19) into effectively the same representation in Frail would be to miss this point:

(9-18)   We cannot dedicate—we cannot consecrate—we cannot hallow—this ground. The brave men, living and dead, who struggled here, have consecrated it far above our poor power to add or detract.[12]

(9-19)   Some men who were brave, some of whom are now dead, and who were faced with much adversity at this particular place have already gone and made said place holy, thereby effectively preventing us from doing it now.

How could the difference between (9-18) and (9-19) be detected by Absity and represented in Frail?

Exercise 3.6 [6.2.1, 7.4.3] Discourse comments, such as *frankly* in (9-20):

(9-20)   Frankly, it gives me a headache.
        (i.e., I am frank in saying this: it gives me a headache.)

---

[10]"Esquire's dubious achievement awards for 1976." *Esquire,* **87**(1), January 1977, 49–55.

[11]It also helps that *pet rock* has become an unambiguous canned phrase. When it was novel, however, interpreting it involved exactly the same problems of trading off metaphor for *pet* and literal interpretation for *rock*.

[12]LINCOLN, Abraham. 19 November 1863.

are not part of the literal interpretation of a sentence but operate at a different level. How may they be detected and correctly handled by Absity? Consider also the related problem of EPITHET INSERTION, in which a word is inserted whose literal interpretation should be ignored, its presence instead serving as an intensifier:

(9-21)   I fucking hate this fucking assignment![13]

Exercise 3.7 [3.8, 8.2.3, exercise 1.5] An interlingua for machine translation must represent much more than literal meaning. Other necessities include non-literal meaning (*i.e.*, intent of speaker), the topic or emphasis, and the tenor or tone. A sentence representation thus becomes an *n*-tuple, of which the Frail semantic representation is just one component. We would like the processes that produce the other components to be as closely related to Absity as possible. Discuss the architecture of such a system.

Exercise 3.8 [3.8] Make a full inventory of words such as *again*, *even*, and *let alone* which are problematic for compositional semantics. What patterns do you see? Can Absity be improved to deal with these words, possibly by treating them as functions instead of passive objects? If you believe that a separate pragmatic process is necessary to handle them, design such a process. How can the import of such words be carried through a language-independent interlingua in a machine translation system? Make a cross-linguistic study of these words, and look for universals.

9.4 Lexical ambiguity

Exercise 4.1 [1.1.2] The Boots-And-All Theory of Language Comprehension (Hirst 1981a[1]: 49, footnote 28) says that language tends to evolve so that every available cognitive faculty is used in its comprehension. Therefore, if there were a real cognitive distinction between polysemy and homonymy, as Panman's work (1982) suggests, we would expect that at least some languages, if not all of them, would exploit the distinction in some way, and that this would be reflected in any formal description of such a language. Find such a language, or, better still, show that English is such a language. Alternatively, show that a language could make use of the distinction without it being "noticeable" in a formal description.

Exercise 4.2 Some words are ambiguous at the morphological level. For example, an *undoable knot* could be one that can be undone or one that cannot be done—that is, *undo-able* or *un-doable*.[14] It is probably not adequate simply to mark all such words in the lexicon, as affixes such as *un-* and *-able* are highly productive. Examine the size of the class of words for which this is a problem,

---

[13] Jim Hendler, personal communication, 22 September 1983.

[14] I am grateful to Martin Kay for this example.

and see if simple lexical ambiguity really has to be ruled out. Could novel words of this class be reliably identified by Polaroid Words in order that they be given special treatment? What treatment?

Exercise 4.3 [1.1.1] In English, ambiguous verbs tend to be polysemous, while ambiguous nouns tend to be homonymous; adjectives show less ambiguity than nouns and verbs. Is this true in other languages? Run an experiment to test the hypothesis that polysemy is "cognitively easy" for verbs and homonymy "cognitively hard", while the reverse is true for nouns.

Exercise 4.4 If a polysemous PW is unable to choose between two or more of its meanings, one strategy it could use is to take the "central concept" common to these senses (*cf.* Marslen-Wilson and Tyler 1980). In a frame system such as Frail, this central concept might be the nearest frame dominating both candidate senses in the ISA hierarchy. Test this suggestion by implementing it. Note the trade-offs in deciding whether to dynamically search for this frame when it is needed, or to store it in the lexical entry for the PW; the latter case, though faster, would be difficult if the frame sought depended on exactly which senses remained, and would be awkward if the frame system were frequently changing. In either event, the PW would have to be marked to indicate whether use of the strategy is permitted, since applying it to a homonym could be disastrous.

Exercise 4.5 [4.2.4, 4.3, 4.3.3, 4.3.4] Small's word experts (1980, 1983; Small and Rieger 1982) each contain a discrimination net for deciding on the word's meaning (if it is ambiguous). Thus, word experts correspond to a form of the ordered-search hypothesis in which the search is controlled not by frequency but by a net structure that, presumably, minimizes the average distance from the root to a leaf; that is, minimizes the number of questions that have to be asked in order to choose the right meaning. Could failure to control for this possibility explain the experimental results of Tanenhaus, Leiman, and Seidenberg (1979) and Seidenberg, Tanenhaus, Leiman and Bienkowski (1982)? What predictions does the discrimination net model make that would distinguish it from the competing hypotheses? Construct and run a suitable experiment.

Exercise 4.6 [4.3, 4.3.4, 5.6, 5.6.2] Using the experimental method of Swinney (1979), test for activation and decay of the senses of words that are not disambiguated by the preceding context. When (if ever) is the final choice made? Consider the effects of dominant meanings, of phrase, clause, and sentence boundaries, and of subsequent disambiguating information of various types. Look at the work of Garrod and Sanford (1985), who addressed the similar question of when an anaphor is resolved. Explain the apparent conflict of the results of Hudson and Tanenhaus (1984) with those of Granger, Holbrook, and Eiselt (1984). If Granger *et al* are correct, then is there a psychological reality to paragraphs?

Exercise 4.7 [5.1] Lexical disambiguation can be added to Montague's PTQ formalism (1973) by "hiding" it in the translation function g. This implies, however, that g has access to the information it needs, such as certain other words in the sentence (*cf.* the concept of visibility in Polaroid Words). Can this be done by modifications to the top level of the formalism, or is a back-door method like Polaroid Words, semi-transparent to the translation level, required? In either event, provide a suitable formalization.

Exercise 4.8 [5.3.2, 8.3.3] Polaroid Words bear a superficial similarity to a simulated annealing system, or Boltzmann machine (Kirkpatrick, Gelatt and Vecchi 1983; Fahlman, Hinton and Sejnowski 1983; Smolensky 1983; Feldman 1985). What are the similarities and differences? (*Hint:* consider time.) Program a simulated annealing model of lexical disambiguation, in which all words are disambiguated at the same time. In the graph view of simulated annealing, nodes of the system will be Polaroid Words and arcs will represent visibility. Labels on the arcs will note syntactic and selectional constraints on meaning. Can the system be modified so that the nodes can be added one at a time as the sentence is processed from left to right, the system being re-annealed for each new word?[15]

Exercise 4.9 [5.3.4, 7.2.7] Develop a principled way of deciding when a PW should be required to make its final decision, even if it has to guess.

Exercise 4.10 [4.3.1, 4.3.2, 5.2.2, 5.6.1–3] [16]People's semantic associations don't always seem to be what marker passing in an elegantly organized frame system says they ought to be. In particular, people have WORD ASSOCIATIONS, which are not usually based on semantic closeness but rather on vaguer relationships such as "frequently-associated-with". These associations are generally strong and reliable, and much the same across individuals. The following examples are from Jenkins 1970:

(9-22)	priest–church	music–song	red–white
	quiet–loud	moon–stars	command–order
	doctor–nurse	eagle–bird	citizen–U.S.A.
	cheese–crackers	cabbage–head	stem–flower
	whistle–stop	working–hard	

Some of the associations, such as *doctor–nurse*, may be due to the frequency with which the two concepts named co-occur; but others are synonym or antonym pairs (*quiet–loud*, *command–order*), or phrase completions (*whistle–stop*).

We can thus distinguish two possible types of spreading activation: that between semantically close concepts, and that between associates such as those above. Two questions arise: Most of the research on semantic priming effects used stimulus

---

[15]For approaches to parsing in a connectionist system, see Jones 1983, Selman 1985, Selman and Hirst 1985, 1987, Pollack and Waltz 1982, Cottrell 1985b, Waltz and Pollack 1985, Jones and Driscoll 1985.

[16]I am grateful to Gary Cottrell, Rusty Bobrow, Margery Lucas, Mike Tanenhaus, and Ken Forster for discussion on the points in this exercise.

pairs many or all of which were associates rather than close concepts; is there in fact any spreading activation at all between the latter? If there are two separate kinds of spreading activation, are both of them used in lexical disambiguation?

Evidence that activation spreads between both kinds of pairs is given by the work of Fischler (1977), who found semantic priming effects both for associates such as *jump–rope* and for semantically related pairs, such as *cave–mine*, which were not associates but which shared more semantic features than control pairs such as *bread–stem*. Evidence that association links are used for disambiguation comes from semantic garden-path sentences *(section 4.3.2)*. However, it may well be that the kind of activation is different in the two cases. De Groot (1983) found no facilitation for associates of associates; that is, the associations *bull–cow* and *cow–milk* did NOT facilitate *bull–milk*. This kind of activation may thus spread a distance of exactly one link. Lupker (1984) found that semantic facilitation was much smaller than associative facilitation; Kintsch and Mross (1985) had similar results comparing associative facilitation with that from words that were thematically related but not particularly close semantically, such as *plane–gate* (**aircraft–airport-doorway**). Moreover, it seems that semantic garden paths occur just when the misleading prime is an associate to the ambiguous word, and not when there is only semantic closeness (Michael Tanenhaus, personal communication).

At present, Polaroid Words have no access to association norms. If these could be added to the Frail knowledge base, with appropriate marker passing between them, would they help or hinder disambiguation? What other effects, good or bad, could they have in the knowledge base? What would the effects be of a rule that allowed PWs to jump to a conclusion only in the case of a link by association and not one of general semantic closeness?

Experiment: Test for word association links between the negative prime and the misinterpreted word in the garden-path examples of section 4.3.2. Can you use the word association norms of Postman and Keppel (1970) to construct new semantic garden paths? Can you construct any garden-paths that don't have an associate link? What purpose (if any) does word association serve in the human mind; or of what is it an artifact? What side-effects does it have on cognitive processes?

9.5 Structural ambiguity

Exercise 5.1 [1.1.3, 6.3.2, 6.3.3] Marcus (1980: 228–234) has suggested that if semantic and syntactic biases of equal strength conflict in a sentence, the sentence is ill-formed. Test this suggestion experimentally. Since such biases vary widely from one individual to another, you will first need to devise a method for measuring the strength of an individual's syntactic and semantic biases. In your experiment, the subjects' biases are measured and then their judgments are taken on a set of sentences with bias conflicts. You will be looking to see whether a sentence is judged ill-formed whenever the same subject rated each of its component biases equal. Careful construction of the experimental materials will be crucial. You must also take care to avoid the inherent pitfalls of a within-subjects experimental design.

Exercise 5.2 [6.2.1, 6.2.3, 7.3, 7.4.3] Punctuation can be an important cue to structural disambiguation—compare (9-23) and (9-24):

(9-23)   Despite Ross's promises, to Nadia he seems as unreliable as ever.

(9-24)   Despite Ross's promises to Nadia, he seems as unreliable as ever.

but Absity and the Semantic Enquiry Desk do not use it at present. Make an inventory of cases in which punctuation can be helpful or critical to disambiguation, considering in particular clause-final participles and when they do and don't require a preceding comma. Show how the SED could take account of punctuation.

Exercise 5.3 [6.2.5] I have hypothesized that a closed constituent may be reopened if no presently open constituents admit the attachment of the current constituent:

(9-25)   ?Many students failed that were expected not to.

This is not a sufficient condition, however:

(9-26)   *Many students failed of the negligent professor.

What are necessary and sufficient conditions for reopening a constituent? How may a Marcus parser be modified so that it can reopen constituents when necessary? What are the ramifications of reopening constituents for Absity, Polaroid Words, and the Semantic Enquiry Desk?

Discontinuous constituents are a particular problem for Absity, which is always eager to close a constituent and add it to the sentence structure, since Polaroid Words and the Semantic Enquiry Desk need well-formed partial results to do their work. This is not a good strategy for flat-structured languages such as Warlpiri and Guugu Yimidhirr, in which constituents may be fragmented arbitrarily, and one cannot know until the sentence is over whether or not more pieces of a constituent may turn up. For example, in the Warlpiri sentence (9-27) (from Nash 1980), the case filler **small child** is expressed by two words that have much of the sentence in between them; the case markings serve to tie the two words together.

(9-27)   kurdu-jarra-rlu   ka-pala   maliki   wajili-pi-nyi wita-jarra-rlu
          child-dual-erg   aux:pres-3dual(subj) dog   chase-NPast   small-dual-erg
          'The two small children are chasing the dog.'

What changes need to be made to Absity so that it can keep its partial results well-formed but allow later modifications to them?[17] Do the changes reduce the available information that PWs and the SED need? If so, what problems are created?

---

[17] See Brunson 1986b for a deterministic parser for Warlpiri; see also Johnson 1985 on parsing discontinuous constituents in Guugu Yimidhirr.

Do speakers of such languages avoid ambiguities that this might otherwise make difficult? Do they create ambiguities that are easy to resolve in these languages but would be difficult in English?

Exercise 5.4 [6.3.3] Is Ford, Bresnan, and Kaplan's theory of closure (1982) falsifiable?

Exercise 5.5 [7.2.2] We have said that PPs with prepositions such as *despite* can never be NP-attached and that in apparent exceptions the PP is attached to a nominalized verb with the attachment taking place before the nominalization. To parse these exceptions we will need a mechanism for detecting them. This entails having pointers from nominalizations to their verbs—from *sale* to *sell*, for example. The SED could then check for PP attachment to the nominalization by testing for its attachment to the corresponding verb. Implement a mechanism for handling nominalizations. Notice that in nominalization, pseudo-prepositions are translated to genitive constructions; thus (9-28) becomes (9-29):

(9-28) <u>SUBJ</u> Ross sold <u>OBJ</u> the book to Nadia.

(9-29) Ross<u>'s</u> sale <u>of</u> the book to Nadia

Exercise 5.6 [6.3.3] Brunson (1985, 1986a) has observed that preference for verb phrase or noun phrase attachment of a locative prepositional phrase varies according as the subject of the sentence is an AGENT or an EXPERIENCER or both. (Brunson assumes Chomsky's (1982) theory of government and binding, in which an NP can play more than one THETA-ROLE—in our terms, be in more than one case slot.) This effect is especially strong with causative verbs, for which the preference for VP attachment if the subject is an AGENT overrides semantic anomaly. Examples:

(9-30) Ross baked the cake <u>in the freezer</u>.
(Ross is the AGENT of bake; the PP is VP-attached, i.e., the baking took place in the freezer.)

(9-31) Ross saw the man <u>in the park</u>.
(Ross is both AGENT and EXPERIENCER; there is no preference in the attachment of the PP.)

(9-32) Ross knew the man <u>in the park</u>.
(Ross is the EXPERIENCER of know; the PP is NP-attached to the man.)

Brunson's explanation is that verbs that take an AGENT tend to be more concrete actions that can be more easily located spatially, while verbs that take EXPERIENCER subjects tend to express more abstract relations that are harder to locate in any spatial sense. Is there any similar effect caused by the concrete–abstract continuum for nouns, and, if so, how does it interact with the effect of the agentive–experiential verb continuum (Brunson 1985, 1986a)?

Exercise 5.7 [7] We have said nothing about the effects in structural disambiguation of the length of the constituents involved. Frazier (1978) noted that VP attachment is preferred for (9-33):

(9-33)   Joe returned the book for Susan.
          (i.e., it was for Susan that Joe returned the book.)

but lengthening the intervening NP seems to change the preference:

(9-34)   Joe returned the sunglasses, the wok, some gaudy posters, and the book for Susan.
          (i.e., the book for Susan, the wok, etc, were returned by Joe.)

That is, there is a preference for local right attachment over distant minimal attachment, distance being measured in words, not constituents.

Frazier (1978; Frazier and Fodor 1978) proposed a two-stage model to account for this effect; the first stage was limited in its dealings to a short stretch of words. This model has been heavily criticized (*e.g.*, Wanner 1980; Ford, Bresnan, and Kaplan 1982). However, there seems to be something essentially right about incorporating an account of the effects of constituent length in a model of disambiguation, but neither the present work nor other critics of Frazier do this. Make a study of these effects. Can they be accounted for within the framework of the Semantic Enquiry Desk? How would its rules have to be modified? Are changes to the parser itself called for?

Exercise 5.8 [5.5, exercise 1.7] It may be regarded as an inconsistency that in section 5.5 we were insistent upon taking selectional restrictions out of the lexicon and putting them in the knowledge base, while in sections 7.2 and 7.3 we had no qualms about putting case preference information in the lexicon rather the knowledge base. We did this, of course, because we were using Ford, Bresnan, and Kaplan's results (1982). But the question obviously arises as to whether the preferences are a strictly lexical matter, or whether they actually reside in the concept underlying the lexeme.

Evidence that the latter is correct comes from the work of Kurtzman (1984). In Kurtzman's experiments, the verb of a structurally ambiguous sentence was replaced by a made-up word:

(9-35)   The official <u>shemlarked</u> the student that the teacher had failed.

Subjects, told that the experiments concerned the teaching of foreign vocabulary, were given one of two definitions for the novel word:

(9-36)   *(a)* to shemlark: to inform a person of some very upsetting news.
          (b) to shemlark: to inform a very upset person of news.

Subjects who received definition *(a)*, which emphasized the news, tended to interpret (9-35) as *the student was shemlarked by the official the news that the teacher had failed*—that is, their preference was:

(9-37)   [AGENT *shemlark* PATIENT MESSAGE]

By contrast, the second definition, focusing on the person, produced a preference for the other structure: *the student that the teacher failed was shemlarked*:

(9-38)   [AGENT *shemlark* PATIENT]

The claim is that when parsing the sentences with novel words, subjects did not merely take the lexical preferences of a corresponding English word—the definitions were constructed so that there was no such word—but rather assigned sentence structure on the basis of what information might reasonably be provided in a sentence referring to the novel concept.

This result is intuitively appealing. It predicts that two verbs whose underlying concepts are the same, or nearly so, should have the same preferences, and, moreover, that preferences should be the same across languages. Are these predictions borne out? Can you find counterexamples? Clearly no significant change need be made to the Semantic Enquiry Desk to have it look to Frail instead of the lexicon for preferences, but what are the ramifications for Frail? Regardless of the psychological reality of conceptual preferences, is perhaps the lexicon still the best place to store case preferences in an NLU system?

Exercise 5.9 [5.6.2] When looking at lexical ambiguity, we considered at length the question of when the final choice of meaning is made. We didn't look at the same question for structural ambiguity because there the resolution point came as a given: resolution occurs exactly when the parser asks for the advice of the Semantic Enquiry Desk. However, there are many other models that could be conceived and there is much disagreement among researchers in the area. On the basis of his experiments, Kurtzman (1984) proposed a model in which competing structures are built in parallel; the point at which one is selected as the final interpretation depends on the concepts and context involved. On the other hand, Ferreira (1985) provides experimental evidence for a contrary model, in which a syntactically preferred structure is built first; if it is found implausible, or if the parser is garden-pathed, the system backs up and attempts another structure.

Ferreira's experimental material was somewhat flawed.[18] However, she makes the interesting suggestion that her results support a model in which the processor may look in the discourse model for a potential referent for a possible NP such as *the horse raced past the barn* much as the Semantic Enquiry Desk, with the Principle of Referential Success, will ask Frail if it can find a referent.

Investigate the question of at what point structural disambiguation occurs in humans. Are there speed differences that may be attributable to the need in some cases to access world knowledge to test for referential success? Could Kurtzman's conceptual factors also affect the point at which lexical disambiguation occurs?

---

[18] Ferreira claimed that the presuppositions of reduced relative clause sentences such as:

(i)   The horse raced past the barn fell in a puddle.

were satisfied in her 'neutral context' condition; in the example she gives, they are not.

Exercise 5.10 [7.3.1, 7.3.2] Experiments by Tanenhaus, Stowe, and Carlson (1985) suggest how lexical expectations may be used by our gap-finding procedure. Subjects were given sentences with a false gap after the verb, and their reading times were measured at that point. There were four kinds of sentence tested: those in which the available filler was plausible at the false gap and those in which it was not, crossed with those with a verb whose lexical expectations were for an object to be supplied, and those in which the preference for the verb was intransitive. Examples (the false gap is marked ♦; the true gap is marked ◊):

(9-39)   *Transitive expectations, plausible filler:*
         I wonder which story the teacher told ♦ the children about ◊.

(9-40)   *Transitive expectations, implausible filler:*
         I wonder which book the teacher told ♦ the children about ◊.

(9-41)   *Intransitive expectations, plausible filler:*
         I wonder which patient the nurse hurried ♦ the doctor towards ◊.

(9-42)   *Intransitive expectations, implausible filler:*
         I wonder which bed the nurse hurried ♦ the doctor towards ◊.

When the verb expectations were transitive, reading times were longer for the implausible filler; when they were intransitive, plausibility did not affect reading time.

This suggests a model in which the parser hypothesizes a gap after the verb only if the verb is expecting a case flagged by object position. Thus the false gap was never considered in (9-41) or (9-42). In (9-39) and (9-40), it IS considered, and the attempt to fill it with something implausible, in (9-40), takes longer. Later on in these sentences, the parser discovers the true gap and, presumably, adjusts its analysis.

We have seen that because Paragram is deterministic, it has to stake everything on the SED being able to correctly accept or reject a potential gap on semantic grounds, without knowing whether or not another gap is available further to the right. Since the SED has insufficient information to always do this correctly, Paragram sometimes finds itself embarrassed. Paragram could not adopt the model suggested by the results of Tanenhaus, Stowe, and Carlson, described above, because they imply non-determinism (*cf.* exercise 6.3). However, the number of errors could perhaps be reduced if the SED, following this model, took lexical expectations into account in its gap-finding deliberations. Would this in fact be the case, or would it simply result in a different (but not smaller) set of errors? Could expectations for cases flagged by prepositions also be used by the SED for gap-finding?

9.6 None of the above

Exercise 6.1 [4.3.4] Just as Seidenberg, Tanenhaus, Leiman, and Bienkowski (1982) found that selectional restrictions are not used to inhibit access to inappropriate meanings of a word, so Frazier, Clifton, and Randall (1983) found that some information carried on the verb that could be used in gap finding apparently isn't. Is this a trend, or what? Perhaps accessing a word or word sense does not provide immediate access to its syntactic or semantic features. How would you test this hypothesis? (See also Frazier, Clifton, and Randall's discussion (1983: 211–216), and the conflicting results of Crain and Fodor (1985) and Stowe (1984).)

Exercise 6.2 A language generation program should try to avoid producing sentences that are gratuitously ambiguous or misleading. For example, Lytinen's MOP-TRANS (1984: 112–113) *(see section 8.3.1)* translated (9-43) as (9-44):

(9-43)   deux jeunes filles, dont les mains avaient été blessées par suite d'une bombe

(9-44)   two young women injured by a bomb in the hands

wrongly saying that the women were holding the bomb. A better translation would have been one of these:

(9-45)   two young women injured in the hands by a bomb

(9-46)   two young women whose hands were injured by a bomb

To avoid this sort of error, a system should check its proposed output for ambiguity and ambiguity resolvability before "uttering" it, and, ideally, it should be able to do this with the same ambiguity-handling mechanisms used for processing input. Take your favorite language generation program and add a mechanism that lets it use Polaroid Words and the Semantic Enquiry Desk in this manner.[19]

Exercise 6.3 [7.3, 7.4] Existing grammars for Marcus parsers are unable to handle several of the syntactic constructions that we looked at in chapter 7. Add the necessary grammar rules. What changes to the parsers' structure do you find necessary? Consider in particular the gap-finding problems of section 7.3.1, which, I claim, are proof that parsing without backtracking is impossible in principle.

---

[19] See also Taha 1983 for a few heuristics for out-of-context ambiguity avoidance.

References
and
Indexes

References

The thesis had been virtually unexamined, since nobody could be found willing to waste their time [on it] ... However, her footnoting and her bibliography had been found to conform in an exemplary fashion to the commandments of the MLA style-sheet, and she had been granted her doctorate like many another, through a sort of academic exhaustion.
—Robert Barnard[1]

AKMAJIAN, Adrian and HENY, Frank W (1975). *An introduction to the principles of transformational syntax.* Cambridge, MA: The MIT Press, 1975.

AKMAJIAN, Adrian and LEHRER, Adrienne (1976). "NP-like quantifiers and the problem of determining the head of an NP." *Linguistic analysis*, 2(4), 1976, 395-413.

ALI, Yawar B (1985). *Understanding adjectives.* [1] MSc thesis, Department of Computer Science, University of Toronto, January 1985. [2] Technical report 167, Computer Systems Research Institute, University of Toronto, January 1985.

ALLEN, James Frederick (1979). *A plan-based approach to speech act recognition.* Doctoral dissertation [available as technical report 131/79], Department of Computer Science, University of Toronto, February 1979.

ALLEN, James Frederick (1983a). "ARGOT: A system overview." In Cercone 1983, 97–109.

ALLEN, James Frederick (1983b). "Recognizing intentions from natural language utterances." In BRADY, Michael and BERWICK, Robert Cregar (editors). *Computational models of discourse.* Cambridge, MA: The MIT Press. 107–166.

ALLEN, James Frederick and PERRAULT, Charles Raymond (1980). "Analyzing intention in utterances." *Artificial intelligence*, 15(3), December 1980, 143–178.

AMSLER, Robert A (1980). *The structure of the* Merriam-Webster Pocket Dictionary. Doctoral dissertation, University of Texas at Austin, December 1980.

AMSLER, Robert A (1981). "A taxonomy of English nouns and verbs." *Proceedings, 19th Annual Meeting of the Association for Computational Linguistics*, Stanford, July 1981. 133–138.

AMSLER, Robert A (1982a). "Experimental research on knowledge representations for lexical disambiguation of full-text sources." MS, 1982.

---

[1] BARNARD, Robert. *Death of an old goat.* Harmondsworth, Middlesex: Penguin, 1977.

AMSLER, Robert A (1982b). "Computational lexicology: A research program." *AFIPS conference proceedings*, **51**, 1982 (National Computer Conference), 657–663.

ANDERSON, John Robert (1976). *Language, memory, and thought*. Hillsdale, NJ: Lawrence Erlbaum Associates, 1976.

ANDERSON, John Robert (1983). "A spreading activation theory of memory." *Journal of verbal learning and verbal behavior*, **22**(3), June 1983, 261–295.

ARCHBOLD, Armar A; GROSZ, Barbara Jean and SAGALOWICZ, Daniel (1981). "A TEAM user's guide." Technical note 254, Artificial Intelligence Center, SRI International, 21 December 1981.

AUBLE, Pamela and FRANKS, Jeffery J (1983). "Sentence comprehension processes." *Journal of verbal learning and verbal behavior*, **22**(4), August 1983, 395–405.

BAKER, Carl Lee (1978). *Introduction to generative-transformational syntax*. Englewood Cliffs, NJ: Prentice-Hall, 1978.

BARWISE, Jon (1981). "Some computational aspects of situation semantics." *Proceedings, 19th Annual Meeting of the Association for Computational Linguistics*, Stanford, CA, June 1981. 109–111.

BARWISE, Jon and PERRY, John R (1983). *Situations and attitudes*. Cambridge, MA: The MIT Press / Bradford Books, 1983.

BATES, Madeleine (1978). "The theory and practice of augmented transition network grammars." In BOLC, Leonard (editor). *Natural language communication with computers* (Lecture notes in computer science 63). Berlin: Springer-Verlag, 1978. 191–259.

BAUER, Laurie (1979). "On the need for pragmatics in the study of nominal compounding." *Journal of pragmatics*, **3**(1), February 1979, 45–50.

BECKER, Joseph D (1975). "The phrasal lexicon." In *Proceedings, [Interdisciplinary workshop on] Theoretical issues in natural language processing*, Cambridge, MA, June 1975. 70–73.

BENJAMIN, Thomas B and WATT, Norman F (1969). "Psychopathology and semantic interpretation of ambiguous words." *Journal of abnormal psychology*, **74**(6), 1969, 706–714.

BERKOVITS, Rochele (1982). "On disambiguating surface-structure ambiguity." *Linguistics*, **20**(11/12), 1982, 713–726.

BEVER, Thomas G (1970). "The cognitive basis for linguistic structures." In HAYES, John R (editor). *Cognition and the development of language*. New York: John Wiley, 1970. 279–362.

BEVER, Thomas G; CARROLL, John M and MILLER, Lance A (editors) (1984). *Talking minds: The study of language in cognitive science*. Cambridge, MA: The MIT Press, 1984.

BLANK, Michelle A and FOSS, Donald J (1978). "Semantic facilitation and lexical access during sentence processing." *Memory and cognition*, **6**(6), November 1978, 644–652.

BOBROW, Daniel Gureasko and WINOGRAD, Terry Allen (1977). "An overview of KRL, a knowledge representation language." [1] *Cognitive science*, **1**(1), January–March 1977, 3–46. [2] Technical report CSL–76–4, Xerox Palo Alto Research Center, 4 July 1976. [3] Memo AIM–293, Artificial Intelligence Laboratory, Stanford University. [4] In Brachman and Levesque 1985, 263–285.

BOBROW, Daniel Gureasko and WINOGRAD, Terry Allen (1979). "KRL: Another perspective." *Cognitive science*, **3**(1), January–March 1979, 29–42.

BOBROW, Robert J and WEBBER, Bonnie Lynn (1980a). "PSI-KLONE: Parsing and semantic interpretation in the BBN natural language understanding system." *Proceedings, Third Biennial Conference, Canadian Society for Computational Studies of Intelligence / Société canadienne pour études d'intelligence par ordinateur*, Victoria, May 1980. 131–142.

BOBROW, Robert J and WEBBER, Bonnie Lynn (1980b). "Knowledge representation for syntactic/semantic processing." *Proceedings, First Annual National Conference on Artificial Intelligence*, Stanford, August 1980. 316–323.

BODEN, Margaret A (1977). *Artificial intelligence and natural man.* Hassocks: Harvester Press, 1977.

BOGURAEV, Branimir Konstantinov (1979). *Automatic resolution of linguistic ambiguities.* Doctoral dissertation [available as technical report 11], Computer Laboratory, University of Cambridge. August 1979.

BOGURAEV, Branimir Konstantinov; SPARCK JONES, Karen and TAIT, John I (1982). "Three papers on parsing." Technical report 17, Computer Laboratory, University of Cambridge, 1982.

BOYD, Julian and FERRARA, S (1979). *Speech acts ten years after.* Milan: Versus, 1979.

BRACHMAN, Ronald Jay (1978). [1] "A structural paradigm for representing knowledge." Report 3605, Bolt, Beranek and Newman, Cambridge, MA, May 1978. [2] *A structural paradigm for representing knowledge.* Norwood, NJ: Ablex Publishing, 1984. [3] An earlier version: Doctoral dissertation, Division of Engineering and Applied Physics, Harvard University, May 1977.

BRACHMAN, Ronald Jay (1982). "What 'ISA' is and isn't." [1] *Proceedings, Fourth Biennial Conference of the Canadian Society for Computational Studies of Intelligence / Société canadienne pour études d'intelligence par ordinateur.* Saskatoon, Saskatchewan, May 1982, 212–221. [2] Revised version: "What IS-A is and isn't: An analysis of taxonomic links in semantic networks." *Computer*, **16**(10), October 1983, 30–36.

BRACHMAN, Ronald Jay and LEVESQUE, Hector Joseph (1982). "Competence in knowledge representation." *Proceedings of the National Conference on Artificial Intelligence*, Pittsburgh, August 1982. 189–192.

BRACHMAN, Ronald Jay and LEVESQUE, Hector Joseph (editors) (1985). *Readings in knowledge representation.* Los Altos, CA: Morgan Kaufmann Publishers, 1985.

BRESNAN, Joan Wanda (editor) (1982a). *The mental representation of grammatical relations.* Cambridge, MA: The MIT Press, 1982.

BRESNAN, Joan Wanda (1982b). "Polyadicity." In Bresnan 1982a, 149–172.

BRESNAN, Joan Wanda (1982c). "The passive in lexical theory." In Bresnan 1982a, 3–86.

BROWN, Gretchen P (1979). "Toward a computational theory of indirect speech acts." Technical report 223, Laboratory for Computer Science, Massachusetts Institute of Technology. September 1979.

BROWN, Gretchen P (1980). "Characterizing indirect speech acts." *American journal of computational linguistics*, **6**(3–4), July–December 1980, 150–166.

BROWSE, Roger Alexander (1978). "Knowledge identification and metaphor." *Proceedings, Second Biennial Conference of the Canadian Society for Computational Studies of Intelligence / Société canadienne pour études d'intelligence par ordinateur,* Toronto, Ontario, July 1978. 48–54.

BRUNSON, Barbara Anne (1985). "Prepositional phrase attachment." MS, May 1985.

BRUNSON, Barbara Anne (1986a). "Thematic argument structure." MS, May 1986.

BRUNSON, Barbara Anne (1986b). *A processing model of Warlpiri syntax and implications for linguistic theory.* [1] MA thesis, Department of Linguistics, University of Toronto, August 1985. [2] To appear as a technical report, Computer Systems Research Institute, University of Toronto, 1987.

CAIRNS, Helen Smith and KAMERMAN, Joan (1975). "Lexical information processing during sentence comprehension." *Journal of verbal learning and verbal behavior,* **14**(2), April 1975, 170–179.

CARBONELL, Jaime Guillermo, Jr (1981). "Metaphor comprehension." Technical report CMU–CS–81–115, Department of Computer Science, Carnegie–Mellon University, 4 May 1981.

CARPENTER, Patricia A and DANEMAN, Meredyth (1981). "Lexical retrieval and error recovery in reading: A model based on eye fixations." *Journal of verbal learning and verbal behavior,* **20**(2), April 1982, 137–160.

CATER, Arthur William Sebright (1981). *Analysis and inference for English.* Doctoral dissertation [available as technical report 19, Computer Laboratory], University of Cambridge, September 1981.

CATER, Arthur William Sebright (1982). "Request-based parsing with low-level syntactic recognition." In Sparck Jones and Wilks 1982, 141–147.

CERCONE, Nicholas Joseph (editor) (1983). *Computational linguistics.* [1] published as special issue of *Computers and mathematics with applications,* **9**(1), 1983, 1–244. [2] New York: Pergamon Press, 1983.

CHAPMAN, Loren J; CHAPMAN, Jean P and MILLER, Glenn A (1964). "A theory of verbal behavior in schizophrenia." In MAHER, Brendan Arnold (editor). *Progress in experimental personality research, volume 1.* New York: Academic Press, 1964. 49–77.

CHARNIAK, Eugene (1976). "Inference and knowledge." [1] In Charniak and Wilks 1976, 1–21 and 129–154. [2] An earlier version appears as "Organization and inference in a frame-like system of common sense knowledge." *Proceedings, [Interdisciplinary workshop on] Theoretical issues in natural language processing,* Cambridge, MA, June 1975. 46–55. [3] A shorter, revised version appears as "Inference and knowledge in language comprehension." *Machine intelligence,* **8**, 1977, 541–574.

CHARNIAK, Eugene (1981a). "A common representation for problem-solving and language-comprehension information." [1] *Artificial intelligence,* **16**(3), July 1981, 225–255. [2] Technical report CS–59, Department of Computer Science, Brown University, Providence, RI, July 1980.

CHARNIAK, Eugene (1981b). "Passing markers: A theory of contextual influence in language comprehension." [1] Technical report CS–80, Department of Computer Science, Brown University, Providence, RI, 1981. [2] *Cognitive science,* **7**(3), July–September 1983, 171–190.

CHARNIAK, Eugene (1981c). "The case–slot identity theory." *Cognitive science*, **5**(3), July–September 1981, 285–292.

CHARNIAK, Eugene (1982). "Context recognition in language comprehension." In Lehnert and Ringle 1982, 435–454.

CHARNIAK, Eugene (1983a). "A parser with something for everyone." [1] In King 1983, 117–149. [2] Technical report CS–70, Department of Computer Science, Brown University, Providence, RI, April 1981.

CHARNIAK, Eugene (1983b). "A reverse transformational parser." MS, January 1983.

CHARNIAK, Eugene (1984). "Cognitive science is methodologically fine." In KINTSCH, Walter; MILLER, James R and POLSON, Peter G (editors). *Methods and tactics in cognitive science*. Hillsdale, NJ: Lawrence Erlbaum Associates, 1984. 263–274.

CHARNIAK, Eugene (1985). "A single-semantic-process theory of parsing." MS, Department of Computer Science, Brown University, 1985.

CHARNIAK, Eugene; GAVIN, Michael Kevin and HENDLER, James Alexander (1983). "The Frail/NASL reference manual." Technical report CS–83–06, Department of Computer Science, Brown University, Providence, RI, February 1983.

CHARNIAK, Eugene and McDERMOTT, Drew Vincent (1985). *Introduction to artificial intelligence*. Reading, MA: Addison-Wesley, 1985.

CHARNIAK, Eugene; RIESBECK, Christopher Kevin and McDERMOTT, Drew Vincent (1980). *Artificial intelligence programming*. Hillsdale, NJ: Lawrence Erlbaum Associates, 1980.

CHARNIAK, Eugene and WILKS, Yorick Alexander (1976). *Computational semantics: An introduction to artificial intelligence and natural language comprehension* (Fundamental studies in computer science 4). Amsterdam: North-Holland, 1976.

CHIERCHIA, Gennaro (1982). "Nominalization and Montague grammar: A semantics without types for natural languages." *Linguistics and philosophy*, **5**, 1982, 303–354.

CHIERCHIA, Gennaro (1983). *Topics in the syntax and semantics of infinitives and gerunds*. Doctoral dissertation, Department of Linguistics, University of Massachusetts, Amherst, 1983.

CHOMSKY, Noam Avram (1965). *Aspects of the theory of syntax*. Cambridge, MA: The MIT Press, 1965.

CHOMSKY, Noam Avram (1975). *Reflections on language*. New York: Pantheon Press, 1975.

CHOMSKY, Noam Avram (1982). *Lectures on government and binding: The Pisa lectures* (Studies in generative grammar), second edition. Dordrecht: Foris Publications, 1982.

CHURCH, Kenneth W and PATIL, Ramesh S (1982). "Coping with syntactic ambiguity or how to put the block in the box on the table." [1] *American journal of computational linguistics*, **8**(3–4), July–December 1982, 139–149. [2] Technical report MIT/LCS/TM–216, Laboratory for Computer Science, Massachusetts Institute of Technology, April 1982.

CLARK, Herbert H and CLARK, Eve V (1977). *Psychology and language: An introduction to psycholinguistics*. New York: Harcourt Brace Jovanovich, 1977.

CLIFTON, Charles Jr; FRAZIER, Lyn and CONNINE, Cynthia (1984). "Lexical expectations in sentence comprehension." *Journal of verbal learning and verbal behavior*, **23**(6), December 1984, 696-708.

COLE, Peter and MORGAN, Jerry L (editors) (1975). *Syntax and semantics 3: Speech acts.* New York: Academic Press, 1975.

COLLINS, Allan M and LOFTUS, Elizabeth F (1975). "A spreading-activation theory of semantic processing." *Psychological review*, **82**(6), November 1975, 407–428.

CONNINE, Cynthia; FERREIRA, Fernanda; JONES, Charlie; CLIFTON, Charles Jr and FRAZIER, Lyn (1984). "Verb frame preferences: Descriptive norms." *Journal of psycholinguistic research*, **13**(4), July 1984, 307–319.

COOPER, Robin (1983). *Quantification and syntactic theory* (Synthese language library 21). Dordrecht: D. Reidel, 1983.

COOPER, Robin (editor) (1985). Special issue on situation semantics. *Linguistics and philosophy*, **8**(1), February 1985, 1–161.

COOPER, William E and WALKER, Edward C T (editors) (1979). *Sentence processing: Studies presented to Merrill Garrett.* Hillsdale, NJ: Lawrence Erlbaum Associates, 1979.

COTTRELL, Garrison Weeks (1985a). *A connectionist approach to word sense disambiguation.* Doctoral dissertation [available as technical report 154], Department of Computer Science, University of Rochester, May 1985.

COTTRELL, Garrison Weeks (1985b). "Connectionist parsing." *Proceedings of the Seventh Annual Conference of the Cognitive Science Society*, Irvine, CA, August 1985. 201–211.

COWIE, A P and MACKIN, R (1975). *Oxford dictionary of current idiomatic English. Volume 1: Verbs with prepositions and particles.* Oxford University Press, 1975.

CRAIN, Stephen and FODOR, Janet Dean (1985). "How can grammars help parsers?" In Dowty, Karttunen, and Zwicky 1985, 94–128.

CRAIN, Stephen and STEEDMAN, Mark (1985). "On not being led up the garden path: The use of context by the psychological syntax processor." In Dowty, Karttunen, and Zwicky 1985, 320–358.

CULLINGFORD, Richard Edward (1978). *Script application: Computer understanding of newspaper stories.* Doctoral dissertation [available as research report 116], Department of Computer Science, Yale University, January 1978.

CUTLER, Anne (1982). "Prosody and sentence perception in English." In Mehler, Walker, and Garrett 1982, 201–216.

DANEMAN, Meredyth and CARPENTER, Patricia A (1983). "Individual differences in integrating information between and within sentences." *Journal of experimental psychology: Learning, memory and cognition*, **9**(4), October 1983, 561–581.

DE GROOT, Annette M B (1983). "The range of automatic spreading activation in word priming." *Journal of verbal learning and verbal behavior*, **22**(4), August 1983, 417–436.

DEJONG, Gerald Francis and WALTZ, David Leigh (1983). "Understanding novel language." In Cercone 1983, 131–147.

DOWNING, Pamela (1977). "On the creation and use of English compound nouns." *Language*, **53**(4), December 1977, 810–842.

DOWTY, David R; KARTTUNEN, Lauri Juhani and ZWICKY, Arnold M (editors) (1985). *Natural language parsing: Psychological, computational, and theoretical perspectives* (Studies in natural language processing). Cambridge, England: Cambridge University Press, 1985.

DOWTY, David R; WALL, Robert Eugene and PETERS, Stanley (1981). *Introduction to Montague semantics* (Synthese language library 11). Dordrecht: D. Reidel, 1981.

DRURY, Donald (1983). "A harvest of heteronyms." *Verbatim*, **9**(3), Winter 1983, 10–11. [Addenda and corrigenda: *Verbatim*, **10**(1), Summer 1983, 11–12.]

DYER, Michael George (1983). *In-depth understanding: A computer model of integrated processing for narrative comprehension.* [1] (MIT Press series in artificial intelligence). Cambridge, MA: The MIT Press, 1983. [2] An earlier version, without index or appendices: Doctoral dissertation [available as research report 219], Department of Computer Science, Yale University, May 1982.

FAHLMAN, Scott Elliot (1979). *NETL: A system for representing and using real-world knowledge.* [1] (MIT Press series in artificial intelligence). Cambridge, MA: The MIT Press, 1979. [2] A slightly earlier version: Doctoral dissertation, Artificial Intelligence Laboratory, Massachusetts Institute of Technology, September 1977.

FAHLMAN, Scott Elliot; HINTON, Geoffrey E and SEJNOWSKI, Terrence J (1983). "Massively parallel architectures for AI: NETL, Thistle, and Boltzmann machines." *Proceedings of the National Conference on Artificial Intelligence*, Washington, August 1983. 109–113.

FANTY, Mark A (1986). "Context-free parsing with connectionist networks." MS, Department of Computer Science, University of Rochester, 1986.

FAWCETT, Brenda Louise (1985). *The representation of ambiguity in opaque constructs.* [1] MSc thesis, Department of Computer Science, University of Toronto, October 1985. [2] Technical report 178, Computer Systems Research Institute, University of Toronto, April 1986.

FAWCETT, Brenda Louise and HIRST, Graeme (1986). "The detection and representation of ambiguities of intension and description." *Proceedings, 24th Annual Meeting of the Association for Computational Linguistics*, New York, June 1986. 192–199.

FELDMAN, Jerome Arthur (editor) (1985). Special issue on connectionist models and their applications. *Cognitive science*, **9**(1), January–March 1985, 1–169.

FELDMAN, Jerome Arthur and BALLARD, Dana H (1982). "Connectionist models and their properties." *Cognitive science*, **6**(3), July–September 1982, 205–254.

FENSTAD, Jens Erik; HALVORSEN, Per-Kristian; LANGHOLM, Tore and VAN BENTHAM, Johan (1985). "Equations, schemata and situations: A framework for linguistic semantics." Technical report 85–29, Center for the Study of Language and Information, Stanford University, August 1985.

FERREIRA, Fernanda (1985). "The role of context in resolving syntactic ambiguity." *University of Massachusetts Occasional Papers in Linguistics*, 1985.

FIKES, Richard E and KEHLER, Tom (1985). "The role of frame-based representation in reasoning." *Communications of the ACM*, **28**(9), September 1985, 904–920.

FILLMORE, Charles J (1968). "The case for case." In BACH, Emmon Werner and HARMS, Robert Thomas (editors). *Universals in linguistic theory*, New York: Holt, Rinehart and Winston, 1968. 0–88 [sic].

FILLMORE, Charles J (1975). *Lectures on deixis*. Bloomington, Indiana: Indiana University Linguistics Club, 1975.

FILLMORE, Charles J (1977). "The case for case re-opened." In COLE, Peter and SADOCK, Jerrold M (editors). *Syntax and semantics 8: Grammatical relations*. New York: Academic Press, 1977. 59–81.

FININ, Timothy Wilking (1980). *The semantic interpretation of nominal compounds*. Doctoral dissertation, Department of Computer Science, [available as report T–96, Coordinated Science Laboratory], University of Illinois at Urbana-Champaign.

FISCHLER, Ira (1977). "Semantic facilitation without association in a lexical decision task." *Memory and cognition*, 5(3), 1977, 335–339.

FODOR, Janet Dean (1977). *Semantics: Theories of meaning in generative grammar.* New York: Thomas Y Crowell Company, 1977. Cambridge, MA: Harvard University Press, 1980.

FODOR, Janet Dean (1978). "Parsing strategies and constraints on transformations." *Linguistic inquiry*, 9(3), Summer 1978, 427–473.

FODOR, Janet Dean and FRAZIER, Lyn (1980). "Is the human sentence parsing mechanism an ATN?" *Cognition*, 8(4), December 1980, 417–459.

FODOR, Jerry Alan (1978). "Tom Swift and his procedural grandmother." *Cognition*, 6(3), September 1978, 229–247.

FODOR, Jerry Alan (1979). "In reply to Philip Johnson-Laird." *Cognition*, 7(1), March 1979, 93–95.

FOLLETT, Wilson (1966). *Modern American usage: A guide*. New York: Hill and Wang, 1966.

FORD, Marilyn; BRESNAN, Joan Wanda and KAPLAN, Ronald M (1982). "A competence-based theory of syntactic closure." In Bresnan 1982a, 727–796.

FORSTER, Kenneth I (1979). "Levels of processing and the structure of the language processor." In Cooper and Walker 1979, 27–85.

FOSS, Donald J (1970). "Decision processes during sentence comprehension: Effects of lexical item difficulty and position upon decision times." *Journal of verbal learning and verbal behavior*, 9(6), December 1970, 457–462.

FOSS, Donald J and HAKES, David T (1978). *Psycholinguistics: An introduction to the psychology of language*. Englewood Cliffs, NJ: Prentice-Hall, 1978.

FOSS, Donald J and JENKINS, Charles M (1973). "Some effects of context on the comprehension of ambiguous sentences." *Journal of verbal learning and verbal behavior*, 12(5), October 1973, 577–589.

FOWLER, Henry Watson (1965). *A dictionary of modern English usage*. Second edition, revised by GOWERS, Ernest. Oxford: Oxford University Press, 1965 [reprinted with corrections, 1968].

FRAZIER, Lyn (1978). *On comprehending sentences: Syntactic parsing strategies*. [1] Doctoral dissertation, University of Connecticut, 1978. [2] Bloomington, Indiana: Indiana University Linguistics Club, February 1979.

FRAZIER, Lyn; CLIFTON, Charles Jr and RANDALL, Janet (1983). "Filling gaps: Decision principles and structure in sentence comprehension." *Cognition*, 13(2), March 1983, 187–222.

FRAZIER, Lyn and FODOR, Janet Dean (1978). "The sausage machine: A new two-stage parsing model." *Cognition*, 6(4), December 1978, 291–325.

FRENCH, Peter A; UEHLING, Theodore E, Jr and WETTSTEIN, Howard K (editors) (1979). *Contemporary perspectives in the philosophy of language.* Minneapolis: University of Minnesota Press, 1979.

FRIEDMAN, Joyce; MORAN, Douglas Bailey and WARREN, David Scott (1978a). "Explicit finite intensional models for PTQ." [1] *American journal of computational linguistics*, 1978: 1, microfiche 74, 3–22. [2] Paper N–3, Computer Studies in Formal Linguistics, Department of Computer and Communication Sciences, University of Michigan, Ann Arbor, MI.

FRIEDMAN, Joyce; MORAN, Douglas Bailey and WARREN, David Scott (1978b). "An interpretation system for Montague grammar." [1] *American journal of computational linguistics*, 1978: 1, microfiche 74, 23–96. [2] Paper N–4, Computer Studies in Formal Linguistics, Department of Computer and Communication Sciences, University of Michigan, Ann Arbor, MI.

FRIEDMAN, Joyce; MORAN, Douglas Bailey and WARREN, David Scott (1978c). "Evaluating English sentences in a logical model: A process version of Montague grammar." [1] *Proceedings of the 7th International Conference on Computational Linguistics*, Bergen, Norway, August 1978. [2] Paper N–15, Computer Studies in Formal Linguistics, Department of Computer and Communication Sciences, University of Michigan, Ann Arbor, MI, August 1978.

FUJISAKI, Tetsunosuke (1984). "A stochastic approach to sentence parsing." *Proceedings, 10th International Conference on Computational Linguistics (COLING-84)*, Stanford, July 1984, 16–19.

GALLIN, Daniel (1975). *Intensional and higher-order modal logic with applications to Montague semantics* (North-Holland Mathematics Series 9). Amsterdam: North-Holland, 1975. [Revised from the author's doctoral dissertation, Department of Mathematics, University of California, Berkeley, September 1972.]

GARROD, Simon and SANFORD, Anthony J (1985). "On the real-time character of interpretation during reading." *Language and cognitive processes*, **1**(1), 1985, 43–59.

GAWRON, Jean Mark; KING, Jonathan J; LAMPING, John; LOEBNER, Egon E; PAULSON, Elizabeth Anne; PULLUM, Geoffrey K; SAG, Ivan A and WASOW, Thomas A (1982). "Processing English with a generalized phrase structure grammar." [1] *Proceedings, 20th Annual Meeting of the Association for Computational Linguistics*, Toronto, June 1982. 74–81. [2] Technical note CSL–82–5, Computer Science Laboratory, Hewlett-Packard, Palo Alto, CA, April 1982.

GAZDAR, Gerald (1982). "Phrase structure grammar." In JACOBSON, Pauline Ida and PULLUM, Geoffrey K (editors). *The nature of syntactic representation.* Dordrecht: D. Reidel, 1982.

GENTNER, Dedre (1981a). "Some interesting differences between nouns and verbs." *Cognition and brain theory*, **4**(2), Spring 1981, 161–178.

GENTNER, Dedre (1981b). "Integrating verb meanings into context." *Discourse processes*, **4**(4), October–December 1981, 349–375.

GERSHMAN, Anatole V (1979). *Knowledge-based parsing.* Doctoral dissertation [available as research report 156], Department of Computer Science, Yale University, April 1979.

GODDEN, Kurt Sterling (1981). *Montague grammar and machine translation between English and Thai.* Doctoral dissertation, Department of Linguistics, University of Kansas, 1981.

GRANGER, Richard H, Jr (1977). "FOUL-UP: A program that figures out meanings of words from context." *Proceedings, 5th International Joint Conference on Artificial Intelligence*, Cambridge, MA, August 1977. 172–178.

GRANGER, Richard H, Jr; HOLBROOK, Jennifer K and EISELT, Kurt P (1984). "Interaction effects between word-level and text-level inferences: On-line processing of ambiguous words in context." *Proceedings of the Sixth Annual Conference of the Cognitive Science Society*, Boulder, June 1984. 172–178.

GRANGER, Richard H, Jr; STAROS, Chris J; TAYLOR, Gregory B and YOSHII, Rika (1983). "Scruffy text understanding: Design and implementation of the NOMAD system." *Proceedings, Conference on Applied Natural Language Processing*, Santa Monica, February 1983. 104–106.

GRICE, H Paul (1975). "Logic and conversation." In Cole and Morgan 1975, 41–58.

GROSZ, Barbara Jean (1977a). "The representation and use of focus in a system for understanding dialogs." [1] *Proceedings, 5th International Joint Conference on Artificial Intelligence*, Cambridge, MA, August 1977. 67–76. [2] Technical note 150, Artificial Intelligence Center, SRI International, June 1977. [3] In Grosz, Sparck Jones, and Webber 1986, 353–362.

GROSZ, Barbara Jean (1977b). *The representation and use of focus in dialogue understanding.* [1] Doctoral dissertation, Department of Computer Science, University of California, Berkeley, June 1977. [2] Slightly revised as Technical note 151, Artificial Intelligence Center, SRI International, July 1977. [3] Another revised version appears as section 4 of WALKER, Donald E (editor). *Understanding spoken language* (The computer science library, Artificial intelligence series 5). New York: North-Holland, 1978.

GROSZ, Barbara Jean (1978). "Focusing in dialog." [1] *TINLAP–2: [Proceedings of the 2nd workshop on] Theoretical Issues in Natural Language Processing*, Urbana, 25–27 July 1979. 96–103. [These proceedings were republished as *Proceedings of the 1978 meeting of the Association for Computational Linguistics, American journal of computational linguistics*, 1978: 3, microfiche 78–80.] [2] Technical note 166, Artificial Intelligence Center, SRI International, July 1978.

GROSZ, Barbara Jean (1981). "Focusing and description in natural language dialogues." [1] In Joshi, Webber, and Sag 1981, 84–105. [2] Technical note 185, Artificial Intelligence Center, SRI International, April 1979.

GROSZ, Barbara Jean (1983). "TEAM: A transportable natural-language interface system." *Proceedings, Conference on Applied Natural Language Processing*, Santa Monica, February 1983. 39–45.

GROSZ, Barbara Jean; HAAS, Norman; HENDRIX, Gary Grant; HOBBS, Jerry Robert; MARTIN, Paul; MOORE, Robert Carter; ROBINSON, Jane J and ROSENSCHEIN, Stanley Joshua (1982). "DIALOGIC: A core natural-language processing system." Technical note 270, Artificial Intelligence Center, SRI International, 9 November 1982.

GROSZ, Barbara Jean; SPARCK JONES, Karen and WEBBER, Bonnie Lynn (1986). *Readings in natural language processing.* Los Altos, CA: Morgan Kaufmann, 1986.

GUINDON, Raymonde (1985). "Anaphora resolution: Short-term memory and focusing." *Proceedings, 23rd Annual Meeting of the Association for Computational Linguistics*, Chicago, July 1985. 218–227.

HAMBLIN, C L (1973). "Questions in Montague English." [1] *Foundations of language*, **10**(1), May 1973, 41–53. [2] In Partee 1976, 247–259.

HAUSSER, Roland R (1984). *Surface compositional grammar* (Studies in theoretical linguistics 4). Munich: Wilhelm Fink Verlag, 1984.

HAVILAND, Susan E and CLARK, Herbert H (1974). "What's new? Acquiring new information as a process in comprehension." *Journal of verbal learning and verbal behavior*, **13**(5), October 1974, 512–521.

HAYES, Philip J (1976). "A process to implement some word-sense disambiguations." [1] Working paper 23, Institut pour les études sémantiques et cognitives, Université de Genève. 1976. [2] Technical report 6, Department of Computer Science, University of Rochester, no date.

HAYES, Philip J (1977a). *Some association-based techniques for lexical disambiguation by machine*. [1] Doctoral dissertation, Département de Mathématiques, École polytechnique fédérale de Lausanne. [2] Technical report 25, Department of Computer Science, University of Rochester, June 1977.

HAYES, Philip J (1977b). "On semantic nets, frames and associations." *Proceedings of the 5th International Joint Conference on Artificial Intelligence*, Cambridge, MA, August 1977. 99–107.

HAYES, Philip J (1978). "Mapping input onto schemas." Technical report 29, Department of Computer Science, University of Rochester, June 1978.

HEIDORN, George E (1982). "Experience with an easily computed metric for ranking alternative parses." *Proceedings, 20th Annual Meeting of the Association for Computational Linguistics*, Toronto, June 1982. 82–84.

HENDLER, James Alexander (1985). "Integrating marker-passing and problem solving." [1] *Proceedings of the Seventh Annual Conference of the Cognitive Science Society*, Irvine, CA, August 1985. 130–139. [2] Technical report 85-08, Department of Computer Science, Brown University, 1985.

HENDLER, James Alexander (1986a). *Integrating marker-passing and problem-solving: A spreading-activation approach to improved choice in planning*. Doctoral dissertation [available as technical report CS–86–01], Department of Computer Science, Brown University, January 1986.

HENDLER, James Alexander (1986b). "Issues in the design of marker-passing systems." [1] Technical report 1636, Department of Computer Science, University of Maryland, February 1986. [2] A shorter version published in: JERNIGAN, R; HAMILL, B and WEINTRAUB, D (editors). *The Role of Language in Problem Solving—II*, June 1986.

HENDLER, James Alexander and PHILLIPS, Brian (1981). "A flexible control structure for the conceptual analysis of natural language using message-passing." Technical report TR–08–81–03, Computer Science Laboratory, Texas Instruments Incorporated, Dallas, TX, 1981.

HENDRIX, Gary Grant (1977a). "The LIFER manual: A guide to building practical natural language interfaces." Technical note 138, Artificial Intelligence Center, SRI International, February 1977.

HENDRIX, Gary Grant (1977b). "Human engineering for applied natural language research." *Proceedings of the 5th International Joint Conference on Artificial Intelligence*, Cambridge, MA, August 1977. 181–191.

HILLIER, Bevis (1974). *Punorama, or the best of the worst.* Andoversford, Gloucestershire: The Whittington Press, 1974.

HIRST, Graeme (1976). "Artificial intelligence and computational linguistics II: Methodology and problems." MS, Department of Computer Science, University of British Columbia, April 1976.

HIRST, Graeme (1981a). *Anaphora in natural language understanding: A survey.* [1] (Lecture notes in computer science 119). New York: Springer-Verlag, 1981. [2] Technical report 79–2, Department of Computer Science, University of British Columbia, 1 May 1979. [3] MSc thesis, Department of Engineering Physics, Australian National University. June 1979.

HIRST, Graeme (1981b). "Discourse-oriented anaphora resolution in natural language understanding: A review." *American journal of computational linguistics,* 7(2), April–June 1981, 85–98.

HIRST, Graeme (1983a). "A foundation for semantic interpretation." [1] *Proceedings, 21st Annual Meeting of the Association for Computational Linguistics,* Cambridge, MA, June 1983. 64–73. [2] Technical report CS–83–03, Department of Computer Science, Brown University, Providence, RI, January 1983.

HIRST, Graeme (1983b). *Semantic interpretation against ambiguity.* Doctoral dissertation [available as technical report CS–83–25], Department of Computer Science, Brown University, 1983.

HIRST, Graeme (1984). "Jumping to conclusions: Psychological reality and unreality in a word disambiguation program." *Proceedings of the Sixth Annual Conference of the Cognitive Science Society,* Boulder, June 1984. 179–182.

HIRST, Graeme (1985). Review of van Bakel 1984. *Computational linguistics,* 11(2–3), April–September 1985, 185–186.

HIRST, Graeme (1988). "Humorous information processing: Why artificial intelligence and cognitive science must consider humor as a cognitive phenomenon." Technical report, Computer Systems Research Institute, University of Toronto, in preparation.

HIRST, Graeme and CHARNIAK, Eugene (1982). "Word sense and case slot disambiguation." *Proceedings, National Conference on Artificial Intelligence,* Pittsburgh, August 1982. 95–98.

HOBBS, Jerry Robert (1979). "Metaphor, metaphor schemata, and selective inferencing." Technical note 203, Artificial Intelligence Center, SRI International, December 1979.

HOBBS, Jerry Robert (1983). "An improper treatment of quantification in ordinary English." *Proceedings, 21st Annual Meeting of the Association for Computational Linguistics,* Cambridge, MA, June 1983. 57–63.

HOBBS, Jerry Robert (1985). "Ontological promiscuity." *Proceedings, 23rd Annual Meeting of the Association for Computational Linguistics,* Chicago, July 1985. 61–69.

HOBBS, Jerry Robert and ROSENSCHEIN, Stanley Joshua (1977). "Making computational sense of Montague's intensional logic." *Artificial Intelligence,* 9(3), December 1977, 287–306.

HOGABOAM, Thomas W and PERFETTI, Charles A (1975). "Lexical ambiguity and sentence comprehension." *Journal of verbal learning and verbal behavior,* 16(3), June 1975, 265–274.

HOLMES, Virginia M (1984). "Parsing strategies and discourse context." *Journal of psycholinguistic research*, **13**(3), May 1984, 237–257.

HOWE, Adele (1983). "HOW? A customizable, associative network based help facility." Technical report MS–CIS–83–14, Department of Computer and Information Science, University of Pennsylvania, 16 July 1983.

HOWE, Adele and FININ, Timothy Wilking (1984). "Using spreading activation to identify relevant help." *Proceedings, Fifth Biennial Conference, Canadian Society for Computational Studies of Intelligence / Société canadienne pour études d'intelligence par ordinateur*, London, Ontario, May 1984. 25–27.

HUDSON, Susan B and TANENHAUS, Michael K (1984). "Ambiguity resolution in the absence of contextual bias." *Proceedings of the Sixth Annual Conference of the Cognitive Science Society*, Boulder, CO, June 1984. 188–192.

ISRAEL, David J (1983). "A prolegomenon to situation semantics." *Proceedings, 21st Annual Meeting of the Association for Computational Linguistics*, Cambridge, MA, June 1983. 28–37.

JACKENDOFF, Ray S (1972). *Semantic interpretation in generative grammar.* Cambridge, MA: The MIT Press, 1972.

JACKENDOFF, Ray S (1983). *Semantics and cognition.* Cambridge, MA: The MIT Press, 1983.

JACKENDOFF, Ray S (1984). "Sense and reference in a psychologically based semantics." In Bever, Carroll, and Miller 1984, 49–72.

JENKINS, James J (1970). "The 1952 Minnesota word association norms." In Postman and Keppel, 1970, 1–38.

JOHNSON, Mark (1985). "Parsing with discontinuous elements." *Proceedings, 23rd Annual Meeting of the Association for Computational Linguistics*, Chicago, July 1985. 127–132.

JOHNSON, Roderick (1983). "Parsing with transition networks." In King 1983, 59–72.

JOHNSON-LAIRD, Philip Nicholas (1977). "Procedural semantics." *Cognition*, **5**(3), September 1977, 189–214.

JOHNSON-LAIRD, Philip Nicholas (1978). "What's wrong with Grandma's guide to procedural semantics: A reply to Jerry Fodor." *Cognition*, **6**(3), September 1978, 249–261.

JONES, Mark A (1983). "Activation-based parsing." *Proceedings of the 8th International Joint Conference on Artificial Intelligence*, Karlsruhe, August 1983. 678–682.

JONES, Mark A and DRISCOLL, Alan S (1985). "Movement in active production networks." *Proceedings, 23rd Annual Meeting of the Association for Computational Linguistics*, Chicago, July 1985. 161–166.

JONES, Mark A and WARREN, David Scott (1982). "Conceptual dependency and Montague grammar: A step toward conciliation." *Proceedings, National Conference on Artificial Intelligence*, Pittsburgh, August 1982. 79–83.

JOSHI, Aravind K; WEBBER, Bonnie Lynn and SAG, Ivan A (editors) (1981). *Elements of discourse understanding.* Cambridge, England: Cambridge University Press, 1981.

JUST, Marcel Adam and CARPENTER, Patricia A (1980). "Inference processes during reading: From eye fixations to comprehension." *Psychological review*, **87**(4), July 1980, 329–354.

KAPLAN, David (1978). "Dthat." [1] In COLE, Peter (editor). *Syntax and semantics 9: Pragmatics*. New York: Academic Press, 1978. [2] In French *et al* 1979, 383–400.

KAPLAN, David (1979). "The logic of demonstratives." In French *et al* 1979, 401–412.

KARTTUNEN, Lauri Juhani and PETERS, Stanley (1979). "Conventional implicature." In Oh and Dinneen 1979, 1–56.

KATZ, Jerrold Jacob (1972). *Semantic theory.* New York: Harper, 1972.

KATZ, Jerrold Jacob and FODOR, Jerry Alan (1963). "The structure of a semantic theory." *Language*, **39**(2), June 1963, 170–210.

KELLY, Edward F and STONE, Philip J (1975). *Computer recognition of English word senses* (North-Holland linguistic series 13). Amsterdam: North-Holland, 1975.

KEMPSON, Ruth (1977). *Semantic theory* (Cambridge textbooks in linguistics). Cambridge: Cambridge University Press, 1977.

KESS, Joseph F and HOPPE, Ronald A (1981). *Ambiguity in psycholinguistics* (Pragmatics and beyond II:4). Amsterdam: John Benjamins, 1981.

KIMBALL, John (1973). "Seven principles of surface structure parsing in natural language." *Cognition.* **2**(1), 1973, 15–47.

KING, Margaret (editor) (1983). *Parsing natural language.* London: Academic Press, 1983.

KINTSCH, Walter and MROSS, Ernest F (1985). "Context effects in word identification." *Journal of memory and language*, **24**(3), June 1985, 336–349.

KIRKPATRICK, Scott; GELATT, C D, Jr and VECCHI, M P (1983). "Optimization by simulated annealing." [1] *Science*, **220**(#4598), 13 May 1983, 671–680. [2] An earlier version appeared as: Research report RC 9355 (#41093), IBM Thomas J. Watson Research Center, 2 April 1982.

KURTZMAN, Howard Steven (1984). *Studies in syntactic ambiguity resolution.* Doctoral dissertation, Department of Psychology, Massachusetts Institute of Technology, 13 September 1984. Indiana University Linguistics Club.

LAITIN, David D (1977). *Politics, language, and thought.* Chicago: The University of Chicago Press, 1977.

LANGENDOEN, D Terence; KALISH-LANDON, Nancy and DORE, John (1973). "Dative questions: A study in the relation of acceptability to grammaticality of an English sentence type." *Cognition*, **2**(4), 1973, 451–478.

LANHAM, Richard A (1974). *Style: An anti-textbook.* New Haven: Yale University Press, 1974.

LEHNERT, Wendy Grace and RINGLE, Martin H (editors) (1982). *Strategies for natural language processing.* Hillsdale, NJ: Lawrence Erlbaum Associates, 1982.

LESK, Michael Edward (1986). "Automatic sense discrimination: How to tell a pine cone from an ice cream cone." MS, 1986.

LESPÉRANCE, Yves (1986). "Toward a computational interpretation of situation semantics." [1] *Computational intelligence*, **2**(1), February 1986, 9–27. [2] Technical report 181, Computer Systems Research Institute, University of Toronto, July 1986.

LEVI, Judith N (1978). *The syntax and semantics of compound nominals.* New York: Academic Press, 1978.

LEVINE, Donald Nathan (1965). *Wax and gold: Tradition and innovation in Ethiopian culture.* Chicago: The University of Chicago Press, 1965.

LEVINE, Donald Nathan (1985). *The flight from ambiguity: Essays in social and cultural theory.* Chicago and London: The University of Chicago Press, 1985.

LEVINSON, Stephen C (1983). *Pragmatics* (Cambridge textbooks in linguistics). Cambridge University Press, 1983.

LORCH, Robert F, Jr (1982). "Priming and search processes in semantic memory: A test of three models of spreading activation." *Journal of verbal learning and verbal behavior,* **21**(4), August 1982, 468–492.

LUCAS, Margery M (1983). "Lexical access during sentence comprehension: Frequency and context effects." *Proceedings, Fifth annual conference of the Cognitive Science Society,* Rochester, New York, May 1983. [unpaginated]

LUCAS, Margery M (1984). "Frequency and context effects in lexical ambiguity resolution." Cognitive Science technical report URCS–14, Department of Psychology, University of Rochester, February 1984.

LUPKER, Stephen J (1984). "Semantic priming without association: A second look." *Journal of verbal learning and verbal behavior,* **23**(6), December 1984, 709–733.

LYTINEN, Steven Leo (1984). *The organization of knowledge in a multi-lingual, integrated parser.* Doctoral dissertation [published as research report 340], Department of Computer Science, Yale University, November 1984.

MADHU, Swaminathan and LYTLE, Dean W (1965). "A figure of merit technique for the resolution of non-grammatical ambiguity." *Mechanical translation,* **8**(2), February 1965, 9–13.

MAHOOD, Molly Maureen (1957). *Shakespeare's wordplay.* London: Methuen, 1957.

MAIDA, Anthony S (1982). "Using lambda abstraction to encode structural information in semantic networks." Report 1982–9–1, Center for Cognitive Science, Brown University, 1 September 1982.

MAIDA, Anthony S and SHAPIRO, Stuart C (1982). "Intensional concepts in semantic networks." [1] *Cognitive science,* **6**(4), October–December 1982, 291–330. [2] In Brachman and Levesque 1985, 169–189.

MALLERY, John C (1985). "Universality and individuality: The interaction of noun phrase determiners in copular clauses." *Proceedings, 23rd Annual Meeting of the Association for Computational Linguistics,* Chicago, July 1985. 35–42.

MARCUS, Mitchell P (1980). *A theory of syntactic recognition for natural language.* [1] Cambridge, MA: The MIT Press, 1980. [2] A slightly earlier version: Doctoral dissertation, Artificial Intelligence Laboratory, Massachusetts Institute of Technology, October 1977.

MARCUS, Mitchell P (1984). "Some inadequate theories of human language processing." In Bever, Carroll, and Miller 1984, 253–278.

MARSLEN-WILSON, William D and TYLER, Lorraine Komisarjevsky (1980). "The temporal structure of spoken language understanding." *Cognition,* **8**(1), March 1980, 1–71.

MARTIN, Paul; APPELT, Douglas and PEREIRA, Fernando C N (1983). "Transportability and generality in a natural-language interface system." *Proceedings of the 8th International Joint Conference on Artificial Intelligence,* Karlsruhe, August 1983. 573–581.

MASTERMAN, Margaret (1961). "Semantic message detection for machine translation, using an interlingua." *1961 International Conference on Machine Translation of Languages and Applied Language Analysis*, London: Her Majesty's Stationery Office, 1962. 437–475.

MCCARTHY, John (1979). "First order theories of individual concepts and propositions." [1] In HAYES, Jean Elizabeth; MICHIE, Donald and MIKULICH, L I (editors). *Machine intelligence 9*. Chichester: Ellis Horwood Ltd, 1979. 129–147. [2] In Brachman and Levesque 1985, 523–533.

MCCLELLAND, James L and KAWAMOTO, Alan H (1986). "Mechanisms of sentence processing: Assigning roles to constituents of sentences." In MCCLELLAND, James L; RUMELHART, David E and THE PDP RESEARCH GROUP. *Parallel distributed processing: Explorations in the microstructure of cognition. Volume 2: Psychological and biological models*. Cambridge, MA: The MIT Press / Bradford Books, 1986. 272–325.

MCDERMOTT, Drew Vincent (1978). "Planning and acting." *Cognitive science*, 2(2), April–June 1978, 71–109.

MCDONALD, David Blair (1982). *Understanding noun compounds*. Doctoral dissertation [available as technical report CMU–CS–82–102], Department of Computer Science, Carnegie–Mellon University, January 1982.

MCDONNELL, Cheryl Joanne (1982). *Access of meaning for idiomatic expressions*. Doctoral dissertation, University of South Carolina, 1982.

MEHLER, Jacques; WALKER, Edward C T and GARRETT, Merrill F (editors) (1982). *Perspectives on mental representation: Experimental and theoretical studies of cognitive processes*. Hillsdale, NJ: Lawrence Erlbaum Associates, 1982.

MELLISH, Christopher S (1982a). "Incremental semantic interpretation in a modular parsing system." In Sparck Jones and Wilks 1982, 148–155.

MELLISH, Christopher S (1982b). "Incremental evaluation: An approach to the semantic interpretation of noun phrases." Cognitive Studies Research Paper 001, University of Sussex, September 1982.

MELLISH, Christopher S (1985). *Computer interpretation of natural language descriptions* (Ellis Horwood series in artificial intelligence). Chichester: Ellis Horwood / John Wiley, 1985.

MEYER, David E and SCHVANEVELDT, Roger W (1971). "Facilitation in recognizing pairs of words: Evidence of a dependence between retrieval operations." *Journal of experimental psychology*, 90(2), October 1971, 227–234.

MILLER, George Armitage (1956). "The magical number seven, plus or minus two: Some limits on our capacity for processing information." *Psychological review*, 63(2), March 1956, 81–97.

MILNE, Robert William (1980). "Parsing against lexical ambiguity." [1] *COLING-80: Proceedings of the 8th International Conference on Computational Linguistics*, Tokyo, September 1980. 350–353. [2] Research paper 144, Department of Artificial Intelligence, University of Edinburgh, 1980.

MILNE, Robert William (1982a). "An explanation for minimal attachment and right association." *Proceedings of the National Conference on Artificial Intelligence*, Pittsburgh, August 1982. 88–90.

MILNE, Robert William (1982b). "Predicting garden path sentences." *Cognitive science*, 6(4), October–December 1982, 349–373.

MILNE, Robert William (1986). "Resolving lexical ambiguity in a deterministic parser." *Computational linguistics*, **12**(1), January–March 1986, 1–12.

MOHANTY, Ajit K (1983). "Perceptual complexity of lexical, surface structure, and deep structure types of ambiguous sentences and change in heart rate." *Journal of psycholinguistic research*, **12**(3), May 1983, 339–352.

MONTAGUE, Richard (1973). "The proper treatment of quantification in ordinary English." [1] In HINTIKKA, Kaarlo Jaakko Juhani; MORAVCSIK, Julius Matthew Emil and SUPPES, Patrick Colonel (editors). *Approaches to natural language: Proceedings of the 1970 Stanford workshop on grammar and semantics*. Dordrecht: D. Reidel, 1973. 221–242. [2] In THOMASON, Richmond Hunt (editor). *Formal philosophy: Selected papers of Richard Montague*. New Haven: Yale University Press, 1974. 247–270.

MOORE, Robert Carter (1981). "Problems in logical form." [1] *Proceedings, 19th Annual Meeting of the Association for Computational Linguistics*, Stanford, July 1981. 117–124. [2] Technical note 241, Artificial Intelligence Center, SRI International, April 1981. [3] In Grosz, Sparck Jones, and Webber 1986, 285–292.

MORTON, John (1969). "Interaction of information in word recognition." *Psychological review*, **76**(2), March 1969, 165–178.

NASH, David (1980). *Topics in Warlpiri grammar*. Doctoral dissertation, Massachusetts Institute of Technology, 1980.

NATHAN, Ruth (1984). "The effects of semantic and syntactic context on ongoing word recognition: A test of the interactive–compensatory model." MS, 1984.

NEWMAN, Jean E and DELL, Gary S (1978). "The phonological nature of phoneme monitoring: A critique of some ambiguity studies." *Journal of verbal learning and verbal behavior*, **17**(3), June 1978, 359–374.

NIDA, Eugene Albert (1975). *Componential analysis of meaning: An introduction to semantic structures* (Approaches to semiotics 57). The Hague: Mouton, 1975.

NISHIDA, Toyoaki (1983). *Studies on the application of formal semantics to English–Japanese machine translation*. Doctoral dissertation, Department of Information Science, Faculty of Engineering, Kyoto University, October 1983.

NISHIDA, Toyoaki (1985). "The application of Montague semantics to natural language processing." MS, 9 February 1985.

ODEN, Gregg C (1978). "Semantic constraints and judged preferences for interpretations of ambiguous sentences." *Memory and cognition*, **6**(1), January 1978, 26–37.

ODEN, Gregg C and SPIRA, James L (1983). "Influence of context on the actuation and selection of word senses." *Quarterly journal of experimental psychology, Section A: Human experimental psychology*. **35A**(1), February 1983, 51–64.

OH, Choon-Kyu and DINNEEN, David A (editors) (1979). *Syntax and semantics 11: Presupposition*. New York: Academic Press, 1979.

ONIFER, William and SWINNEY, David A (1981). "Accessing lexical ambiguities during sentence comprehension: Effects of frequency of meaning and contextual bias." *Memory and cognition*, **9**(3), May 1981, 225-236.

ORTONY, Andrew; SCHALLERT, Diane L; REYNOLDS, Ralph E and ANTOS, Stephen J (1978). "Interpreting metaphors: Some effects of context on comprehension." [1] *Journal of verbal learning and verbal behavior*, **17**(4), August 1978, 465–477. [2] Technical report 93, Center for the Study of Reading, University of Illinois at Urbana-Champaign,

July 1978.

PANMAN, Otto (1982). "Homonymy and polysemy." *Lingua*, **58**(1–2), September–October 1982, 105–136.

PARTEE, Barbara Hall (1973). "Some transformational extensions of Montague grammar." [1] *Journal of philosophical logic*, **2**, 1973, 509–534. [2] In Partee 1976, 51–76.

PARTEE, Barbara Hall (1975). "Montague grammar and transformational grammar." *Linguistic inquiry*, **6**(2), Spring 1975, 203–300.

PARTEE, Barbara Hall (editor) (1976). *Montague grammar*. New York: Academic Press, 1976.

PAZZANI, Michael K and ENGELMAN, Carl (1983). "Knowledge based question answering." *Proceedings, Conference on Applied Natural Language Processing*, Santa Monica, February 1983. 73–80.

PERICLIEV, Vladimir (1984). "Handling syntactical ambiguity in machine translation." *Proceedings, 10th International Conference on Computational Linguistics (COLING-84)*, Stanford, July 1984. 521–524.

PERRAULT, Charles Raymond and ALLEN, James Frederick (1980). "A plan-based analysis of indirect speech acts." *American journal of computational linguistics*, **6**(3–4), July–December 1980, 167–182.

PHILLIPS, Brian (1975). *Topic analysis*. Doctoral dissertation, Department of Computer Science, State University of New York at Buffalo, 1975.

PHILLIPS, Brian (1983). "An object-oriented parser for text understanding." *Proceedings of the 8th International Joint Conference on Artificial Intelligence*, Karlsruhe, August 1983, 690–692.

PHILLIPS, Brian and HENDLER, James Alexander (1982). "A message-passing control structure for text understanding." In HORECKÝ, Ján (editor). *COLING 82: Proceedings of the Ninth International Conference on Computational Linguistics, Prague, July 5–10, 1982* (North-Holland Linguistic Series 47). Amsterdam: North-Holland, 1982. 307–312.

PLANTINGA, Edwin Peter Owen (1986). "Who decides what metaphors mean?" *Pre-proceedings of the Conference on Computers and the Humanities: Today's research, tomorrow's teaching*, Toronto, April 1986.

POLLACK, Jordan B and WALTZ, David Leigh (1982). "Natural language processing using spreading activation and lateral inhibition." *Proceedings, Fourth Annual Conference of the Cognitive Science Society*, Ann Arbor, MI, August 1982. 50–53.

POPOWICH, Fred (1984). "SAUMER: Sentence analysis using metarules." Technical report LCCR 84–2 / CMPT 84–10, Laboratory for Computer and Communications Research, Simon Fraser University, 23 August 1984.

POSTMAN, Leo and KEPPEL, Geoffrey (editors) (1970). *Norms of word association*. New York: Academic Press, 1970.

PUTNAM, Hilary (1970). "Is semantics possible?" [1] In MUNITZ, M K and KIEFER, H K (editors). *Contemporary philosophical thought: The International Philosophy Year conferences at Brockport. Volume 1: Language, belief and metaphysics*. Albany: State University of New York Press, 1970. 50–63. [2] In MARGOLIS, J (editor). *An introduction to philosophical enquiry* (second edition). New York: Knopf, 1978. 462–473.

QUILLIAN, M Ross (1962). "A revised design for an understanding machine." *Mechanical translation*, 7(1), July 1962, 17–29.

QUILLIAN, M Ross (1967). "Word concepts: A theory and simulation of some basic semantic capabilities." [1] *Behavioral science*, 12, 1967, 410–430. [2] In Brachman and Levesque 1985, 97–118.

QUILLIAN, M Ross (1968). "Semantic memory." [1] In MINSKY, Marvin Lee (editor). *Semantic information processing*. Cambridge, MA: The MIT Press, 1968. 227–270. [2] Doctoral dissertation, Carnegie Institute of Technology [Carnegie–Mellon University], October 1966. Published as report 2, project 8668, Bolt, Beranek and Newman Inc., October 1966.

QUILLIAN, M Ross (1969). "The teachable language comprehender: A simulation program and theory of language." *Communications of the ACM*, 12(8), August 1969, 459–476.

QUIRK, Randolph; GREENBAUM, Sidney; LEECH, Geoffrey and SVARTVIK, Jan (1972). *A grammar of contemporary English*. London: Longman, 1972 [corrected 8th impression, 1979].

RAKOWSKY, Amy Bonnie (1985). "Processing of dual idiomatic meanings." *Brown University Working Papers in Linguistics*, 5, June 1985, 134–146.

RAPAPORT, William J (1985). "Meinongian semantics for propositional semantic networks." *Proceedings, 23rd Annual Meeting of the Association for Computational Linguistics*, Chicago, July 1985. 43–48.

RASKIN, Victor (1985). *Semantic mechanisms of humor* (Synthese language library 24). Dordrecht: D. Reidel, 1985.

RAYNER, Keith; CARLSON, Marcia and FRAZIER, Lyn (1983). "The interaction of syntax and semantics during sentence processing: Eye movements in the analysis of semantically biased sentences." *Journal of verbal learning and verbal behavior*, 22(3), June 1983, 358–374.

REDER, Lynne M (1983). "What kind of pitcher can a catcher fill? Effects of priming in sentence comprehension." *Journal of verbal learning and verbal behavior*, 22(2), April 1983, 189–202.

REIMOLD, Peter Michael (1976). *An integrated system of perceptual strategies: Syntactic and semantic interpretation of English sentences*. Doctoral dissertation, Columbia University, 1976.

RICHENS, R H (1958). "Interlingual machine translation." *Computer journal*, 1(3), October 1958, 144–147.

RIESBECK, Christopher Kevin (1974). *Computational understanding: Analysis of sentences and context*. Doctoral dissertation [available as memo AIM–238 Artificial Intelligence Laboratory (= report STAN–CS–74–437)], Computer Science Department, Stanford University, May 1974.

RIESBECK, Christopher Kevin (1975). "Conceptual analysis." In Schank 1975, 83–156.

RIESBECK, Christopher Kevin and SCHANK, Roger Carl (1978). "Comprehension by computer: Expectation-based analysis of sentences in context." [1] In LEVELT, Willem J M and FLORES D'ARCAIS, Giovanni B (editors). *Studies in the perception of language*. New York: John Wiley, 1978. [2] Research report 78, Department of Computer Science, Yale University, October 1976.

RINGLE, Martin H (1983). "Psychological studies and artificial intelligence." *The AI Magazine*, **4**(1), Winter/Spring 1983, 37–43.

RIPS, Lance J; SHOBEN, Edward J and SMITH, Edward E (1973). "Semantic distance and the verification of semantic relations." *Journal of verbal learning and verbal behavior*, **12**(1), February 1973, 1–20.

RITCHIE, Graeme Donald (1980). *Computational grammar: An artificial intelligence approach to linguistic description* (Harvester studies in cognitive science 15). Brighton: Harvester; Towata, NJ: Barnes and Noble, 1980.

ROSENSCHEIN, Stanley Joshua and SHIEBER, Stuart M (1982). "Translating English into logical form." *Proceedings, 20th Annual Meeting of the Association for Computational Linguistics*, Toronto, June 1982. 1–8.

RUSSELL, Sylvia Weber (1976). "Computer understanding of metaphorically used verbs." *American journal of computational linguistics*, 1976: 2, microfiche 44.

RYDER, Joan and WALKER, Edward C T (1982). "Two mechanisms of lexical ambiguity." In Mehler, Walker, and Garrett 1982, 134–149.

SAMPSON, Geoffrey R (1983). "Deterministic parsing." In King 1983, 91–116.

SAPIR, Edward (1921). *Language: An introduction to the study of speech*. New York: Harcourt, Brace, and World, 1921.

SCHANK, Roger Carl (1973). "Identification of conceptualizations underlying natural language." In Schank and Colby 1973, 187–247.

SCHANK, Roger Carl (editor) (1975). *Conceptual information processing* (Fundamental studies in computer science 3). Amsterdam: North-Holland, 1975.

SCHANK, Roger Carl (1982a). "Reminding and memory organization: An introduction to MOPs." [1] In Lehnert and Ringle 1982, 455–494. [2] Research Report 170, Department of Computer Science, Yale University, New Haven, CT, December 1979.

SCHANK, Roger Carl (1982b). *Dynamic memory: A theory of reminding and learning in people and computers*. Cambridge University Press, 1982.

SCHANK, Roger Carl and ABELSON, Robert Paul (1977). *Scripts, plans, goals and understanding: An enquiry into human knowledge structures*. Hillsdale, NJ: Lawrence Erlbaum Associates, 1977.

SCHANK, Roger Carl and BIRNBAUM, Lawrence (1980). "Meaning, memory, and syntax." [1] Research report 189, Department of Computer Science, Yale University, 1980. [2] in Bever, Carroll, and Miller 1984, 209–251.

SCHANK, Roger Carl and COLBY, Kenneth Mark (editors) (1973). *Computer models of thought and language*. San Francisco: W H Freeman and Company, 1973.

SCHANK, Roger Carl; GOLDMAN, Neil Murray; RIEGER, Charles J, III and RIESBECK, Christopher Kevin (1975). "Inference and paraphrase by computer." *Journal of the Association for Computing Machinery*, **22**(3), July 1975, 309–328.

SCHANK, Roger Carl and THE YALE AI PROJECT (1975). "SAM—A story understander." Research report 43, Department of Computer Science, Yale University, August 1975.

SCHUBERT, Lenhart K and PELLETIER, Francis Jeffry (1982). "From English to logic: Context-free computation of 'conventional' logical translation." [1] *American journal of computational linguistics*, **8**(1), January–March 1982, 26–44. [2] In Grosz, Sparck Jones, and Webber 1986, 293–312.

SEARLE, John R (1969). *Speech acts: An essay in the philosophy of language.* Cambridge University Press, 1969.

SEIDENBERG, Mark S and TANENHAUS, Michael K (1980). "Chronometric studies of lexical ambiguity resolution." *Proceedings, 18th Annual Meeting of the Association for Computational Linguistics*, Philadelphia, June 1980. 155–158.

SEIDENBERG, Mark S; TANENHAUS, Michael K; LEIMAN, James Mehner and BIENKOWSKI, Marie A (1982). "Automatic access of the meanings of ambiguous words in context: Some limitations of knowledge-based processing." [1] *Cognitive psychology*, **14**(4), October 1982, 489–537. [2] Technical report 240, Center for the Study of Reading, University of Illinois at Urbana-Champaign, April 1982.

SELMAN, Bart (1985). *Rule-based processing in a connectionist system for natural language understanding.* [1] MSc thesis, Department of Computer Science, University of Toronto, January 1985. [2] Technical report 168, Computer Systems Research Institute, University of Toronto, April 1985.

SELMAN, Bart and HIRST, Graeme (1985). "A rule-based connectionist parsing system." *Proceedings of the Seventh Annual Conference of the Cognitive Science Society*, Irvine, CA, August 1985. 212–221.

SELMAN, Bart and HIRST, Graeme (1987). "Parsing as an energy minimization problem." In DAVIS, David (editor). *Genetic algorithms and simulated annealing* (Research notes in artificial intelligence), Pitman, 1987.

SHALLICE, Tim; WARRINGTON, Elizabeth K and MCCARTHY, Rosaleen (1983). "Reading without semantics." *Quarterly journal of experimental psychology, Section A: Human experimental psychology*, **35A**(1), February 1983, 111–138.

SHIEBER, Stuart M (1983). "Sentence disambiguation by a shift-reduce parsing technique." [1] *Proceedings, 21st Annual Meeting of the Association for Computational Linguistics*, Cambridge, MA, June 1983. 113–118. [2] Technical note 281, Artificial Intelligence Center, SRI International, 1983. [3] *Proceedings of the 8th International Joint Conference on Artificial Intelligence*, Karlsruhe, August 1983. 699–703.

SIMMONS, Robert F and BURGER, John F (1968). "A semantic analyzer for English." *Mechanical translation*, **11**(1–2), March–June 1968, 1–13.

SIMPSON, Greg B (1981). "Meaning dominance and semantic context in the processing of lexical ambiguity." *Journal of verbal learning and verbal behavior*, **20**(1), February 1981, 120–136.

SIMPSON, Greg B (1984). "Lexical ambiguity and its role in models of word recognition." *Psychological bulletin*, **96**(2), 1984, 316–340.

SIMPSON, Greg B and BURGESS, Curt (1985). "Activation and selection processes in the recognition of ambiguous words." *Journal of experimental psychology: Human perception and performance*, **11**(1), 1985, 28–39.

SMALL, Steven Lawrence (1980). *Word expert parsing: A theory of distributed word-based natural language understanding.* Doctoral dissertation [available as technical report 954], Department of Computer Science, University of Maryland, September 1980.

SMALL, Steven Lawrence (1983). "Parsing as cooperative distributed inference: Understanding through memory interactions." In King 1983, 247–275.

SMALL, Steven Lawrence and RIEGER, Charles J, III (1982). "Parsing and comprehending with word experts (a theory and its realization)." In Lehnert and Ringle 1982, 89–147.

SMALL, Steven Lawrence; COTTRELL, Garrison Weeks and SHASTRI, Lokendra (1982). "Toward connectionist parsing." *Proceedings of the National Conference on Artificial Intelligence*, Pittsburgh, August 1982. 247–250.

SMITH, Brian Cantwell (1979). "Intensionality in computational contexts." MS, Artificial Intelligence Laboratory, Massachusetts Institute of Technology, Cambridge, MA, December 1979.

SMITH, Edward E; SHOBEN, Edward J and RIPS, Lance J (1974). "Structure and process in semantic memory: A featural model for semantic decisions." *Psychological review*, **81**(3), May 1974, 214–241.

SMOLENSKY, Paul (1983). "Schema selection and stochastic inference in modular environments." *Proceedings of the National Conference on Artificial Intelligence*, Washington, August 1983. 378–382.

SOMERS, Harry L (1983). "The use of verb features in arriving at a 'meaning representation'." *Linguistics*, **20**(3/4), 237–265.

SOMERS, Harry L (1984). "On the validity of the complement–adjunct distinction in valency grammar." *Linguistics*, **22**, 507–530.

SONDHEIMER, Norman K; WEISCHEDEL, Ralph M and BOBROW, Robert J (1984). "Semantic interpretation using KL-ONE." *Proceedings, 10th International Conference on Computational Linguistics (COLING-84)*, Stanford, July 1984. 101–107.

SOWA, John F (1984). *Conceptual structures: Information processing in mind and machine.* Reading, MA: Addison-Wesley, 1984.

SOWA, John F (1985). "Using a lexicon of canonical graphs in a conceptual parser." MS, 1985.

SPARCK JONES, Karen and WILKS, Yorick Alexander (editors) (1982). [1] *Automatic natural language parsing: Proceedings of a workshop.* Memorandum 10, Cognitive Studies Centre, University of Essex, June 1982. [2] *Automatic natural language parsing.* Chichester: Ellis Horwood / John Wiley, 1983.

STANOVICH, Keith E (1980). "Toward an interactive-compensatory model of individual differences in the development of reading fluency." *Reading research quarterly*, **16**(1), 1980, 32–71.

STANOVICH, Keith E (1984). "The interactive-compensatory model of reading: A confluence of developmental, experimental, and educational psychology." *Remedial and special education*, **5**(3), May–June 1984, 11–19.

STANOVICH, Keith E and WEST, Richard F (1983a). "The generalizability of context effects on word recognition: A reconsideration of the roles of parafoveal priming and sentence context." *Memory and cognition*, **11**(1), 1983, 49–58.

STANOVICH, Keith E and WEST, Richard F (1983b). "On priming by a sentence context." *Journal of experimental psychology: General*, **112**(1), March 1983, 1–36.

STANOVICH, Keith E; CUNNINGHAM, Anne E and FEEMAN, Dorothy J (1984). "Relation between early reading acquisition and word decoding with and without context: A longitudinal study of first-grade children." *Journal of educational psychology*, **76**(4), 1984, 668–677.

STANOVICH, Keith E; WEST, Richard F and FEEMAN, Dorothy J (1981). "A longitudinal study of sentence context effects in second-grade children: Tests of an interactive–compensatory model." *Journal of experimental child psychology*, **32**, 1981, 185–199.

STEEDMAN, Mark (1982). "Natural and unnatural language processing." In Sparck Jones and Wilks 1982, 132–140.

STEINACKER, Ingeborg and TROST, Harald (1983). "Structural relations—A case against case." *Proceedings of the 8th International Joint Conference on Artificial Intelligence*, Karlsruhe, August 1983. 627–629.

STOWE, Laurie A (1984). *Models of gap-location in the human language processor.* Doctoral dissertation, University of Wisconsin–Madison, 1984. Bloomington, Indiana: Indiana University Linguistics Club.

STRUNK, William, Jr and WHITE, Elwyn Brooks (1979). *The elements of style* (third edition). New York: Macmillan, 1979.

SWINNEY, David A (1979). "Lexical access during sentence comprehension: (Re)Consideration of context effects." *Journal of verbal learning and verbal behavior*, **18**(6), December 1979, 645–659.

SWINNEY, David A (1982). "The structure and time-course of information interaction during speech comprehension: Lexical segmentation, access, and interpretation." In Mehler, Walker, and Garrett 1982, 151–167.

SWINNEY, David A and HAKES, David T (1976). "Effects of prior context upon lexical access during sentence comprehension." *Journal of verbal learning and verbal behavior*, **15**(6), December 1976, 681–689.

TAHA, Abdul Karim (1983). "Types of syntactic ambiguity in English." *IRAL: International review of applied linguistics in language teaching*, **21**(4), November 1983, 251–266.

TAIT, John I (1982). "Semantic parsing and syntactic constraints." [1] In Boguraev *et al* 1982, 15–22. [2] Revised version in Sparck Jones and Wilks 1982, 169–177.

TANENHAUS, Michael K and DONNENWERTH-NOLAN, Suzanne (1984). "Syntactic context and lexical access." Cognitive Science technical report URCS-17, Department of Psychology, University of Rochester, May 1984.

TANENHAUS, Michael K; LEIMAN, James Mehner and SEIDENBERG, Mark S (1979). "Evidence for multiple stages in the processing of ambiguous words in syntactic contexts." *Journal of verbal learning and verbal behavior*, **18**(4), August 1979, 427–440.

TANENHAUS, Michael K; STOWE, Laurie A and CARLSON, Greg (1985). "The interaction of lexical expectation and pragmatics in parsing filler–gap constructions." *Proceedings of the Seventh Annual Conference of the Cognitive Science Society*, Irvine, CA, August 1985. 361–365.

TARNAWSKY, George Orest (1982). *Knowledge semantics.* Doctoral dissertation, Department of Linguistics, New York University, 1982.

TAYLOR, Brock Harold (1975). *A case-driven parser.* MSc thesis, Department of Computer Science, University of British Columbia, May 1975.

TAYLOR, Brock Harold and ROSENBERG, Richard Stuart (1975). "A case-driven parser for natural language." [1] *American journal of computational linguistics*, 1975: 4, microfiche 31. [2] Technical report 75–5, Department of Computer Science, University of British Columbia, October 1975.

TOMITA, Masaru (1984). "Disambiguating grammatically ambiguous sentences by asking." *Proceedings, 10th International Conference on Computational Linguistics (COLING-84)*, Stanford, July 1984, 476–480.

TYLER, Lorraine Komisarjevsky and MARSLEN-WILSON, William D (1982). "Speech comprehension processes." In Mehler, Walker, and Garrett 1982, 169–184.

UNDERWOOD, Geoffrey (1981). "Lexical recognition of embedded unattended words: Some implications for reading processes." *Acta psychologica*, **47**, 1981, 267–283.

VAN BAKEL, Jan (1984). *Automatic semantic interpretation: A computer model of understanding natural language.* Dordrecht: Foris Publications, 1984.

WALES, Roger J and TONER, Hugh (1979). "Intonation and ambiguity." In Cooper and Walker 1979, 135–158.

WALPOLE, Ronald E (1974). *Introduction to statistics* (2nd edition). New York: Macmillan, 1974.

WALTZ, David Leigh (1978). "On the interdependence of language and perception." *Proceedings, TINLAP–2: [Second interdisciplinary workshop on] Theoretical issues in natural language processing*, Urbana, IL, July 1978. 149–156. [These proceedings were reprinted in: *American journal of computational linguistics*, 1978: 3, microfiche 78–80.]

WALTZ, David Leigh (1982). "Event shape diagrams." *Proceedings of the National Conference on Artificial Intelligence*, Pittsburgh, August 1982. 84–87.

WALTZ, David Leigh and POLLACK, Jordan B (1985). "Massively parallel parsing: A strongly interactive model of natural language interpretation." *Cognitive science* , **9**(1), January–March 1985, 51–74.

WANNER, Eric (1980). "The ATN and the Sausage Machine: Which one is baloney?" *Cognition*, **8**(2), June 1980, 209–225.

WARREN, Beatrice (1978). *Semantic patterns of noun-noun compounds* (Gothenburg studies in English 41). Göteborg, Sweden: Acta Universitatis Gothoburgensis, 1978.

WARREN, David Scott (1983). "Using λ-calculus to represent meanings in logic grammars." [1] Technical report 83/045, Department of Computer Science, State University of New York at Stony Brook, January 1983. [2] *Proceedings, 21st Annual Meeting of the Association for Computational Linguistics*, Cambridge, MA, June 1983. 51–56.

WARREN, David Scott (1985). "Using Montague semantics in natural language understanding." *Proceedings, Workshop on theoretical approaches to natural language understanding*, Halifax, May 1985.

WEBSTER (1983). *Webster's ninth new collegiate dictionary.* Springfield, MA: G. & C. Merriam Company, 1983.

WEISCHEDEL, Ralph M (1979). "A new semantic computation while parsing: Presupposition and entailment." [1] In Oh and Dinneen 1979, 155–182. [2] In Grosz, Sparck Jones, and Webber 1986, 313–326.

WEISCHEDEL, Ralph M (1983). "Mapping between semantic representations using Horn clauses." *Proceedings of the National Conference on Artificial Intelligence*, Washington, August 1983. 424–428.

WEST, Richard F and STANOVICH, Keith E (1978). "Automatic contextual facilitation in readers of three ages." *Child development*, **49**, 1978, 717–727.

WEST, Richard F; STANOVICH, Keith E; FEEMAN, Dorothy Jand CUNNINGHAM, Anne E (1983). "The effect of sentence context on word recognition in second- and sixth-grade children." *Reading research quarterly*, **19**(1), Fall 1983, 6–15.

References   WHITLEY • WINOGRAD   249

WHITLEY, M Stanley (1983). *"Hopefully:* A shibboleth in the English adverb system."
  American speech, **58**(2), Summer 1983, 126–149.
WILENSKY, Robert and ARENS, Yigal (1980a). "PHRAN: A knowledge-based approach to
  natural language analysis." Memo UCB/ERL M80/34, Electronics Research Laboratory, University of California, Berkeley, 12 August 1980.
WILENSKY, Robert and ARENS, Yigal (1980b). "PHRAN: A knowledge-based natural language understander." *Proceedings, 18th Annual Meeting of the Association for Computational Linguistics*, Philadelphia, June 1980. 117–121.
WILKS, Yorick Alexander (1968). "On-line semantic analysis of English texts." *Mechanical
  translation*, **11**(3–4), September–December 1968, 59–72.
WILKS, Yorick Alexander (1973). "An artificial intelligence approach to machine transla-
  tion." In Schank and Colby 1973, 114–151.
WILKS, Yorick Alexander (1975a). "Primitives and words." *Proceedings, [Interdisciplinary
  workshop on] Theoretical issues in natural language processing*, Cambridge, MA,
  June 1975. 42–45.
WILKS, Yorick Alexander (1975b). "Preference semantics." [1] In KEENAN, Edward Louis,
  III (editor). *Formal semantics of natural language.* Cambridge University Press, 1975.
  329–348. [2] Memo AIM–206, Artificial Intelligence Laboratory (= Report CS–377,
  Computer Science Department), Stanford University, July 1973.
WILKS, Yorick Alexander (1975c). "An intelligent analyzer and understander of English."
  [1] *Communications of the ACM*, **18**(5), May 1975, 264–274. [2] In Grosz, Sparck
  Jones, and Webber 1986, 193–204.
WILKS, Yorick Alexander (1975d). "A preferential, pattern-seeking semantics for natural
  language inference." *Artificial Intelligence*, **6**, 1975, 53–74.
WILKS, Yorick Alexander (1975e). "Methodology in AI and natural language understand-
  ing." *Proceedings, [Interdisciplinary workshop on] Theoretical issues in natural language processing*, Cambridge, MA, June 1975. 144–147.
WILKS, Yorick Alexander (1977). "Making preferences more active." [1] *Artificial intelligence*, **11**(3), December 1978, 197–223. [2] In FINDLER, Nicholas V (editor). *Associative networks: Representation and use of knowledge by computers.* New York,
  Academic Press, 1979. 239–266. [3] An early version appears as Research report 32,
  Department of Artificial Intelligence, University of Edinburgh. April 1977. Reprinted
  as Research paper 131. 1980. [4] A shorter version appears as "Knowledge structures
  and language boundaries." *Proceedings of the 5th International Joint Conference on
  Artificial Intelligence*, Cambridge, MA, August 1977, 151–157.
WILKS, Yorick Alexander (1982a). "Some thoughts on procedural semantics." [1] In Lehn-
  ert and Ringle 1982, 494–516. [2] Technical report CSCM-1, Cognitive Studies Cen-
  tre, University of Essex, Wivenhoe Park, Colchester, November 1980.
WILKS, Yorick Alexander (1982b). "Does anyone really still believe this kind of thing?" In
  Sparck Jones and Wilks 1982, 182–189.
WILKS, Yorick Alexander; HUANG, Xiuming and FASS, Dan (1985). "Syntax, preference
  and right attachment." *Proceedings of the 9th International Joint Conference on Artificial Intelligence*, Los Angeles, August 1985, 779–784.
WINOGRAD, Terry Allen (1970). "Procedures as a representation for data in a computer
  program for understanding natural language." [1] Doctoral dissertation, Department of
  Mathematics, Massachusetts Institute of Technology, 21 August 1970. [2] Technical

report 17, Artificial Intelligence Laboratory, Massachusetts Institute of Technology, February 1971.

WINOGRAD, Terry Allen (1972). [1] "Understanding natural language." *Cognitive psychology*, **3**(1), 1972, 1–191. [2] *Understanding natural language*. New York: Academic Press. 1972.

WINOGRAD, Terry Allen (1976). "Towards a procedural understanding of semantics." [1] Memo 292, Artificial Intelligence Laboratory, Stanford University, November 1976. [2] *Revue internationale de philosophie*, number 117–118, 1976, 260–303.

WINOGRAD, Terry Allen (1984). "Moving the semantic fulcrum." [1] Technical report CSLI–84–17, Center for the Study of Language and Information, Stanford University, December 1984. [2] *Linguistics and philosophy*, **8**(1), February 1985, 91–104.

WINSTON, Patrick Henry (1978). "Learning by creating and justifying transfer frames." *Artificial intelligence*, **10**(2), April 1978, 147–172.

WONG, Douglas (1981a). "Language comprehension in a problem solver." *Proceedings of the 7th International Joint Conference on Artificial Intelligence*, Vancouver, 24–28 August 1981. 7–12.

WONG, Douglas (1981b). *On the unification of language comprehension with problem solving*. Doctoral dissertation [available as technical report CS-78], Department of Computer Science, Brown University, 1981.

WOODS, William Aaron (1967). *Semantics for a question-answering system.* [1] Doctoral dissertation, Harvard University, August 1967. [2] Reprinted as a volume in the series Outstanding dissertations in the Computer Sciences. New York: Garland Publishing, 1979.

WOODS, William Aaron (1968). "Procedural semantics for a question-answering machine." *AFIPS conference proceedings*, **33** (Fall Joint Computer Conference), 1968, 457–471.

WOODS, William Aaron (1970). "Transition network grammars for natural language analysis." *Communications of the ACM*, **13**(10), October 1970, 591–606.

WOODS, William Aaron (1975). "What's in a link: foundations for semantic networks." [1] In BOBROW, Daniel Gureasko and COLLINS, Allan M (editors). *Representation and understanding: Studies in cognitive science*. New York: Academic Press, 1975. 35–82. [2] In Brachman and Levesque 1985, 217–241.

WOODS, William Aaron (1981). "Procedural semantics as a theory of meaning." In Joshi, Webber, and Sag 1981, 300–334.

WOODS, William Aaron; KAPLAN, Ronald M and NASH-WEBBER, Bonnie Lynn (1972). "The Lunar Sciences Natural Language Information System: Final report." Report 2378, Bolt, Beranek and Newman, Inc., Cambridge, MA, 15 June 1972.

YATES, Jack (1978). "Priming dominant and unusual senses of ambiguous words." *Memory and cognition*, **6**(6), November 1978, 636–643.

ZADEH, Lotfi A (1983). "Commonsense knowledge representation based on fuzzy logic." *Computer*, **16**(10), October 1983, 61–65.

Index of names

Subject index